God Incarnate

God Incarnate
Explorations in Christology

Oliver D. Crisp

t&t clark

Published by T&T Clark International
A Continuum Imprint
The Tower Building, 11 York Road, London SE1 7NX
80 Maiden Lane, Suite 704, New York, NY 10038

www.continuumbooks.com

British Library Cataloguing-in-Publication Data
A catalogue record for this book is available from the British Library

ISBN: 978-0-567-03347-5 (Hardback)
       978-0-567-03348-2 (Paperback)

Typeset by Newgen Imaging Systems Pvt Ltd, Chennai, India
Printed and bound in Great Britain by Athenauem Press Ltd, Gateshead, Tyne and Wear

For John and Jean,
Who believed in me, when I did not

CONTENTS

Acknowledgements

I should like to thank the following individuals who have provided their advice and assistance in the preparation of this volume: Richard Bauckham, Gavin D'Costa, Christopher Eberle, Thomas Flint, Simon Gathercole, Tee Gatewood, David Gibson, Alan Gomes, Paul Helm, Daniel Hill, Stephen Holmes, Anthony Lane, Bruce McCormack, Benjamin Myers, Robin Parry, Susan Parsons, Myron Penner, Michael Rea, Ian Stackhouse, Alan Torrance, Eddy Van der Borght and John Webster. I am particularly grateful to William Storrar, Thomas Hastings and the staff and other resident members of the Center of Theological Inquiry, Princeton, where the book took shape during my period as the William H. Scheide Research Fellow in Theology in 2008–2009. As ever, special thanks must go to my wife, Claire, and to Liberty, Elliot and Mathilda who have supported me throughout the ups and downs of writing of this material in England and New Jersey. Finally, I offer thanks to my editor Thomas Kraft, whose enthusiasm for the project was most welcome.

Earlier versions of a number of chapters were given their first outing in various learned journals and, in one case, a Feschrift. They have all been revised since then, some substantively. I am grateful to the following editors and publishers for permission to use material from the following essays:

1. 'Robert Jenson on the Pre-Existence of Christ' in *Modern Theology* 23 (2007): 27–45.
2. 'Was Christ Sinless or Impeccable?' in *Irish Theological Quarterly* 72 (2007): 169–187.
3. 'On the 'Fittingness' of the Virgin Birth' in *Heythrop Journal* 49. 2 (2008): 197–221.
4. 'The Election of Jesus Christ' in *Journal of Reformed Theology* 2. 2 (2008): 131–150.
5. 'Multiple Incarnations' in M. W. F. Stone, ed. *Reason, Faith and History: Essays in Honour of Paul Helm* (Aldershot: Ashgate, 2008) 217–236.

This book is dedicated to my parents-in-law John and Jean Wright with great affection.

INTRODUCTION

This volume deals with a cluster of central doctrinal problems concerning the person of Christ. I have chosen to do so via engagement with a number of theologians, past and present, all of whom are concerned with what we might call classical Christology, that is, Christology pursued within the dogmatic boundaries set by the great ecumenical symbols (i.e. creeds) of the Church, including the so-called 'definition' of the person of Christ found in the canons of the Council of Chalcedon of AD 451. But this book is not an exercise in historical theology. It is an attempt to offer a constructive account of a number of central dogmatic issues in Christology that are the subject of ongoing discussion amongst theologians.

This study is also an exercise in *analytic theology*. By this I mean the method used to scrutinize the subject matter of each chapter involves deploying some of the techniques and rigour of current analytical philosophy in order to make sense of properly theological problems. Some theologians seem to think that analytical philosophy suffers from a certain intellectual myopia, focusing in on particular issues with such intensity and logical rigour that the organic whole is sometimes lost in the pursuit of the minutiae of a given argument. This need not be the case, and I hope that the treatment of the issues contained in this volume offer some reason to think analytical *theology* does not necessarily suffer from such short-sightedness, even if some analytical philosophy of religion might. In fact, the reverse may be true: such a theological method might provide one useful way of making clear certain interconnections between different aspects of theology as parts of an organic whole. Still, the theologian could be suspicious that analytic theology is a philosophical, rather than a theological exercise.[1] But this need not be the case. The use of certain philosophical apparatus does not govern the theological conclusions reached in the chapters of this book, nor does it motivate the discussion. Rather, the theological issues under scrutiny are made clearer using methods borrowed and adapted

---

1. I have set out what analytic theology may and may not entail in 'On Analytic Theology' in Oliver D. Crisp and Michael Rea, eds *Analytic Theology, New Essays in the Philosophy of Theology* (Oxford: Oxford University Press, 2009).

from philosophy for a theological purpose. In my way of thinking, one of the principal tasks of analytic theology is to provide a theological method that makes clearer the 'internal logic' of a particular doctrinal matter. In this way analytical theology (again, on my construal of this term) is primarily, though not exclusively, concerned with what might be called a procedural, rather than substantive use of reason, where the deliverances of reason are subordinate to, and in the service of, a particular theological end.[2] Hence, this is a modern instance of a venerable theological method, where a particular philosophical tradition and the tools it has to offer are used as a handmaid to theology. Or, to coin a phrase, analytic theology is (or at least, can be) an instance of a faith seeking understanding programme of theology.

I hope, by examining the cluster of problems in Christology that make up this volume, to 'road test' analytic theology as a way of approaching particular doctrinal questions in Christian theology.[3] However, what follows is not merely a series of closely connected but distinct studies in Christology; it is not offered as a collection of methodologically related essays. This book is united by a common methodological concern. But it is also a step along the way towards setting out a comprehensive account of the main contours of Christology.[4] Most of the issues I have focused on here are either dogmatically central to the doctrine of the Incarnation, or are matters raised by what we might call core-commitments of Christology, such as the relationship between Christ's human nature and our human natures with respect to the question of when a human embryo becomes a human person – a problem discussed in the fourth chapter, after considering the dogmatically prior issue of the viability of the virgin birth. This is also true of several chapters that tackle matters that reflect some current concerns in the analytical philosophical–theological literature on Christology, which have roots deep in the tradition. Here I am thinking of the seventh and eighth chapters, which address the question of materialist accounts of human persons and classical Christology, and whether multiple incarnations are possible – this last being a matter that is considered in the tradition by St Thomas Aquinas, amongst others. In this way, I have tried to indicate the virtues of analytic theology, by showing how the analytic theologian might deal with some central topics in Christology and with several matters that commitment to classical Christology raise, pertinent to contemporary theological discourse.

---

2. I owe the distinction between 'substantive' and 'procedural' uses of reason to Paul Helm. See his *Faith and Understanding* (Edinburgh: Edinburgh University Press, 1997), ch. 1.

3. I suppose one could have an analytic Jewish theology, or an analytical Islamic theology. But as a Christian theologian I am responsible to the Christian community, not to the communities of other religious traditions, though Jewish and Muslim theologians may wish to make use of similar analytical methods.

4. The first step along this road was taken in my *Divinity and Humanity: The Incarnation Reconsidered* (Cambridge: Cambridge University Press, 2007) which is also a piece of analytic theology, although I did not speak of it as such there.

I have said that this is a book that engages with classical theologians and the Christology of the catholic creeds and deploys an analytic theological method to that end. It is also worth pointing out that this mode of doctrinal engagement is commensurate with what John Webster has recently called 'theology of retrieval'. He says '"Retrieval", then, is a mode of theology, an attitude of mind and a way of approaching theological tasks which is present with greater or lesser prominence in a range of different thinkers, not all of them self-consciously "conservative" or "orthodox".' He goes on to suggest that one important characteristic of theologies of retrieval is that they treat 'pre-modern Christian theology as resource rather than problem'.[5] This certainly fits with the strategy employed here. As a theological method analytic theology need not be a theology of retrieval – the two terms are not co-terminus. It is possible to do theology in this analytical mode and be much more revisionist in outlook than this book is.[6] But my own theological sympathies are in many respects very similar to Webster's account of theological retrieval.[7]

Finally, this book is offered as a piece of *Reformed* analytic theology that is engaged in theological retrieval. Like an increasing number of historical theologians and systematicians, I do not think the term 'Reformed Catholic' is an oxymoron; far from it.[8] This book is an attempt to set out one way of thinking about a cluster of issues in Christology through the lens of Reformed thought in particular. But it is also engaged with the wider catholic (i.e., 'universal', and, in this book, primarily western) tradition to which Reformed theology belongs. Hence, in addition to the foregoing, it could be said that this book is an exercise in ecumenical theology of a certain sort – a theology that is, I hope, a properly 'generous orthodoxy'.

---

5.   John Webster, 'Theologies of Retrieval' in John Webster, Kathryn Tanner and Iain Torrance, eds *The Oxford Handbook of Systematic Theology* (Oxford: Oxford University Press, 2007), pp. 584 and 585 respectively.

6.   As I have indicated in 'On Analytic Theology'. One recent Christology that is both 'analytic' and in some respects more revisionist than that offered here is Marilyn Adams *Christ and Horrors* (Cambridge: Cambridge University Press, 2006), which repays careful study.

7.   Webster places a wide range of current approaches to theology under the umbrella term 'theologies of retrieval', not all of which are mutually reinforcing, or even compatible. Nevertheless, he thinks that theologies of retrieval can be characterized by, amongst other things, theological realism (there is a divine reality to which we can and do refer); indebtedness to creedal orthodoxy and classical theology; the recognition that theology ought to be properly ecclesial; and recognition that the norms of theology are established by the object of theology, that is, by God, not by some discipline outside of theology, for example, the natural sciences. See Webster, 'Theologies of Retrieval', p. 584. This is very much in keeping with the analytic theological method used here.

8.   The Reformed tradition was an historic attempt to reform catholic Christianity, which is why it is perfectly appropriate to speak of 'Reformed Catholics'. For this reason, I am wary of talking of 'Catholics' as opposed to 'Protestants'. There are catholic Christians: some Catholics are Romans (i.e. Roman Catholics); others are Reformed (i.e. 'Reformed Catholics'). And, of course, there are other ecclesial bodies besides these, such as the Lutherans and the Orthodox, which are also catholic, in the sense intended here.

1. *The Shape of Things to Come*

The format follows what might be called a traditional dogmatic ordering of Christological topics. The first chapter deals with questions of authority and method in Christology. Theology is often divided into two broad categories: natural and revealed. Here I am concerned only with the latter. Christology is not a subject that natural theology has very much (if anything) to contribute to;[9] it is a concern of revealed theology, since only via revelation can we know that Jesus of Nazareth was God Incarnate. But given that this is the case, how should theologians weight different sources of authority, and different witnesses to this divine revelation? In this chapter I offer an account of how different sources of authority should be weighted when dealing with matters Christological – although the reasoning here has application beyond Christology to other theological topics as well. Scripture is the 'norming norm' in all matters concerning revealed theology, but there are subordinate norms, like creedal and conciliar statements, as well as confessional statements and the work of particular Doctors of the Church that have to be accounted for. I also offer some discussion of the place of reason and experience in revealed theology. It seems to me that theology that fails to wrestle with the tradition as well as scripture is in some important sense defective. By giving an account of how the theologian might think about the different sources of testimony to which she must appeal in considering the subject matter of Christology, I hope to show how the theologian can deal with the tradition and scripture responsibly and with respect, as well as in a manner that displays appropriate critical engagement with the data of revelation. Although analytic theology does not commit one to this particular model of dealing with authority in Christology, I think it is a way of dealing with these matters that will be appealing to those engaged in constructive systematic theology, and is consistent with an analytical-theological approach that is understood in term of a 'theology of retrieval'. The second part of the opening chapter turns to consider 'high' and 'low' Christology as well as Christologies said to be 'from above' and 'from below'. I argue that there is a need to get a clearer understanding of these terms, and that Christology should begin with the data of revelation and the creeds, taking into consideration the findings of biblical criticism, but using the tradition as a 'control' on what is considered theologically acceptable biblical scholarship.

The second chapter considers the question of the election of Christ. This is a subject that has been much discussed in contemporary theology, in the wake of Karl Barth's reformulation of the doctrine of election in his magisterial *Church Dogmatics*. Often discussion of this matter within the Reformed tradition is cast in terms of either a traditional Reformed doctrine of election, as per Calvin and his intellectual progeny, or a revisionist account of election, such as

---

9. Although see Adams, *Christ and Horrors*, ch. 1 for a rather different view.

that offered by Barth. In this chapter, I argue that this polarization is mistaken. As recent historical scholarship has demonstrated, there was a vigorous debate about the doctrine of election in Post-Reformation Reformed theology, and a variety of views on the matter tolerated within Reformed confessional thought. Barth's account of election may be seen as one recent way of rethinking this doctrine from within that tradition. But it is not the only creative way of thinking about the doctrine. Focusing on the election of Christ and the place of Christ's election in the ordering of the divine decrees, I set out a moderate Reformed position on this matter, drawing on the Post-Reformation discussion in an attempt to set out a contemporary account of the doctrine that is rooted in the Reformed tradition, remains cognizant of the carefully circumscribed doctrinal plurality that characterized that discussion and manages to say much that seemed important in Barth's account, without commitment to his revisionist views about the problems into which he thought Post-Reformation theology descended.

In the third chapter, we turn to the doctrine of Christ's pre-existence. I begin by outlining one construal of the traditional account of this doctrine. With this in mind, I then turn to consider the account of Christ's pre-existence recently set out by the American ecumenical Lutheran theologian, Robert Jenson. In his *Systematic Theology*, he offers a novel way of construing the pre-existence of Christ, which, I argue, is not wholly satisfactory. The main problem underlying what he has to say on this matter is that Jenson, like a number of contemporary Protestant theologians, thinks that theology must be done in the teeth of philosophical thinking, which has tainted systematic theology. It seems to me that Jenson's take on the role philosophy has played in theology is contentious, and skews his treatment of Christ's pre-existence in important ways. I suggest that a more traditional account of Christ's pre-existence that has a more positive approach to western metaphysics (Jenson's 'Olympian-Parmenidean religion') would succeed where Jenson's account fails. This sort of positive approach is, of course, part of my larger commitment to analytic theology, although one need not be a partisan of analytical theology to agree that Jenson's disparaging of the role philosophical metaphysics may play in theology is mistaken.

The fourth chapter deals with the Virgin Birth. This doctrine has been the subject of considerable discussion in modern theology, and a number of prominent theologians and biblical scholars have rejected it. I set out a version of the doctrine that follows one particular strand of the tradition, whilst updating it to take account of contemporary biological advances. (This means distancing my account of the Virgin Birth from some aspects of one influential reading of the Virgin Birth, namely, the reading of St Thomas Aquinas.) In the process of setting forth one version of a traditional doctrine of the Virgin Birth, Emil Brunner's attack upon the doctrine is also dealt with. I contend that Brunner is right to claim the Incarnation does not require a virgin birth, but wrong to think that the Virgin Birth is false. Then, at the end of the chapter, I turn to St Anselm of Canterbury, and his account of the 'fittingness' of the Virgin Birth. It seems to me that with certain qualifications, St Anselm's way of thinking about the Virgin Birth is a positive and helpful contribution to Christology.

As already mentioned, the fifth chapter is a kind of theological *excursus*, or pause in our treatment of central dogmatic issues in Christology to consider what the ethical implications of one particular view of Christ's human nature – mentioned in setting out the argument of the chapter on the Virgin Birth – might be. I argue that commitment to a particular way of thinking about Christ's human nature that maintains Christ had a human body and rational soul, and that he was a complete human from conception, has important bearing upon what we think about the development of human embryos, and the vexed bio-ethical question of whether embryos are human persons or not. These are difficult ethical questions and I do not presume to have offered a solution to all the aspects of the matter that are currently pressing concerns in bioethics. But this does show that certain dogmatic and metaphysical commitments have ethical implications that it is incumbent upon the theologian to think through with care and sensitivity. And I also think that the argument offered here is a good Christological basis for thinking about the development of human embryos – which may help inform discussion of this matter amongst Christian ethicists.

Chapter 6 offers an account of Christ's impeccability. A number of recent scholars, including a number of theologians sympathetic to Chalcedonian Chris-tology have shied away from the idea that Christ is impeccable, that is, incapable of committing sin. In order to retain a robust account of Christ's humanity – spe-cifically, that he was like us in every way sin excepted (Heb. 4. 15) – these theologians have thought it important to claim that though Christ was without sin, he was capable of sinning (i.e., was sinless but not impeccable). The sup-posed virtue of this weaker account of Christ's sinlessness is that it means Christ really struggled with sin; he really could have succumbed to temptation, though he did not. I argue that this weaker account of Christ's sinlessness has undesirable theological consequences and requires the theologian to make adjustments to the doctrine of God that many will find unacceptable. Moreover, the traditional view, that Christ is impeccable, is perfectly capable of incorpo-rating the idea that Christ really felt the pull of temptation, and yet resisted. Hence, the traditional view is able to deliver all that the weaker view of Christ's sinlessness promises, without the need for changes to the doctrine of God.

Chapter 7 deals with the important recent literature that has developed in various branches of theology in response to work being done in the philosophy of mind: an increasing number of theologians are dissatisfied with a traditional account of the metaphysics of human beings, claiming that humans are not normally composed of a body and soul, rightly related, but are material beings which have no immaterial substance distinct from the matter of which they are composed. I set out what materialism concerning human beings requires and then ask whether this is consistent with classical Christology, according to which Christ is composed of a human body and a 'rational soul'. It turns out that there are plausible renderings of a materialist account of human persons that can make sense of this requirement of classical Christology. I set forth one such account, and argue that this version of materialism does not entail Apollinarianism, the heresy according to which the human nature of Christ consists of a human body, the divine nature taking the place usually occupied by a human soul. This means that at least one way of thinking about materialism with respect to human persons avoids an obvious theological error and appears to be creedally orthodox – although I myself do not endorse materialism about human persons. Yet I think there is merit in placing more than one account of the metaphysics of human persons at the disposal of theologians, which other divines might usefully explore. This is also an example of the way in which attention to particular doctrinal claims in classical Christology can throw new and unexpected light on an area of considerable theological and philosophical debate in the current literature.

The eighth and final chapter deals with the question of multiple Incarnations. There are several ways in which this might be a problem for the traditional doctrine of the Incarnation. First, it might be thought that Christ is only one of several, or perhaps many, divine incarnations, or divine avatars. If this is true, then the traditional claim of religious exclusivity that is implied by the doctrine of the Incarnation is jeopardized. Alternatively, it might be objected that Christ's Incarnation does not have cosmic significance. Christ might atone for the sin of human beings on this world, but this says nothing about possible life on other worlds, and their salvation. Finally, it might be thought that the Incarnation is too restrictive. What is there to prevent God from becoming Incarnate more than once? And why only in a human being – why not an ass, as some medieval theologians argued, or, perhaps, an ape? And, if it is somehow important that the Word of God is Incarnate as a human being, why should he become incarnate in only *one* human being? Why not the entire race? The Anglican theologian Brian Hebblethwaite has addressed some of these problems. He has done much to defend the traditional account of the Incarnation in his long and distinguished career. In this chapter, we shall assess to what extent his argument against the idea that there might be multiple Incarnations is successful. I argue that his analysis fails: there is reason to think multiple Incarnations are metaphysically possible. However, there are also reasons for thinking that as a matter of fact there is only one Incarnation – reasons having to do with the suitability of this particular arrangement.

In a short afterword I commend analytic theology as a powerful means by which to make sense of theological problems such as those considered in this book.

Chapter 1

CHRISTOLOGICAL METHOD

For I do not seek to understand so that I might believe; but I believe so that I may understand. For I believe this also, that 'unless I believe I shall not understand'
[Is. 7. 9].

St Anselm of Canterbury, *Proslogion 1*

All theology involves dialogue. It is a conversation in which contemporary theologians are in dialogue with each other, their intellectual forebears, the confessions and creeds of Christendom and Holy Scripture. How one weights these different sources of authority, indeed, whether one thinks of all these as sources of authority, is also a matter of debate. This is a question of theological method, usually thought to belong to the prolegomena of systematic theology. However, something should be said at the beginning of a book like this about *Christological* method. To the extent that the question of authority arises for other theological *loci* and for theology as a science (i.e., as an organized body of knowledge, a *wissenschaft*), it also arises for Christology as a particular aspect of theological science. One might think that, because Christology is so central to Christian theology, the issue of authority for Christological statements is even more pressing than it might be for other doctrines that may be thought to be less central to the Christian faith, or less definitive for the content of Christian theology (e.g., the mode of baptism, or marriage; the former is arguably less central, the latter is arguably not definitive for Christian theology – it is an institution shared with other religious traditions and the state). So, we shall begin by considering the question of the weighting of these different sources of authority, and their bearing upon the formation of orthodox Christology.

Having laid out some parameters on this issue, I shall then turn to consider problems with Christological method that have been raised in the recent literature, focusing my attention on the terms 'high' and 'low' Christology and the related phrases, Christology 'from above' and 'from below'. Making sense of how the theologian engages Scripture and tradition is an important methodological consideration about what we might call the trajectory of Christology, where it begins and where it is headed. Such issues are logically prior to substantive questions pertaining to this doctrinal *locus*, such as whether the two-natures doctrine of the hypostatic union is coherent or not, or what we mean by terms like 'person', 'nature' and so forth.

1. *Weighting Authority*

1.1 *Holy Scripture*

I take it that Holy Scripture is normative for all matters of faith and practice, and therefore, for all matters doctrinal. It is the *norma normans,* that is, the norm which stands behind and informs all the subordinate 'norms' of catholic creeds, or the confessional documents of particular ecclesial traditions. I will not enter into the difficult issue of the inspiration of Holy Scripture here. It is sufficient for our purposes to see that in the history of the church, Scripture has been regarded as revelation. This too is an ambiguous statement. Is it that the words of the original autographs of Scripture are revelation? Or are the propositions we can find in Scripture, or derive from Scripture, revelation? Or is Scripture the vehicle for revelation, the means by which the Holy Spirit brings about an event of revelation to the reader of Scripture now, as he or she reads the record of a previous event of revelation (where the written record of that original revelation is not itself a revelation), as it was experienced by the apostles and prophets who penned the Scriptures? Or, perhaps, it is revelation in some other sense – perhaps God somehow 'owns' the whole message, although not necessarily every word, written down in Scripture by the apostles and prophets and delivered to the saints, and, through the work of the Holy Spirit, Christians come to see this. In which case Scripture as a whole is revelation, although it does not necessarily follow from this that each word, phrase or proposition derived from Scripture is itself revelation. This is rather like an author who regards the motion picture adaptation of her book as a faithful representation of the whole work even though some plot details may have been omitted or altered.

For our purposes, we will not need to decide which, if any, of these views represents the truth of the matter, important though this undoubtedly is. All of the positions just alluded to (and the different views I allude to are not necessarily mutually exclusive or exhaustive) represent what we shall call *high views of Scripture.* They all share a reverence for Holy Scripture and regard it as the particular place in which God now reveals himself to his people. Those who share such a high view of Scripture think that the fact it is the particular place in which God reveals himself to his people sets it apart from all other sorts of literature. Even great works of art such as Shakespeare's tragedies, or Homer's *Iliad,* though 'inspired' in some sense, and classic examples of their particular literary genres, cannot be said to have the property 'being the particular place in which God reveals himself to his people'. They are not works in or through which God reveals his plan of salvation to those who seek him. This is true even if we think God may use particular examples of literature to inspire us, or to motivate us to act in certain sorts of ways. It is even consistent with the notion that God may take up certain human literary creations and 'own' them as part of his special revelatory work in or through Scripture. This is just what we find occurring in Acts 17.28, when Paul, in his speech to the Athenian

Areopagus, uses a phrase from the pagan Cretan poet Epimenides in order to make a particular point about an unknown god some of the religious Athenians worshipped. Rather than undermining the distinction between the special revelatory status of Scripture and other sorts of literature, this underlines the fact that there is a distinction to be made between the sort of writings God somehow superintends, in order to convey a message revealing something about the nature of salvation, and those sorts of writings God enables human authors to write, but where God does not superintend the writing process in such a way as to convey a particular message about the nature of salvation to his people that constitutes a divine *revelation*. God may be said to be involved in the bringing about of both sorts of writing. But in the first, he so superintends whatever is written that what is conveyed is either a report of revelation, which God may then use as the basis for an event of revelation today, or is itself something that conveys, or perhaps contains, propositions that are revelation. This cannot be said of the works of Shakespeare and Homer, which contain no trace of any divine intention to convey through the works of these authors something about himself or his message of salvation.[1]

In short, God may be said to enable certain authors to write the most beautiful or profound literature. But revealing something about God or something about the nature of salvation is a rather different matter and requires a correspondingly different literary output. Here the difference is rather like that between an author taking a creative writing workshop where he helps those present to produce their own pieces of work, and a situation in which the author conveys a message to a particular person, asking them to commit it to paper for him and pass it on to posterity as *his* (i.e. the author's) message.[2]

There are other views of Scripture that may be said to have a certain reverence for Scripture, but do not regard Scripture as the particular place in which God reveals himself to his people. Such views are not high views of Scripture, in the sense I am using that term here. So, for instance, if someone were to say that Scripture is a collection of wise sayings and teachings gathered over hundreds of years by sages, prophets and religious teachers for the edification of the church, this would not be sufficient to count it as a high view of Scripture as I am using the term – indeed, probably, as most theologians use the term. Those who deny that Scripture is either (a) a divine revelation of what is otherwise unknown, or (b) the particular place wherein God reveals himself and his

---

1.   How then are the works of Shakespeare or Homer said to be inspired, as previously asserted? In this sense: that they convey certain deep truths about what is sometimes called, rather misleadingly, the 'human condition'. Naturally, God brings it about that these works contain such truths as they do, including deep truths about the human condition. But this is qualitatively different from thinking of these works as in some sense revelation, or the locus of divine revelation.

2.   Gavin D'Costa has suggested to me that this sounds rather more like an Islamic doctrine of revelation than a Christian one. But this image of the author and his amanuensis need not be thought of in terms of a dictation theory, which I would certainly want to resist.

message of salvation to his people through the work of the Holy Spirit, do not have a high view of Scripture in this fashion. They may have great respect for Scripture, just as I have great respect for the works of Shakespeare or Homer. But respect for a piece of great literature falls far short of regarding that piece of literature as a divine revelation, or the vehicle for divine revelation, even if it is particularly insightful, or conveys truths that are said to be 'of universal' or 'enduring' significance.

In what follows, we shall assume a high view of Scripture. But we will not need to commit ourselves to one particular high view of Scripture. This is a deliberate strategy, with the intention of attracting a wider sympathetic readership than might otherwise be the case were we to commit ourselves at the outset to one particular high view of Scripture. Nevertheless, there are limits to a properly catholic approach to theology. Hence, the approach envisaged here also excludes certain revisionist accounts of Christology. If a particular theologian begins with the assumption that Scripture is not, strictly speaking, anything more than classical literature of its type (whatever that is), and is subject to the same sorts of literary, historical and critical considerations attending other sorts of classical literature, then this will inevitably have an impact upon what that theologian thinks about Scripture's portrayal of the person and work of Christ.

Conversely, theologians who have a high view of Scripture will approach issues in Christology with certain assumptions about what we can know about the person and work of Christ. This is true even if, as I suppose, most modern theologians who hold to a high view of Scripture are happy to use the tools of historical biblical criticism to make sense of the origin and formation of the biblical canon. However, this does not necessarily mean that a theologian with a low view of Scripture ('low' in the sense of regarding Scripture as classic literature but not as divine revelation) will inevitably end up with a correspondingly 'thin' or meagre Christology. But it would be fair to say that those who take a low view of Scripture tend to adopt Christological views that are sceptical about many traditional dogmatic claims concerning the person and work of Christ. Similarly, those with a high view of Scripture tend to develop a Christology in keeping with this, which is invariably much less sceptical about traditional dogmatic claims about the person and work of Christ.

There are those in the Christian tradition who have held a high view of Scripture, but ended up with an unorthodox Christology. For some this is because they have understood Scripture to be teaching things contrary to the catholic faith, such as that Christ was not God Incarnate. For others this is because they have exercised certain critical views about which parts of the canon convey the truth of the gospel, and which do not and should be rejected.

This latter view might be consistent with a high view of Scripture if one thought that Scripture was divine revelation but that not all the books in the canon were divine revelation. Perhaps some canonical books have been mistakenly or maliciously included in the canon by certain religious authorities.

Then one would think it important to 'weed out' those books that did not correspond to the pure doctrine of divine revelation one found in certain canonical books, but not others. This is consistent with a high view of Scripture, even if it is a procedure that, in the case of theologians like Marcion in the early church, leads away from orthodoxy.[3]

Theologians who have held both a high view of Scripture and unorthodox Christological views – allegedly derived from, or compatible with, Scripture – include Arius, the Nestorians (although probably not Nestorius) and, perhaps, Origen. So a high view of Scripture does not guarantee an orthodox Christology. But it does foreclose certain ways of thinking about Christology that are theologically unpalatable. For instance, someone with a high view of Scripture is probably less likely to think that Christ is merely a human being (given statements Christ makes about himself and his relationship to the Father, or statements made about him in the New Testament documents), or that his work is less than the means by which God reconciles human beings to himself (again, given what the New Testament says about Christ being the means by which salvation is brought about).

1.2 Creeds and Confessions

Secondly, what follows assumes that the creeds of the ecumenical councils of the church have a special place in Christian thinking. They act as a sort of hermeneutical bridge between Scripture and the church.[4] By this I mean the creeds of the ecumenical councils help us to understand what Scripture is, or is not, saying about a particular doctrine. To change the metaphor, they offer a dogmatic framework for subsequent theological reflection on the matters they deal with. John Webster has recently written of creeds and confessional formulae as acts of confessing the gospel, whereby 'the church binds itself to the gospel'.[5] There is certainly something to be said for this observation, although

---

3. As is well known, Martin Luther adopted a similar procedure in the sixteenth century, as he compiled the translated portions of his German Bible. He placed certain canonical books in an appendix because he did not think they represented the 'pure' doctrine of the gospel as effectively as other books did (notoriously, he considered James to be 'a right strawy epistle'). This does reflect a high view of Scripture, on my accounting. Nevertheless, such a procedure is no more acceptable than Marcion's mutilated canon.

4. The role of the Church in the formation of the Creeds has historically been the subject of some dispute between different ecclesial bodies. My own view is that the Fathers of the ecumenical councils laboured under the guidance of the Holy Spirit, as they reflected on the truth of Holy Scripture, producing documents that have a special status in the life of the Church as a consequence of this.

5. John Webster, *Confessing God, Essays in Christian Dogmatics II* (Edinburgh: T&T Clark, 2005) p. 69. Later in the same essay, Webster puts it like this: '*a creed or confessional formula is a public and binding indication of the gospel set before us in the scriptural witness, through which the church affirms its allegiance to God, repudiates the falsehood by which the church is threatened, and assembles around the judgement and consolation of the gospel*'. Ibid., pp. 73–74, italics in the original.

care must be taken in using theologically loaded verbs like 'binding'.[6] Creeds are not merely a means to making dogmatic sense of, say, the Incarnation. They are also – just as fundamentally – a means of confessing faith in the Christ to whom the creeds bear witness, as they are attempts to make sense of the gospel accounts of who Christ is. This underlines the fact that the creeds of the Church, and the ecumenical creeds in particular, have several functions that run together: they bear witness to the gospel in Scripture, they tease out aspects of the doctrine of the gospel, and because they do this, they have served a doxological and liturgical purpose in the life of the Church, as a means by which Christians may affirm what it is that they believe, and what it is that holds the Church together.

Only the first seven councils of the Church count as truly ecumenical. For only these seven councils are held in common by eastern and western Christians, being councils that were truly representative of the whole undivided Church, prior to the great schism of AD 1054.[7] There are communions that reject one or more of the creeds these councils authorized. One of these is the Coptic Church, which has never reconciled herself to the symbol of the Council of Chalcedon of AD 451. Many Protestant communions also reject some of the canons of the later ecumenical councils, particularly with respect to the use of icons and images in Christian worship. That said, almost all Christians whether Protestant, Roman Catholic or Eastern Orthodox, affirm the four great creedal statements of the councils of Nicea in AD 325, Constantinople in AD 381, Ephesus in AD 431 and Chalcedon as, in some important sense, theologically normative.[8] Exactly what the nature of this authority consists in has been a matter of dispute. In the chapters that follow, we shall assume that those ecumenical councils that touch upon matters Christological are theologically binding because they are repositories of dogmatic reflection upon Scripture by the undivided Church, under the guidance of the Holy Spirit.[9]

6.   For instance, Roman Catholic Christians will think of the ecumenical creeds as 'binding' in a way that might be theologically unacceptable to some theologically conservative Protestants, for whom no dogmatic statement that is not a proposition of Scripture can be said to be theologically binding. By contrast, theologically liberal Protestants might object that no theological statement, perhaps not even a given statement in Scripture, is theologically binding because all theology is potentially revisable in light of further experience of the divine.

7.   A similar privileging of the life of the Church prior to AD 1054 can be found in the work of William Abraham, who connects it with his concept of 'Canonical Theism', roughly, the 'canon' of beliefs about God ratified by the whole Church prior to the Great Schism. See his *Crossing the Threshold of Divine Revelation* (Grand Rapids, MI: Eerdmans, 2006) pp. xii–xiii.

8.   Compare D. H. Williams who says that the Creed of Nicea as amended by the Council of Constantinople in 381, forming the Nicene-Constantinopolitan Creed, was the touchstone for all later symbols, particularly after Chalcedon. No creed after Chalcedon shares 'the same foundational character as the patristic creeds of the fourth and fifth centuries'. Williams, *Evangelicals and Tradition* (Grand Rapids, MI: Baker Academic and Milton Keynes: Paternoster, 2005) p. 43.

9.   Dispute about how the canons of one of the ecumenical councils are theologically binding depends in large part upon one's ecclesiology. Roman Catholics may think it inconceivable that an

We shall also assume that the symbols of the four great councils held in common by all catholic Christians have a special place of theological honour and importance, and should be taken with great seriousness in matters doctrinal. With respect to Christology in particular, it seems to me that the Nicene-Constantinopolitan Creed of AD 381, the Chalcedonian definition of AD 451 and the canons of the Third Council of Constantinople in AD 680–681, are rightly seen as dogmatic pronouncements that were worked out in the teeth of various attempts to revise what was believed to be the biblical view of the person and work of Christ. These particular conciliar statements are of considerable dogmatic significance for what follows. Although they are not revelation, nor the place wherein God reveals himself by his Spirit (although some might want to claim this), they bind together the one, holy, catholic and apostolic Church with Christological bands that reflects the teaching of Scripture.

This does not mean that the ecumenical councils say *everything* that needs to be said about the person and work of Christ (or, about other central and defining doctrines of the faith). There is nothing about the nature of the atonement in the ecumenical creeds, which has led to considerable controversy in subsequent church history. But where the creeds do touch on matters Christological, what they say should be weighed very carefully. In fact, I would suggest that in matters concerning Christian doctrine the teaching of an ecumenical creed should only be set to one side if it teaches something contrary to Scripture, or that occludes Scriptural teaching.[10]

There are other confessions and creeds that are held by particular ecclesiastical bodies and denominations that are not agreed upon by the vast majority of the church, as the ecumenical creeds are. One such is the so-called Athanasian Creed, which most Christians believe to be ancient and important, but not on a

---

ecumenical council under the guidance of the Holy Spirit can deliver some falsehood to the Church. But some Protestants will complain that this gives too much weight to ecclesiastical authorities, which might be mistaken in their interpretation of Scripture, as some think was the case respecting the Iconoclastic Controversy. I am inclined to the former of these two views, not because I believe the Church infallible (I do not), but because it seems extremely implausible to think that God would allow the vast majority of the Christian Church to be led into error on matters central to the faith by believing the canons of an ecumenical council, such as that given in, say, the Chalcedonian 'definition' of the person of Christ.

10.   I am not suggesting that if the Council of Chalcedon had declared that all propositions of the form 'p and ~p' are valid, we should believe that. It is not beyond the bounds of possibility for a Church council to be wrong about something – they are not infallible guides in the same way as Scripture is often thought to be. My point is really this: if an ecumenical council were to declare something about a particular doctrine of Christian theology that contradicts the teaching of Scripture, then the word of the council would have to be disregarded: Scripture is normative in a way that not even a church council (even an ecumenical church council) is. But as my previous comments should have made clear, I do not think that ecumenical councils have *in fact* canonized substantive errors, due to the oversight of the Holy Spirit.

par with the ecumenical creeds, because it was never ratified by an ecumenical council. A confession that belongs to a particular ecclesiastical body or polity might be the Westminster Confession, beloved of Presbyterians, although I would also include here pronouncements by councils like Trent and Vatican I or II. All such creeds, confessions and conciliar statements are of less importance than the ecumenical creeds, not least because only a proportion of the Church upholds them. But such confessions are not of negligible worth. They are important repositories of doctrinal reflection, and for my part I am persuaded that such confessions are of more significance than the teaching of any one particular theologian because they represent the 'mind', or collective wisdom of a conclave of theologians and church leaders seeking to make sense of the teaching of Scripture for the Christian community.

To sum up: creedal and confessional documents are *norma normata*, or standardized norms, in the life of the church. They do not have the same authority in matters touching dogma that Scripture has, as the *principium theologiae* that is, the collection of fundamental principles or sources for theology. It was as the church stood against the voices of particular theologians or groups who claimed to have uncovered the real meaning of salvation ostensibly occluded by the emerging theological consensus that the ecumenical creeds were forged. And, in a similar way, it was as particular ecclesial traditions sought to safeguard their own particular theological distinctiveness that they drew up the creedal and confessional statements that we now have. Hence, the authority invested in creeds and confessions is derivative, and dependent on the normative authority of Scripture.[11]

1.3 *Christian Theologians*

This brings us to the teaching of the Doctors and theologians of the Church. Undoubtedly, there are some theologians whose teaching has an enduring significance, and who have left the Church a body of work that offers an important means by which to interrogate, correct and amend contemporary theological myopia. Theologians of the past have their own blind spots, of course. Yet we can often see the motes in their theology much more clearly than the planks in our own. For this reason, we need to listen to the thinkers of

---

11. Compare Article XXI of the Thirty Nine Articles of the Church of England, which states:

General Councils. . . . When they be gathered together, (forasmuch as they be an assembly of men, whereof all be not governed with the Spirit and Word of God) they may err, and sometimes have erred, even in things pertaining unto God. Wherefore things ordained by them as necessary to salvation have neither strength nor authority, unless it may be declared that they be taken out of holy Scripture. (*The Book of Common Prayer* (Cambridge: Cambridge University Press, 1968 [1662]) p. 620)

the past. Theological forebears often help correct the blind spots we might not discover without them. Amongst these theologians are some who are clearly head and shoulders above the rest. I suggest that their thinking should be taken more seriously than, say, the latest theologically fashionable volume or school of thought because their teaching has been tried and tested over time, and granted a measure of authority through being used by large segments of the Church as sources of derivative theological authority in particular doctrinal disputes. In this class of theologians whose work has had a lasting impact upon subsequent theology, and whose views are worthy of serious engagement, I would include the works of theologians like St Augustine of Hippo, St John of Damascus, St Anselm of Canterbury, St Thomas Aquinas, Martin Luther, John Calvin, Luis de Molina, Jonathan Edwards and Karl Barth. (Naturally, this is an indicative, not an exhaustive list that betrays something of my own theological proclivities.)

Nevertheless, the work of individual theologians, even the great Doctors of the Church like St Augustine or St Thomas, is not as important, for the purposes of systematic theology, as confessions or ecumenical creeds.[12] Their views cannot command the same attention that, say, the Council of Chalcedon can, in part because their pronouncements do not have the same 'reach' as Chalcedon. This is not merely a matter of influence. Some theologians have been extremely influential on the shape of theology beyond their own ecclesial community. St Augustine is surely the principal example of this. The difference I have in mind depends on the theological authority invested in what a given theologian says on the one hand, and what a particular ecumenical symbol records, on the other. We might put it like this: theologians offer up their arguments for and against particular theological views. Where those views are not matters that have been defined by an ecumenical council like Chalcedon, and are not iterations on confessional statements of a particular tradition to which they belong, their statements are *theologoumena*. That is, what they are offering is an informed theological *opinion* on a particular matter of doctrine. This is not the case when it comes to an ecumenical symbol, or part thereof, such as the so-called definition of the person of Christ given by the Fathers of Chalcedon. This sort of theological pronouncement has a different order of theological weight from that of even an Augustine, which has been recognized as such by the church down through the ages. What it offers is not doctrine or teaching so much as *dogma*, that is, particular views that are understood to be *de fide*, or deliverances of the faith, upheld by all catholic Christians, codifying

---

12.   In this respect, I part company with Roman Catholic teaching that St Thomas Aquinas is the official theologian of the Church, or Protestant theologians who, if not in theory, nevertheless in fact, act as though Luther, or Calvin or Barth, were the official theologian of the Church. This is not to deny that I have a very high regard for all these theologians. My point here is about the relative authority that should be invested in their teachings, not the individual merits of these particular theologians.

something taught in Scripture. And it should hardly need to be said that the work of any Christian theologian is entirely subordinate to Scripture.

1.4 *The Role of Tradition*

It is time to take stock. In light of the foregoing discussion, I offer the following principles concerning matters of theological authority that, taken together, form a consistent whole:

1. Scripture is the *norma normans,* the *principium theologiae.* It is the final arbiter of matters theological for Christians as the particular place in which God reveals himself to his people. This is the first-order authority in all matters of Christian doctrine.
2. Catholic creeds, as defined by an ecumenical council of the Church, constitute a first tier of *norma normata,* which have second-order authority in matters touching Christian doctrine. Such norms derive their authority from Scripture to which they bear witness.
3. Confessional and conciliar statements of particular ecclesial bodies are a second tier of *norma normata,* which have third-order authority in matters touching Christian doctrine. They also derive their authority from Scripture to the extent that they faithfully reflect the teaching of Scripture.
4. The particular doctrines espoused by theologians including those individuals accorded the title Doctor of the Church which are not reiterations of matters that are *de fide,* or entailed by something *de fide,* constitute *theologoumena,* or theological opinions, which are not binding upon the Church, but which may be offered up for legitimate discussion within the Church.

The ascending order of *norma normata,* including *theologoumena* at the very bottom of this hierarchy of doctrine, are all norms that are subordinate to the authority of Scripture. And, on my way of thinking, the descending order of subordinate norms has a doctrinal value and status equivalent to the place each possesses in that descending order. So the material content of each standard of authority determines the order of dependence envisaged, yielding a distinctively, and richly Christian theological pattern or order of norms. For this reason catholic creeds are of more value than confessional statements, and *theologoumena* are of less value than either confessional statements or catholic creeds, although they are not without value.

It seems to me that this way of thinking about the relationship between the *norma normata* and the *norma normans* holds no terror for the theologian committed to Reformation principles like the perspicacity and final authority of Scripture in all matters of Christian doctrine. And this, I suggest, is one way of making sense of the Reformation principle *sola scriptura.* Scripture alone is the final arbiter in matters of doctrine, but (somewhat paradoxically) Scripture is never alone. It is always read within the context of a given ecclesial community, which is, as it were, surrounded by a great cloud of theological witnesses and informed by the Christian tradition.[13] This tradition includes the subordinate norms belonging to the whole Church that have been believed *ubique, semper, et ab omnibus*[14] (everywhere, always and by all), as well as the norms which express the particular beliefs of a given ecclesial body, or denomination, to which a given ecclesial community belongs. At the very least, any credible *theologoumenon* must take seriously the tradition, including the *norma normans*. Failure to do so is not only theologically naïve, but potentially destructive of the life of the Church. For in a similar way many heretics of the past have begun their own journey away from orthodox Christian belief.[15]

So those who claim their own views comport with Scripture but not these *norma normata* should be treated with a healthy dose of scepticism by the theological community.[16] For the Church catholic, dogmatic authority is a top-down affair, generated by Scripture as *norma normans*, and in a subordinate sense guarded or preserved by the *norma normata*. It is not something generated from the bottom-up, that is, from the opinions of private individuals or

13.   For a recent statement of this sort of view, see John Webster *Holy Scripture, A Dogmatic Sketch* (Cambridge: Cambridge University Press, 2002).

14.   Vincent of Lérins, *Commonitorium* I. 2. 6., The wider context in which Vincent's famous dictum is situated is worth citing: 'in the Catholic Church itself, all possible care must be taken, that we hold that faith that has been believed everywhere, always, by all [*ubique, semper, ab omnibus*].' He goes on, '[t]his rule we shall observe if we follow universality, antiquity, consent.' (Cited from *A Select Library of Nicene and Pos-Nicene Fathers of the Christian Church, Second Series, Vol. XI Sulpitius Severus, Vincent of Lerins, John Cassian,* trans. C. A. Heurtley, eds Philip Schaff and Henry Wace [Grand Rapids, MI: Eerdmans, 1982 [1886–1889]] p. 132.) All Christians, Protestants, Roman Catholic and Orthodox, have a stake in the catholicity of the church. Useful discussion of the orthodox consensus, and Vincent, can be found in Jaroslav Pelikan, *The Christian Tradition, 1: The Emergence of the Catholic Tradition (100–600)* (Chicago, IL: University of Chicago Press, 1971) ch. 7.

15.   There are also important ways in which doctrine has developed in the history of the Church. The most important dogmatic developments of this kind are, of course, the formal definitions of the doctrines of the Trinity and the theanthropic person of Christ, to be found in the Nicene-Constantinopolitan and Chalcedonian Creeds, respectively. It seems to me that these doctrinal developments of what was eventually understood to be *de fide* (of the faith) were only developments in the Church's understanding of what God had given, either explicitly or implicitly, in Scripture. They are not developments beyond the teaching of Scripture, but more like extrapolations from what Scripture teaches, making plain what, in previous times, was sometimes only partially understood. In this respect, the development of catholic theology is rather like the way in which one comes to see things in a particular work of art after some contemplation that were not immediately apparent at first glance. A classic example of this is the Mona Lisa, a painting full of secrets that are only gradually disclosed through careful study.

16.   Of course this does mean that if my own position does not comport with all the norms listed here, it should be treated with scepticism. However, this objection is not fatal to my position because (a) it is not obvious that my view does fail in this respect, and (b) by my own lights any view I express here is only a *theologoumenon*, or theological opinion. With this in mind I am quite happy to concede that my account of how theological authorities should be weighted may need correction in ways I am currently unable to see.

groups, although private individuals or groups may contribute to the doctrinal life of the church in a modest fashion.

To underline this point, it is worth saying that it is perfectly feasible for someone to hold views that are consistent with the letter of Scripture, but which are false. Indeed, it is perfectly feasible for a particular ecclesial community to hold views consistent with the *letter* of Scripture, which are false. Anyone who doubts this should simply cast his or her mind back to the debacle attending Galileo's publication of a Copernican account of cosmology in 1616. The Roman Catholic theologians who debated whether the heliocentric view of the solar system was correct concluded that it was 'foolish and absurd philosophically, and formally heretical, inasmuch as it expressly contradicts the doctrine of the Holy Scripture in many passages, both in their literal meaning and in the general interpretation of the Fathers and Doctors'.[17] But, as history records, this was a grave mistake. For our purposes the lesson to be learnt here is that particular philosophical views that seem to be plausible, comport with contemporary 'science', and seem consistent with Scripture, may yet turn out to be false in the long run. We might put it like this: the metaphysical truth of the matter is 'out there', so to speak, but our grasp of it is not always as secure as we think it is.

But where creeds or confessions have sought to safeguard a particular dogmatic issue against those who would attack it and who often claim the support of Scripture in so doing, we need to be much more circumspect. After all, it is the canons of the ecumenical councils culminating in Chalcedon in AD 451 and then the Third Council of Constantinople in AD 681 that we have to thank for clarifying what it means to say, with the Apostle, that 'God was in Christ, reconciling the world to himself' (2 Cor. 5.19). To repeat, I am not denying that it is possible for *norma normata* to be wrong on a particular dogmatic question. My point here is that we (individual theologians) need a very considerable theological reason for rejecting a subordinate theological norm that is adhered to by all catholic Christians, such as the so-called Chalcedonian 'definition' of the person of Christ. My own private views about the metaphysics of human persons are not of greater dogmatic authority than the canons of Chalcedon, even if my views are consistent with Scripture. For private arguments, even if logically impeccable, are not the be-all-and-end-all when it comes to central and defining matters of Christian doctrine, and may well turn out to be false. For one can have a logically valid but unsound argument. And one can have a private opinion, which, though internally consistent and beyond logical reproach, is inconsistent with other things, such as the teaching of an

---

17. Cited in Nicholas Wolterstorff, *Reason within the Bounds of Religion, Second Edition* (Grand Rapids, MI: Eerdmans, 1984 [1976]) p. 15. This volume is a classic *exposé* of the intellectual hubris of classical foundationalism, in the course of which the author demonstrates the perils of trying to fit one's theological commitments to a procrustean bed of ideas.

ecumenical council like Chalcedon, or – more importantly – the doctrine of
Scripture.

1.5 *Reason and Experience*

Some theologians, particularly those in the Wesleyan tradition, speak of the
fourfold authority of Scripture, tradition, reason and experience. This is certainly a helpful way of thinking about the nature of theological authority,
provided certain caveats are borne in mind about the supremacy of Scripture
and the derivative and hermeneutical role of tradition.[18] But reason also plays a
role in theology, even in the thought of those theologians who, like Luther,
professed to have a very low view of the place of reason (Luther supposedly
dubbed reason, 'the Devil's whore'). Even Luther expressed his theology in the
form of propositions and arguments that he laid out in a logical fashion,
attempting to avoid fallacies and other missteps in his reasoning as he did so.
It seems to me that this is how philosophy can play a useful role in theology.
Philosophy is sometimes thought of as a rival discipline to theology.[19] And
as practiced by contemporary philosophers that is, at times, true. However,
to suggest that philosophy as a discipline is opposed to theology is rather like
saying the findings of the natural sciences offer a rival account of the world to
that found in Christian theology. There are scientists who are vehemently anti-
Christian, but this does not mean that the natural sciences are anti-Christian.
In fact, it makes no sense to say the natural sciences are anti-Christian. The
body of knowledge the natural sciences have generated is not asking theological questions at all. It is simply a category mistake to think it is.

Similarly, philosophy, at least as it is found amongst most contemporary
Anglo-American practitioners, offers a set of tools by which to make sense
of particular arguments, as well as commitment to certain objectives in intellectual discourse, including the intellectual virtues of clarity, simplicity and
brevity of expression, and a penchant for the construction of metaphysical
world-views. It is foolish to blame these philosophical tools and notions when
they are used for non-theological purposes, just as it is foolish to blame the
screwdriver that punctures a tyre in the hands of a malicious or inept mechanic.
In this volume, and in keeping with the vast majority of the Christian tradition,
we shall deploy the tools of philosophy where appropriate, to lay bare the form

---

18.   For our purposes, tradition corresponds to what has been believed everywhere, by all
Christians, since ancient times, corresponding to Vincent of Lérins' dictum. This includes, but is
not exhausted by, the symbols of the four great creeds, the deliverances of councils, confessional
documents and the teaching of doctors and theologians of the church.

19.   See, for example, Robert Jenson's claim that western philosophy is a secularized theology,
which is a rival discipline to theology and should be resisted. He makes this case in his *Systematic
Theology, Vol. 1, The Triune God* (New York: Oxford University Press, 1997) ch. 1. This is touched
upon in ch. 3 of this volume.

of theological arguments. Only once this is done can we see where the argument in question goes awry.

However, nothing in what follows should be taken as implying that reason, or philosophy for that matter, is the ultimate arbiter of what is theologically acceptable or unacceptable. A tool cannot perform a task without direction or programming, and a particular tool does not dictate the parameters of a task for which it is deployed. True, the wrong tool can be used for a particular job: A hammer will not help examine microscopic organisms in a Petri dish culture. But nothing in what follows assumes that philosophical tools govern what is theologically acceptable. Nor, I hope, do the philosophical tools used skew the sort of theological question being asked. Clear reasoning should be a theological virtue just as it is a virtue in any other academic discipline. It is God who reveals the data of revealed theology and Christology belongs to this branch of theological science. Some of this data can be made sense of (we can understand what God is saying to us). But there is a very real sense in which the central doctrines of Christian theology are deeply mysterious and will forever remain so. Sanctified reason, in the Anselmian and Augustinian tradition of *fides quarens intellectum* (faith seeking understanding) should be used to try to make sense of what can be understood of these divine mysteries, the Incarnation included. But this must be done with an intellectual humility. We cannot pretend to be able to fathom the depths of the Holy Trinity or the Incarnation. This is not a way of avoiding hard questions or covering over weak arguments; it is recognition of the limitations of human ratiocination. Human reason alone cannot make sense of the Trinity or the Incarnation. God has to reveal these things to us. But reason has a function in trying to tease out the logical interrelationships between doctrines that have been revealed, and the inner coherence of each of the doctrines themselves. It is in this Anselmian spirit, that reason is deployed here.

There is also a place for experience in theology. This has always been the case, although it has not always been acknowledged to be the case. The Montanist movement in the early Church, medieval mystical writers like St John of the Cross or Dame Julian of Norwich, theologians of the eighteenth-century Great Awakening, like John Wesley or Jonathan Edwards and charismatic renewal in the twentieth, are perhaps some of the better known examples of experiential (or, as it used to be called, 'experimental') Christian theology. But it would be wrong to think that theologians and churchmen not included in such movements were without such an experiential dimension to their Christian lives or theology. To give just two examples, Augustine famously heard children singing *'tolle, lege'* (take, read) and picked up a copy of the Pauline epistles, read, and was converted. And Thomas, at the close of his life, experienced a profound meeting with God that left him thinking his (unfinished) monumental theological achievements were 'so much straw'. Such stories could be multiplied. What they show is that there is an important experiential dimension to theology. Or, to put it another way, theology is a dead letter without the pneumatic life of religious experience. We might even observe that there is no great theologian in the Christian tradition of whom it can be said that theology was not the product of such experience. In this volume little is said about the experiential side of theology. But it informs much of what is discussed. I assume that religious experience can throw new light on old problems and even, at times, force us to re-think what we thought we knew about the Christian life. But all religious experience should be subordinate to the teaching of Scripture and tradition. Such experience is not normative, as Scripture is. And it is not embedded in Christian thinking like the tradition. Still, it offers valuable insights into the religious life that can be startling and deeply moving.

I say this in order to indicate the positive role experience may play in the formation of the theologian and even themes in the theology that he or she formulates. But in my view it would be a mistake to think that doctrine is merely the codification of religious experience. This view, often associated with Schleiermacher and the nineteenth century liberal theologians who found his thinking persuasive, offers an important insight into the relationship between experience and the formation of doctrine. That much is, I think, indisputable. But this is not equivalent to saying doctrine is derived solely through religious experience, nor that such religious experience may offer reason to revise the doctrine we hold. The Schleiermacherian might claim that doctrine is a means of codifying a religious experience of God for the benefit of the Christian community. And this might be consistent with a critically realist account of theology, where the object of theology (God) brings about such religious experiences which, when codified, approximate to a greater or lesser degree to the object of theology. Then, doctrine is revisable to the extent that it may be replaced with a better approximation to the truth of the matter, and new religious experiences of the right sort may bring about such doctrinal revision. There is much that is attractive about such a proposal. But such attraction is beguiling. Although all doctrine does rest upon religious experience in the final analysis (God *reveals* himself to some individual) this does not necessarily imply that present religious experience may overturn previous experience. For the experience of God codified in Scripture is normative in the way that my experience of God is not, because my experience is not divine revelation in the sense that Scripture is, or becomes, through the work of the Holy Spirit.

2. Method in Christology

Having sketched out some parameters for weighting authority in matters theological, we turn to some specific methodological issues for Christology.

2.1 On Christology from 'Above' and 'Below' and on 'High' and 'Low' Christology

There has been a lot of discussion in modern theology about how one should go about making Christological statements, and particularly, whether one or other method of doing so is to be preferred to another. In this literature, approaches to Christology are often carved up into 'high' and 'low', as well as speaking of 'Christology from above' and 'Christology from below'. Since it is important to be clear just what these words mean, we shall begin with some words of terminological clarification.[20]

I. HIGH CHRISTOLOGY

I take it that a 'high' Christology is a Christology according to which Christ is, minimally, *more than human*. More formally,

High Christology = df. A Christology according to which Christ is (minimally) more than human.[21]

Normally, and in light of Chalcedonian Christology, this is taken to mean Christ is fully but not merely, man – he is also fully divine.[22] This is 'high' in the relevant sense since it means that Christ is *more than* human, although he is also fully human.[23] But some 'high' Christologies might take the claim that Christ is more than human in a rather different direction, meaning by it that Christ is not human at all. His 'human nature' is a sort of facsimile, or similitude of real human nature that he 'wears' as a divine entity. Docetists are the paradigmatic example of this sort of Christology. The docetic Christology claims that Christ appears to be human, though he cannot be human, strictly speaking, because a divine being cannot have anything to do with matter, which would defile it. Assuming possession of a human nature normally includes

20.   Interested readers should consult Wolfhart Pannenberg *Jesus – God and Man* trans. Lewis L. Wilkins and Duane E. Priebe (London: SCM Press, 1968), particularly ch. 1. II, 33–37. According to Stanley Grenz, Pannenberg's later statement in *Systematic Theology Vol. II*, trans. Geoffrey W. Bromiley (Grand Rapids, MI: Eerdmans, 1994), ch. 9 §1 ends up abandoning the distinction between Christology 'from above' and 'from below' as unhelpful. (See Stanley J. Grenz *Reason for Hope, The Systematic Theology of Wolfhart Pannenberg, Second Edition* (Grand Rapids, MI: Eerdmans, 2005) p. 182.) Useful discussion is also to be found in Otto Weber *Foundations of Dogmatics, Vol. II*, trans. Darrell L. Guder (Grand Rapids, MI: Eerdmans, 1983), in which he attempts to get beyond the language of 'above' and 'below' in Christology. See especially, ch. 1, pp. 13–26.

21.   The notation '= df.', culled from contemporary analytical philosophy (and in particular, the work of Roderick Chisholm) means 'is equivalent to the following definition'. I shall use this several times in what follows.

22.   Here I borrow the terms 'fully' and 'merely' human as they occur in Thomas Morris' account of the Incarnation. See *The Logic of God Incarnate* (Ithaca, NY: Cornell University Press, 1986). Although these ideas can be found in catholic Christology, Morris's discussion offers a particularly clear way of making sense of this distinction between being 'merely' and 'fully' human.

23.   A modern theological statement of this view can be found in Adams, *Christ and Horrors*, p. 27. Compare Pannenberg, *Jesus – God and Man*, p. 34; Weber, *Foundation of Dogmatics, Vol. II*, pp. 13–14.

possession of a material human body,[24] Christ's 'body' cannot have been really corporeal, on pain of his being something less than divine. So, Christ's humanity is merely a simulacrum of true humanity. He appears to be human as the angels that met Abraham at Mamre in Gen. 18 appeared to be human, though they were not.[25]

Docetic Christology counts as a high Christology because it is one way of blocking a certain sort of theological reductionism of the person of Christ, where Christ was seen as *merely* human. Arianism might be thought to represent a different unorthodox high Christological trajectory, where Christ is something like a super-angelic being, the first creation of God. I suggest that the convention of regarding the phrase 'high Christology' as semantically equivalent to 'creedally orthodox Christology' is an unfortunate one, because it makes it difficult to place unorthodox Christologies like those offered by docetics and Arians. These are surely 'high' in the sense that they regard Christ as being more than human. (In the case of docetism he is only apparently human, of course.) And we could think of other Christologies that would fit with the definition offered here but which would not be orthodox, for example, that Christ is an incarnate angel, or that Christ is a kind of demi-god, or some other superhuman entity. These Christologies may not be 'high' in the sense of being creedally orthodox. But they are surely 'high' in the sense of regarding Christ as something more than a mere mortal. We might revise our theological vocabulary in light of this. Then 'high Christologies' might, like the definition offered above, include these unorthodox accounts of the person of Christ, with an additional category – 'highest Christology', perhaps – reserved for creedally orthodox Christology. But this is also tendentious, since I suppose those who are docetics might claim that, in one respect, orthodox Christology is not 'high' enough, because it allows that Christ is truly, though not merely, human. The docetic understanding of Christ is 'higher' than this because it denies that the divine can have anything to do with the material world, so Christ being truly divine can only be apparently corporeal. So it looks like in one important respect, orthodox Christology is not the 'highest' Christology one can conceive of. Nor, given the claims of docetic Christology, is it the 'highest' that has been conceived of in the history of Christian thought.

Of course the theologian is perfectly within her rights to respond by saying 'well, this is how *I* define "high Christology"' and proceed to the standard identification of high Christology with creedally orthodox Christology. But that does nothing to alleviate the fact that this is a merely a theological convention,

---

24.   *Pace* idealists like Bishop Berkeley and his modern day epigone, who deny that there is any such thing as a material object.

25.   At one stage (and in my view mistakenly), Jürgen Moltmann even goes as far as saying that as a consequence of adherence to an impassible God 'a mild docetism runs throughout the Christology of the ancient church'! *The Crucified God*, trans. R. A. Wilson and John Bowden (London: SCM Press, 1974), p. 89.

and a rather sloppy one at that. 'High Christology' does not have the semantic *denotation* 'creedally orthodox Christology' as should be obvious given the foregoing. All of which leads me to the conclusion that 'high Christology' is a rather unhelpful term. Though it has a wide currency, it is not semantically or materially equivalent to 'creedally orthodox Christology'. That said, the phrase 'high Christology', as I have defined it, is *consistent* with orthodoxy. The problem is, it is also semantically and (more importantly, perhaps) theologically porous enough to be used to refer to very different views, including docetism and Arianism. Accordingly, we might say that an orthodox Christology includes, but is conceptually richer than, a high Christology. And this does rather diminish the utility of the term for contemporary theology.

II. Low Christology

I take it that a 'low' Christology is, minimally, a Christology according to which Christ is thought to be only a man. He is not in any way superhuman, semi-divine or divine. Put more formally,

Low Christology = df. A Christology according to which Christ is (minimally) fully and merely human.

Unlike the discussion of high Christology, the conventional way in which 'low Christology' is identified with the idea that Christ is fully human is, it seems to me, substantially correct. The Christ of the gospels is clearly a human being – on this all parties to the debate can agree.[26] The theologically controversial issue is whether he is *merely* human. In this regard, our basic definition would need to be augmented in order to deliver a Christology of any theological substance. Interestingly, the rationale for a docetic Christology might also provide the means by which to motivate a low Christology: Christ cannot be divine because he was truly human and God cannot have anything to do with matter, which is inherently evil or otherwise such that God cannot be associated with it. Christ may be an extraordinary human being, but he is fully and merely human.

Similarly, one might accept a low Christology because one is convinced that if there is a God he cannot interfere with a created world that is a closed causal system, such as the one many physicists suppose we inhabit. Thus one might adopt a low Christology motivated by a latter-day version of the sort of concerns that drove eighteenth century deists to adopt the position they did. But in the contemporary academy there will also be those who think a low Christology is the right way to begin thinking about the person of Christ

---

26. Discounting those fanciful suggestions that Christ is an extra-terrestrial life form of some kind. For a literary example of this, see Patrick Tilley's quasi-science fiction novel, *Mission* (New York: Time Warner books 1998 [1981]).

because metaphysical naturalism is true: the only things that exist are material objects. There is, perhaps there can be, no immaterial entity like God. So we must begin our theologizing about Christ with the notion, consistent with this metaphysically naturalist background assumption, that Christ is merely human. As with our brief account of high Christology, I am only concerned here to offer some indications of how one might enrich a commitment to a low Christology (as defined above) so as to deliver the basis of a substantive Christological method. And as before, the sort of assumptions one brings to the theological table will be important in shaping the sort of Christological method one finds most amenable.

III. CHRISTOLOGY FROM ABOVE

Christology from above has an ancient and venerable theological pedigree, being a method that begins with the data of divine revelation, and/or of creedal and confessional symbols and works from that basis to particular dogmatic statements about the person of Christ. In this way, we might frame a definition of Christology from above thus,

> Christology from Above = df. any method in Christology that begins with the data of divine revelation contained in, or generated by Scripture and/or the propositions of the catholic creeds and confessional statements and uses these data to formulate Christological statements.

Such a method presumes what I have been calling a high view of Scripture.[27] It may also include the idea that the catholic creeds offer a norm by which doctrine should be judged. This is not the same as saying that Christology from above assumes *a priori* that Christ is the God-Man. Such an assumption would yield a more robust 'Christology from above' than that just outlined. But, on my way of thinking, the Christologist who adopts the method 'from above' need not be committed at the outset to the notion that Christ is the God-Man.[28] One need only be committed to the weaker claims concerning the high view of Scripture and/or the creeds, both of which as I have already indicated, I take to

27. See the comments made in the previous section of this chapter about what I presume a high view of Scripture to include. I take it that any theologian who thinks Scripture is or contains, or perhaps is witness to and through the action of the Holy Spirit becomes divine revelation, will be able to affirm a Christology from above in the sense I mean here.

28. If one is committed to the idea that Christ is God Incarnate at the outset, then one will begin theological reflection on the person of Christ with a correspondingly robust version of Christology from above. But if one is committed to the weaker claim that Christology from above begins with the data of revelation and the catholic creeds, then one might also have a Christology from above in the sense that one's Christology is formed by the data of divine revelation – it is, quite literally, formed on the basis of what is given 'from above'. But this need not include the additional claim about Christ being God Incarnate. That is the point I am striving to make clear here, and which is overlooked in much of the literature on this matter.

be norms by which we judge matters theological. On this way of thinking Scripture is a kind of norming norm under which stands all other theological authority in matters touching the formation of Christian doctrine. Although, as a matter of fact, by the time many Christologists come to consider the person of Christ they have already acquired the *a priori* assumption that Christ is the God-Man, it is not implausible to think that from consideration of Scripture and/or the creeds one might form the view that Christ is the God-Man, and proceed on that basis to formulate Christian doctrine. And I suppose this is just what many Christians have done, unless one is to believe that all Christians when confronted with Scripture or, say, the canons of the Council of Chalcedon, are already in possession of a clear, well-developed understanding of who Christ is, and all understand what it means to say that Christ is the God-Man, or the Second Person of the Trinity Incarnate, and so forth. But this seems monumentally implausible.[29]

IV. Christology from below

Conversely, 'Christology from below' begins with the data of history and what we can know of the person of Christ from the historical record alone. Such a method is a relative newcomer to the theological scene, having developed in large measure as a consequence of the rise of historical biblical criticism in the early Enlightenment.[30] Normally, this way of thinking presumes a certain methodological naturalism when it comes to historiography, in keeping with current canons by which much of history as an academic discipline is pursued. On this historical basis, dogmatic statements can be made. We might express this method as follows:

> Christology from Below = df. any method in Christology that begins with the data of historical documents that refer to Christ including the New Testament and other extra-biblical materials, and uses these data to formulate Christological statements.

Marilyn Adams thinks that Christology from below 'holds itself responsible to begin with history, or at any rate the New Testament record'.[31] But this

---

29. For this reason, it seems to me that Pannenberg's report that 'It is characteristic of all these attempts to build a "Christology from above" that the doctrine of the Trinity is presupposed and the question posed is: How has the Second Person of the Trinity (the Logos) assumed a human nature?' is simply overdone. For this is not characteristic of *all* Christians who would hold to a 'from above' method in Christology, even if it is characteristic of many theologians by the time they come to the task of serious reflection upon the person of Christ – which is usually after a prolonged period of study and thought. See Pannenberg, *Jesus – God and Man*, p. 34.

30. Useful discussion of the rise of historical biblical criticism can be found in Roy A. Harrisville and Walter Sundberg, *The Bible in Modern Culture: Baruch Spinoza to Brevard Childs, Second Edition* (Grand Rapids, MI: Eerdmans, 2002).

31. Adams, *Christ and Horrors*, p. 27.

seems a little too stringent. The theologian beginning 'from below' need not restrict herself to consideration of the New Testament record alone, though undeniably it is there that the vast majority of historical information about Christ must be gleaned. 'From below' theologians might think that any historical information about Christ is relevant to the task of determining who Christ is, to the extent that any historian can determine such things. It would be a poor historian that excludes certain sorts of data for ideological reasons at the outset of a particular historical inquiry. And the theologian beginning 'from below' might well think that it would be inappropriate to ignore evidence from extra-biblical sources in framing her picture of the historical Jesus. Indeed, the theologian working in this 'Christology from below' tradition might well think there are very good reasons to be suspicious of a picture of Christ formed entirely on the basis of the New Testament documents, since these documents all betray a particular theological assumption about the religious importance of the person and work of Christ that may affect the conclusion they reach about who Christ is. All the more reason to scour classical sources for extra-biblical references to Christ that might balance, or confirm, what is found in the New Testament.

So the 'from below' theologian might adopt Adams' stricture (if indeed Adams meant it as a stricture). This would still count as a 'from below' Christology. Such a theologian would work from what can be gleaned of the historical Jesus from the biblical material, to frame dogmatic statements about Christ. She or he may even assume that the biblical material has a particular claim upon Christian theologians because it has a particular normative status for Christian thought, even if she or he does not subscribe to a high view of Scripture. And, to parse matters more finely still, it is not inconceivable that some 'from below' Christologists do hold a high view of Scripture but think that we must begin with an inductive, historical method by which we may arrive at substantive theological conclusions about the person of Christ. What I am trying to show is that there are various shades of Christology 'from above' and 'from below', depending on the differing theological assumptions one brings along with the methodology one adopts.

That such differences exist under the terms 'Christology from above' and 'Christology from below' has led some theologians to the conclusion that these terms are deeply problematic. To take one well-known example, Nicholas Lash has this to say about the 'from below' method:

> [Christology from] 'below' refers, in different hands (and sometimes even in the same hands) to an exuberant profusion of different 'places'. Sometimes, 'below' seems to refer in very general terms to 'this world' (as distinct from God); sometimes to characteristically twentieth-century patterns of experience ('where we are'); some-times to supposedly 'primitive', as distinct from more fully articulated Christological statements; sometimes to the man Jesus and his human experience; sometimes to history, as distinct from dogma. The point I want to make is simply that these are

different recommendations. To lump them all together, under the general rubric 'begin from below', is an excellent recipe for confusion.[32]

Quite so. It might be thought that my attempt to give some definite scope to these terms offers merely a set of formal distinctions that do not bear much similarity to the sort of conceptual messiness that Lash's paper manages to capture so well. But it is my contention that the sort of confusion Lash thinks is perpetrated by those using these Christological terms in such different ways is at least in part due to the fact that there has not been sufficient attention paid to what is meant by a Christology that is 'high', 'low', 'from above' or 'from below.' When we attempt to pin down what these terms do mean it seems to me that they are much less substantive than has sometimes been thought. Or, perhaps it is that in order to capture as much of the contemporary usage of these terms as possible, one is left with a set of terms that are much less useful than is commonly thought.[33] But it is only when one begins to analyse these things that this becomes apparent.

To these formulations of the two methods in Christology, I would add two further caveats. First, note that these two broad Christological methods could easily be adapted to any particular theological topic. Those who adopt a Christology from above are usually also those who adopt a 'from above' method to doctrine generally, although this is not necessarily the case. And, as Marilyn Adams has recently shown, one can have a rather eclectic approach to matters Christological that does not easily fit with the standard means of differentiating methods in theology.[34] Second, and in amplification of the previous note on Lash's comments about Christology 'from below', note that the way I have framed these two methods in Christology is open-textured enough that one theologian could adopt elements of both in her approach to Christology. This is surely a strength rather than a weakness. As Lash, Adams and a number of other theologians have noted, it is folly to think one can have a method in modern theology that pays no attention to one or other of these two ways of approaching Christology.[35]

---

32. Nicholas Lash 'Up and Down in Christology' in Stephen Sykes and Derek Holmes eds *New Studies in Theology 1* (London: Duckworth, 1980) p. 33.

33. Compare Brian Hebblethwaite who writes that the distinction between Christology 'from above' and 'from below' is 'very confusing' and that the distinction between them is not 'clear cut' and has generated a number of problems for Christology. See his 'The Church and Christology' in *The Incarnation, Collected Essays in Christology* (Cambridge: Cambridge University Press, 1987) p. 80.

34. See Adams, *Christ and Horrors*, particularly chs 1, 3 and 6.

35. Thus Karl Barth, 'the New Testament obviously speaks of Jesus Christ in both these ways: the one looking and moving, as it were, from above downwards, the other from below upwards. . . . Both are necessary. Neither can stand or be understood without the other.' In Geoffrey W. Bromiley and Thomas F. Torrance eds *Church Dogmatics IV/1* (Edinburgh: T&T Clark, 1956) p. 135.

2.2 *Discussion of Methodological Terminology*

The terms just discussed are still in common usage, despite the fact that they have been subject to the verbal stripes of theologians like Lash.[36] The problem with such language, as Lash points out, is that it is simply not specific enough, and can be used on different occasions to refer to different things, or different aspects of Christology.[37] What is more, it is not clear that 'high' Christology is synonymous with 'Christology from above', nor 'low' Christology with 'Christology from below.'

For instance, if a Christology from above is roughly a method that begins with the data of revelation and the catholic creeds and moves from these 'givens' to postulating various things about the person and work of Christ, then the earliest Christians did not have a Christology 'from above' in this sense. They had the testimony of those who had been with Christ, and collections of sayings and stories in circulation, whether orally or in some written form. In other words, they had testimony of some kind, upon which they based their faith in Christ. And it would appear that this testimony included *bona fide* metaphysical claims about who Christ was (rather than being merely the record of some religious experience that might be overturned by further theological reflection). But the testimony was not, at that stage, ecclesiastical dogma nor was it recognized by all to be what theologians today would call 'divine revelation'. Plainly, the earliest Christians simply did not have the conceptual apparatus necessary to make such distinctions because it had yet to be developed in the fires of Christological controversy. Such complex dogmatic equipment is the product of centuries of reflection on the *kerygma* of the Gospel. But there might still be good reason for thinking that many, if not all, the earliest Christians held to a very high Christology – even, perhaps, a Christology according to which Christ was included in the identity of God himself, as has been claimed in recent times by Richard Bauckham and Larry Hurtado, amongst others.[38] But even if we are not favourably disposed to this sort of Early High Christology, it seems plausible to think that from fairly early on in the life of the Church there were Christians moving towards what we would now call a 'high' Christology, even if that Christology was not as dogmatically sophisticated as the main tenets of later orthodox high Christology.

---

36.   To give just two recent examples, see Geoffrey Grogan's essay 'Christology from Below and from Above' in Mark Elliott and John L. McPake eds *Jesus, The Only Hope: Jesus, Yesterday, Today, Forever*. (Fearn: Christian Focus and Edinburgh: Rutherford House, 2001) pp. 59–76 and Colin Gunton, *Yesterday and Today, A Study of Continuities in Christology* (London: Darton, Longman and Todd, 1983), passim.

37.   Lash, 'Up and Down in Christology', pp. 43–44.

38.   See, for example, Richard Bauckham, *God Crucified, Monotheism and Christology in the New Testament* (Grand Rapids, MI: Eerdmans, 1999), and Larry Hurtado, *Lord Jesus Christ, Devotion to Jesus in Earliest Christianity* (Grand Rapids, MI: Eerdmans, 2003). I have discussed the contribution of these so-called Early High Christologists in *Divinity and Humanity*, ch. 6.

That is, early Christians might have had a high view of the person of Christ from the earliest times, although they did not have a 'high Christology' in the technical sense of that phrase.

But saying this makes clear that there is a problem with the term 'high' Christology, just as there is a problem with the corresponding term 'low' Christology. Some Christologists will think that it was precisely a high Christology that led a theologian like Apollinaris to think that the Word of God must assume a human body, taking the place of a human soul. Yet such 'high' Christology is hardly orthodox. Similarly, as we have already had cause to note, it seems reasonable to think that Arius had a high Christology in the sense that he thought Christ could not have been a mere man: something about Jesus of Nazareth meant he must be more than merely human, even if that 'something' did not mean (*could* not mean) Christ was God. Yet the Church anathematized Arius' Christology. Anyone who doubts that Arius had a *high* Christology should read the comments of some contemporary historical biblical critics, like John Dominic Crossan.[39] They will soon find that Arius had a much 'higher' regard for the person of Christ (doctrinally speaking) than someone like Crossan does, even if it was not, at the end of the day, an entirely orthodox high Christology.

So it seems that a high Christology can mean different things. Or at least, the sort of theological sensibility that means a particular theologian begins with the idea that Christ is not a mere man, but is something more – something 'divine' (taken in its broadest sense) – will mean that such a theologian will end up making claims about the person of Christ that are 'high' in the relevant sense. But not all such 'high' Christologies are theologically orthodox.

It is difficult to see how a Christology from above could yield something less than a high Christology (in the sense I am using the term). Could one begin with the data of Scripture and the catholic symbols and end up with a low Christology? I am unclear how this might work in practical terms without some obviously perverse theological gerrymandering, though the 'creativity' of theologians when it comes to such matters should not be underestimated. Still, even if the Christologist who has adopted a Christology from above normally ends up with a high Christology, what I have said indicates that the upshot of such theological reasoning need not be dogmatically acceptable, or orthodox, as the examples of Apollinaris or Arius demonstrate.

And just as earlier in this chapter I intimated that one could have a high view of Scripture and yet end up with a distorted picture of Christ (or other central dogmas of the faith) so one could begin with a Christology from below and yet end up with a surprisingly 'high' Christology – as the Apostles undoubtedly did. They encountered the peasant prophet Jesus of Nazareth, were drawn to

---

39. See, for example, John Dominic Crossan's distillation of much of his earlier scholarship in *Jesus: A Revolutionary Biography* (New York: Harper One, 1995).

him, associated with him, followed him, and eventually, through a series of dramatic and sometimes difficult experiences (including, one presumes, being the recipients of divine revelation) came to view him as much more than another human being. So the distinction between high and low Christology on the one hand, and Christology from above and below on the other are not such that Christology from above entails a high Christology (at least, not a high Christology that is also orthodox), nor that a Christology from below entails a low Christology.

3. *Concluding Thoughts*

But, after all that, which method should the Christologist adopt? Here I am in agreement with Marilyn Adams' general proposal (though not everything about the position she ends up with), that

> any reader of the Bible makes tacit philosophical assumptions, insofar as hermeneutics belongs to the subject matter of philosophy. The implicit philosophical commitments of most theologians go much further. My own contention is that the intellectual quality of theology would improve if theologians made these philosophical assumptions explicit, the better to expose them to discussion and critique . . . [once again taking] responsibility for the philosophical adequacy of their proposals.[40]

The theologian must take seriously the voice of Scripture. She should also take seriously the voice of the tradition, and other theological resources such as those outlined in the first section of this chapter. But theology must also be conscious of the philosophical permutations of a given theological position and make these plain. My own predilection is for a Christology 'from above' that is 'high' in the sense of presuming that Christ is the God-Man (i.e., the conventional sense of this term), whilst taking seriously the results of historical biblical criticism. But to my mind theological tradition must be used to 'control' the theological claims often made on the basis of such historical criticism. Christology that is merely 'from below', which takes the evidence at face value and goes where it leads is as practically impossible for the theologian as it is for the skilled biblical critic.[41] To claim that this is the place from which the 'from below' Christologist begins is nothing short of being intellectually fraudulent. Moreover, and taking my cue from Adams, I think that theology that makes clear the philosophical assumptions with which it is working is better for that. In my view Christology should begin with divine revelation and the catholic creeds. This should yield a 'high' Christology. It should also yield an orthodox Christology – attention to the tradition will

---

40.　Adams, *Christ and Horrors*, p. 25. In this connection, she also advises that 'The attempt to "seal off" theological discourse from the influence of other disciplines flirts with anti-realism.'

41.　As I have tried to intimate elsewhere. See *Divinity and Humanity*, ch. 6.

certainly help in this regard. An *analytic* Christology may take this direction, using the tools of analytical philosophy to make sense of doctrinal claims about Christ in the light of Scripture and the tradition. It is just such an analytical Christology that I will seek to develop in the following chapters. Though the emphasis will be on dogmatic questions and their systematic development, this should not be taken to mean that doctrinal theology takes precedence over biblical theology. The one ought to be informed by the other, in the 'hermeneutical circle'. Systematic theology without biblical theology is surely short-sighted, if not blind. But biblical theology without systematic theology is deaf to the pressing need to give a coherent sense of the whole gospel, once delivered to the saints. Only a theology that engages Scripture and the tradition can see and hear in order to *proclaim* the truth about Christ. For if Christology is not at root about the *euangelion*, if it does not attend to the voice of Scripture and the tradition, then in the spirit of David Hume we should commit it to the flames – for it can contain nothing but sophistry and illusion.

Chapter 2

THE ELECTION OF JESUS CHRIST

[W]e have laid down and developed two statements concerning the election of Jesus Christ. The first is that Jesus Christ is the electing God. This statement answers the question of the Subject of the eternal election of grace. And the second is that Jesus Christ is elected man . . .. Strictly speaking, the whole dogma of predestination is contained in these two statements.

Karl Barth, Church Dogmatics II/2[1]

When in the first two chapters of the Epistle to the Ephesians the Apostle tells us that God has elected 'us in Him before the foundation of the world, that we should be holy and without blame before Him in love, having predestined us to adoption as sons by Jesus Christ according to Himself, according to the good pleasure of His will' or that 'In Him we have redemption through his blood' and that 'now in Christ Jesus' we who were 'far off have been brought near' – does he imply that Christ is the *cause* and *foundation* of election? This is an important theological question that has received a number of different answers in the tradition. Perhaps the most celebrated modern treatment of this issue stems from Karl Barth's discussion of the election of Christ in his *CD* II/2. But there was a lively discussion of this matter in the Post-Reformation period too, and a greater variety of views expressed than is often reported in contemporary discussion of this matter. In keeping with one of the themes of the book, this chapter is an attempt at theological retrieval for the purposes of contemporary doctrinal resourcement. That is, in this chapter I shall be concerned to use the discussion of this matter in the Post-Reformation period, particularly, the Reformed Orthodox theology, to set forth an account of Christ's election which is within the bounds of this confessional tradition, whilst at the same time offering a creative interpretation of Christ's election which owes something to the discussion of this matter by Barth.

The argument falls into four parts. The first, a kind of historical prolegomena, offers some comments on the election of Christ as it has been discussed in Reformed theology, particularly historic Reformed symbols, since they have a

---

1. Karl Barth, *Church Dogmatics II/2*, eds G. W. Bromiley and T. F. Torrance (Edinburgh: T&T Clark, 1957) p. 145. Hereinafter cited as *CD* II/2, followed by page number.

dogmatic status the works of particular theologians do not enjoy. This historical material is important because it establishes that the doctrine of Christ's election – indeed, the doctrine of election *per se* – was not a matter that all Reformed theologians in the post-Reformation period agreed upon. In the second section, we shall set out some of the objections to the idea that Christ is the ground of election, given by Francis Turretin, one of the chief protagonists amongst the Reformed Orthodox[2] for an account of Christ's election often, and mistakenly, identified with Reformed theology *per se*, over and against supposedly 'deviant' forms of Reformed thought in this period, particularly (though not exclusively) that of the theologians at the Academy of Saumur in France. In a third section I shall set out an argument for the conclusion that Christ is the ground of election in one important, though qualified sense. This is not a departure from Reformed theology, but an attempt to parse one of the strands of Reformed thinking on this matter more finely. In the process I hope to offer an olive branch to those who might be more sympathetic to something like the Salmurian view of this matter rather than the view of those Reformed divines who followed Turretin. I also hope that my argument might be of interest to contemporary disciples of Barth's doctrine for reasons that will become clear as the argument unfolds. In a final section I offer some considerations about the relationship between a 'Barthian' account of the election of Christ and this revised view of Christ's election, as a means of indicating the contemporary theological utility of this revised view.

1. *The Election of Christ in Reformed Thought*

This chapter is not primarily a piece of historical theology. Yet it engages the doctrine of Christ's election in dialogue with several prominent thinkers in the Reformed tradition. For this reason, it is worth beginning by clearing away a misconception, still found in works of theology, that there is only one doctrine of election in the Reformed tradition, and only one way of thinking about the relationship between Christ and the doctrine of election that can be properly designated '*the* Reformed position'. To take one prominent example, the Dutch theologian Gerrit Berkouwer speaks of 'the concern of the Reformed view' of the relation between the doctrine of election and Christ, which is 'that Christ

---

2.   In contemporary historical–theological literature on the subject, the term 'Reformed Orthodox' denotes a certain strand of Reformed theology in the Post-Reformation period that utilized the school method of medieval theology. It does not imply any more substantive, doctrinal claims about those who practiced such scholastic theology. I will distinguish between the Reformed Orthodox who followed Turretin and the Salmurians. But this is just a convenient way of distinguishing Turretin and those who took a view similar to him on the matter of Christ's election from the Salmurians. It does not imply that the Salmurians were not scholastic theologians, in the non-pejorative sense of that term.

should not be called the "foundation" and the "cause" of election as if divine election were motivated by Christ's act'.[3] This notion can be found in the work of a number of post-Reformation Reformed divines. Jerome Zanchius puts it succinctly:

> Here let it be carefully observed that not the merits of Christ, but the sovereign love of God only is the cause of election itself, but then the merits of Christ are the alone [sic] procuring cause of that salvation to which men are elected. This decree of God admits of no cause out of Himself.[4]

The central concern of this position is that the sole cause of election is the will and good pleasure of God. Christ's work is merely the means by which this election is brought about. It is not a causal factor motivating the decree of election. Let us call this the *Conservative Reformed Position* or CRP for short.

As recent work on post-Reformation theology has demonstrated, the CRP is only one of several understandings of election, including the election of Christ, to be found in the post-Reformation Reformed tradition, not all of which are commensurate one with another.[5] For instance, the Salmurian theologians

---

3.   G. C. Berkouwer, *Divine Election* trans. Hugo Bekker (Grand Rapids, MI: Eerdmans, 1960) p. 135. Compare Katherine Sonderegger's recent claim that 'the Reformed doctrine of the absolute decree' says that

> Jesus Christ is neither object nor foundation of election nor necessary to the divine internal decree – but rather the instrument or means by which election is carried out. In this light the details of Christ's earthly ministry and passion begin to do explicit work in the doctrine of election. . . . all these [aspects of Christ's work] are the means used by the Son of God to redeem the elect. (Katherine Sonderegger, 'Election' in John Webster, Kathryn Tanner and Iain Torrance eds *The Oxford Handbook of Systematic Theology* (Oxford: Oxford University Press, 2007) p. 114).

An older example of this sort of position can be found in Lorraine Boettner's treatment of election in *The Reformed Doctrine of Predestination* (Philadelphia, PA: Presbyterian and Reformed, 1963), which simply assumes without argument that there is only one properly Reformed doctrine of election. See especially ch. XI.

4.   Jerome Zanchius, *Absolute Predestination* (Evansville, IN: Sovereign Grace Book Club, n. d.) p. 77. There is some dispute about the provenance of this work and its English translation by Augustus Toplady in the eighteenth century. But that this is Zanchius' considered view is established from his other works too.

5.   In an important recent study of this period, G. Michael Thomas has argued that there are three distinct views about how Christ is related to the doctrine of election amongst the Reformed. There are those who subordinate Christ to election; those who subordinate election to Christ; and those (including Calvin) who do not clearly or consistently opt for either of these schemes. See G. Michael Thomas, *The Extent of the Atonement, A Dilemma for Reformed Theology from Calvin to the Consensus (1536–1675)* (Milton Keynes: Paternoster, 1997) passim. See especially the summary on pp. 250–251. See also Stephen Strehle, 'The Extent of the Atonement and The Synod of Dort' in *Westminster Theological Journal* 51(1989): 1–23; Richard A. Muller, *Christ and the Decree, Christology and Predestination in Reformed Theology from Calvin to Perkins* (Durham, NC: Labyrinth Press, 1986) and Jonathan D. Moore, *English Hypothetical Universalism: John Preston and the Softening of Reformed Theology* (Grand Rapids, MI: Eerdmans, 2007).

following the lead of the Scottish theologian John Cameron and his French disciple Moyse Amyraut regarded the election of Christ as part of the grounds of the election of humanity, rather than merely a consequence of the divine decree to elect a particular number of Adam's fallen race. And other theologians in the Reformed tradition took up positions remarkably like that of the Salmurians, including a number of theologians who were amongst the Reformed delegates at the Synod of Dort, which sought to define Reformed thinking on election against the Remonstrants.[6] When one reads works of theology concerned with this period, this difference of opinion amongst the Reformed becomes apparent, even when it is played down (as we shall see when considering what Francis Turretin has to say on this matter presently).

It is also worth noting that the confessional symbols of the Reformed tradition written during the late sixteenth and seventeenth centuries do not appear to speak with one voice concerning the election of Christ. Thus, for instance, Article 16 of the *Belgic Confession* of 1561 states that God 'delivers and preserves from . . . perdition all whom he in his eternal and unchangeable counsel of mere goodness hath elected in Christ Jesus our Lord, without any respect to their works'.[7] This echoes the words of St Paul in Ephesians, but is ambiguous as a statement about the election of Christ. For it is consistent with a Salmurian as well as a more CRP-like rendering of the doctrine, namely, Christ's work being the foundation of election in some sense, or, alternatively, Christ's work being merely a consequence of the divine decree to elect.

Similarly, Chapter Ten of the *Second Helvetic Confession* (1566), entitled 'Of the Predestination of God and the election of the saints' says, 'Therefore, although not on account of any merit of ours, God has elected us, not directly,

---

6. Amongst the British delegation to Dort, John Davenant (1572–1641), Lady Margaret Professor of Divinity in Cambridge and later Bishop of Salisbury espoused a view of Christ's election that bears certain close similarities to the Salmurian position. And amongst the delegation from Bremen, Matthias Martinius (1572–1630), sometime professor and pastor at Herborn and then Professor at Bremen from 1610 until his death held to the notion that Christ is the meritorious cause of the election of individual fallen human beings, allying himself with the idea that Christ died for all, and yet that his death is effectual only for an elect. Martinius' views caused not a little acrimony at the Synod of Dort, but he was not regarded as beyond the bounds of Reformed orthodoxy. Thomas has a useful discussion of this in *The Extent of the Atonement*, ch. 7, and Moore's treatment of Davenant is very interesting in *English Hypothetical Universalism*, ch. 7. See also Richard Muller, *Post-Reformation Reformed Dogmatics Vol. 1* (Grand Rapids, MI: Baker Academic, 2003) pp. 76–77. Richard Baxter's soteriology is another well-known example of an English 'Amyraldian' whose thinking was tolerated within the confessionalism of Reformed thinking. It is also worth pointing out that the Salmurians thought of their own theological 'innovations' as well within the bounds of the Canons of Dort, and that they were not condemned for departing from the letter of Dort by any official ecclesiastical body amongst the Reformed. See Stephen Strehle's paper 'Universal Grace and Amyraldianism' in *Westminster Theological Journal* 51 (1989): 345–357, especially pp. 349–350.

7. From Philip Schaff, ed. *The Creeds of Christendom, With a History and Critical Notes, Vol. III, The Evangelical Protestant Creeds, Sixth Edition* (Grand Rapids, MI: Baker, 1983 [1931]) p. 401.

but in Christ, and on account of Christ, in order that those who are now engrafted into Christ by faith might also be elected.'[8] Once again, at face value this appears commensurate with the claim that election depends in some important and substantive sense upon Christ's merit, not merely on Christ being the means by which election is effected – which is what the Salmurians, amongst others, maintained. For if election is 'in' and 'through' Christ, then this could be construed to mean the cause of election is the work of Christ or the foreseen merit generated by the work of Christ. Then, the Father ordains the election of some number of fallen humanity *because* the foreseen work of Christ merits the election of this number of human beings. In this way, some number of fallen humans is elected 'in' or 'through' Christ. This is not the only construal of the election of Christ consistent with the Confession. But it appears to correspond with what the Confession states, and appears to be rather different from what is allegedly '*the* Reformed view', espoused by theologians adopting the CRP.

Yet when compared with Article 7 of the first *locus* of doctrine on election, in the Canons of the *Synod of Dort* (1619) – the only truly 'ecumenical' Reformed symbol [9] – we read as follows:

> Election is the unchangeable purpose of God, whereby, before the foundation of the world, he hath, out of mere grace, according to the sovereign good pleasure of his own will, chosen, from the whole human race, which had fallen through their own fault, from their primitive state of rectitude, into sin and destruction, a certain number of persons to redemption in Christ, whom He from eternity appointed the Mediator and Head of the elect, and the foundation of salvation.[10]

This sounds much more like the CRP, and is amplified elsewhere. Thus, Article 10 of the first locus tells us that, 'the good pleasure of God is *the sole cause of this gracious election*'.[11]

The language of Dort is very similar to that of the *Westminster Confession* III. V, written almost thirty years later in 1647:

> Those of mankind that are predestined unto life, God, before the foundation of the world was laid, according to his eternal and immutable purpose, and the secret counsel

---

8.   Ibid., p. 252. The Latin text given in Schaff reads 'Ergo non sine medio, licet non propter ullum meritum nostrum, *sed in Christo et propter Christum*, nos elegit Deus, ut qui jam sunt in Christo insiti per fidem, illi ipsi etiam sint electi'. (Emphasis added.)

9.   The Synod of Dort was ecumenical in the sense that it was composed of representatives from a number of Reformed communions in different European countries, present as official delegates. The Arminians did not remain at the synod, because they were not permitted to participate as full delegates – despite the fact that their views were the subject of much of the discussion!

10.   Schaff, *Creeds of Christendom, Vol. III*, 582. Cf. 553 for the Latin original.

11.   Ibid., p. 583, emphasis added. The Latin reads, 'Causa vero hujus gratuitae electionis, est solum Dei beneplacitum', p. 555.

and good pleasure of his will, hath chosen in Christ, unto everlasting glory, out of his mere free grace and love, without any foresight of faith or good works, or perseverance in either of them, or any other thing in the creature, as conditions, or causes moving him thereunto; and all to the praise of his glorious grace.[12]

Here again the apostolic phrase 'chosen in Christ', culled from the opening chapters of Ephesians, might be more naturally construed to mean Christ is merely the means by which the election of some number of fallen humanity is brought about. It is not that Christ, or his work, is some meritorious ground of election, that enables or otherwise facilitates the election of the particular number of fallen humanity God does elect. Like Dort, the Westminster Confession states quite clearly that God's decree to elect depends on 'his mere free grace and love', and the 'secret counsel and good pleasure of his will'. And this seems to be the only grounds for election. So, it would appear that both the Canons of Dort and the Westminster Confession reflect the view that the foundation and ground of election is a matter entirely distinct from the election of Christ, which places it alongside the views of Zanchius and those who follow his lead in adopting the CRP.

It is the *Formula Consensus Helvetica* of 1675 that spells out what I am calling the Conservative Reformed Position on the relationship of Christ to election over and against the Salmurian position, and the views of Reformed theologians more sympathetic to a Saumur-like theology.[13] The reason for this is not hard to find: the framers of the Formula, particularly John Henry Heidegger of Zurich and Francis Turretin, were opposed to the Salmurian theology, and sought, in this statement, to distance their views from those espoused by the Salmurian faculty. This, it should be noted, constitutes an inter-nicene dispute amongst Reformed theologians of the post-Reformation period. It is not evidence for the orthodoxy of Turretin and Heidegger and the heterodoxy of the Salmurians.[14] Several of the canons of the Formula are relevant to our purposes. To begin with, Canon IV states the apostolic doctrine:

Before the creation of the world, God decreed in Christ Jesus our Lord according to his eternal purpose (Eph. 3.11), in which, from the mere good pleasure of his own will, without any prevision of the merit of works or of faith, to the praise of his glorious grace, to elect some out of the human race[.]

12. Schaff, *Creeds of Christendom, Vol. III*, p. 609.
13. Cf. Schaff, *Creeds of Christendom, Vol. I*, p. 478.
14. As already mentioned, the notion that the Salmurian theology represents a deviant, even heretical, Calvinism is a popular misconception. Richard Muller's work has been particularly important in correcting this misinterpretation in the recent literature, although one can find similar sentiments in nineteenth-century studies of Reformed symbols, for example, Schaff, *Creeds of Christendom, Vol. I*, p. 483. Jonathan Moore's recent treatment of Preston's thought in *English Hypothetical Universalism* takes this discussion a step further by demonstrating that there is a distinction between hypothetical universalism and Amyraldianism. There were hypothetical

Canon V spells out the anti-Salmurian construal of this apostolic statement:

> Christ himself is also included in the gracious decree of divine election, not as the meritorious cause, or foundation prior to election itself, but as being himself also elect (1Pet. 2.4, 6). Indeed, he was foreknown before the foundation of the world, and accordingly, as the first requisite of the execution of the decree of election, chosen Mediator, and our first born Brother, whose precious merit God determined to use for the purpose of conferring, without detriment to his own justice, salvation upon us. For the Holy Scriptures not only declare that election was made according to the mere good pleasure of the divine counsel and will (Eph. 1.5, 9; Mt. 11.26), but was also made that the appointment and giving of Christ, our Mediator, was to proceed from the zealous love of God the Father toward the world of the elect.

Finally, in a lengthy paragraph, Canon VI drives the message home:

> Wherefore, we can not agree with the opinion of those [i.e., the Salmurian theologians] who teach: 1) that God, moved by philanthropy, or a kind of special love for the fallen of the human race, did, in a kind of conditioned willing, first moving of pity, as they call it, or inefficacious desire, determine the salvation of all, conditionally, i.e., if they would believe, 2) that he appointed Christ Mediator for all and each of the fallen; and 3) that, at length, certain ones whom he regarded, not simply as sinners in the first Adam, but as redeemed in the second Adam, he elected, that is, he determined graciously to bestow on these, in time, the saving gift of faith; and in this sole act election properly so called is complete. For these and all other similar teachings are in no way insignificant deviations from the proper teaching concerning divine election; because the Scriptures do not extend unto all and each God's purpose of showing mercy to man, but restrict it to the elect alone, the reprobate being excluded even by name, as Esau, whom God hated with an eternal hatred (Rom. 9.11). The same Holy Scriptures testify that the counsel and will of God do not change, but stand immovable, and God in the, heavens does whatsoever he will (Ps. 115.3; Isa. 47.10); for God is infinitely removed from all that human imperfection which characterizes inefficacious affections and desires, rashness repentance and change of purpose. The appointment, also, of Christ, as Mediator, equally with the salvation of those who were given to him for a possession and an inheritance that can not be taken away, proceeds from one and the same election, and does not form the basis of election.[15]

---

unversalists prior to the rise of Salmurian theology, amongst prominent English and Irish divines, like Preston, Davenant and Bishop James Ussher – some of whom did not embrace all the tenets of the later Salmurian position. It appears that there was more doctrinal pluralism tolerated (within certain circumscribed limits) in Post-Reformation Reformed theology regarding the scope of the atonement and the issue of election than has hitherto been acknowledged. The standard work on Amyraldian theology is still Brian G. Armstrong's *Calvinism and The Amyraut Heresy, Protestant Scholasticism and Humanism in Seventeenth-Century France* (Milwaukee, WI: University of Wisconsin Press, 1969), despite the criticisms of it raised by recent revisionist work by Muller and others.

15. The version of the *Formula Consensus Helvetica* used here is taken from the translated by Martin I. Klauber in *Trinity Journal* 11 (1990): 103–123.

It is interesting that neither the Belgic Confession nor the Helvetic Confession offer a view that is unambiguously that identified by advocates of the CRP as *the* orthodox Reformed position on the relationship between the doctrine of election and Christ. That said, what these symbols state is not necessarily inconsistent with the CRP either. The later Reformed confessions offer views more in keeping with the CRP in large part because of the disputes *within* Reformed theology that had generated the differences of opinion on this doctrine in the first place – disputes having to do, at least in part, with the rise and influence of the controversial ideas espoused by the Salmurian theologians. Yet even the *Formula Consensus Helvetica* does not anathematize those who take the Salmurian position on the election of Christ, preferring, in Canon VI, to speak of those 'opinions', that is, *theologoumena*, with which the framers of the Formula cannot agree.[16]

So, there does appear to be evidence that suggests the post-Reformation Reformed community did not speak with one voice on the matter of the election of Christ (or of election *per se*). However, it is also clear that as this discussion developed, a number of influential theologians and confessional statements distanced themselves from the idea that Christ's election might somehow be the cause and foundation of the election of some fraction of the mass of humanity. The Genevan Francis Turretin is an interesting case of an influential theologian and someone involved in drawing up one of the symbols just canvassed. In his magisterial *Institutes of Elenctic Theology*,[17] he offers a robust critique of the notion that Christ's merit is the ground (i.e., cause and foundation) of election. We turn to these next, in order to ascertain why the idea that Christ's election is the cause and foundation of the election of humanity might be thought theologically objectionable.

2. Turretin's Objection to Christ as Cause and Foundation of Election

In his *Institutes,* Turretin is clear that Christ is a necessary condition for bringing about the election of some number of fallen human beings. He agrees that Christ is the 'primary means of its execution' and even says that salvation is brought about by his merit. He observes, 'God, who decreed salvation to us, by the same act destined Christ, the Mediator, to acquire it for us.' The central

---

16.   It is clear from Turretin's *Institutes of Elenctic Theology, 3 Vols.,* trans. George Musgrave Giger, ed. James T. Dennison, Jr (Philipsburg, NJ: Presbyterian and Reformed, 1992–1997) that he does not think of the Salmurians as beyond the bounds of orthodoxy, preferring instead to speak of them (often anonymously and with respect) as part of the Reformed fold who hold views that differ from his own.

17.   Francis Turretin, *Institutes.* All references are to this translation of Turretin's work, cited in the body of the text as 'Inst.' Followed by the Topic number, Question number, and page reference in the Giger translation, e.g. 'Inst. IV. X. 351'.

problem about the ground or reason for election, as he sees it, has to do with
whether Christ entered 'into the decree antecedently as the impulsive and meritorious cause, on account of which it was destined to us?' And this is precisely
the question we are concerned with. He puts it like this:

> Was Christ the foundation and meritorious cause, not of salvation *a posteriori*, but
> of election *a priori*; not on the part of the effect in man, but of the act of willing in
> God? Was the decree absolute, not as to the means, but as to the antecedent cause?
> This we deny; the adversaries [i.e. Arminians, Lutherans and 'papists'] affirm.
> (*Inst.* IV. X. 351)

From the foregoing discussion, it should be clear that Turretin has in mind
those who claim that Christ's foreseen merit is the ground of predestination,
rather than God electing some number of fallen human beings according to
his secret will and good pleasure alone, providing the means of that salvation
through the merits of Christ. The reasoning is something like this (where
'election' is shorthand for 'the divine election of some particular number of
fallen humanity to eternal life'):

1. Either Christ is the ground (i.e., reason, basis) of election or he is not.
2. If he is the ground of election, he is the reason for election; he is the 'cause
   and foundation' of election, as Turretin puts it.
3. If he is the reason for election (i.e., its 'cause and foundation'), God elects
   some number of fallen humanity on account of some foreseen merit of
   Christ, that is, some meritorious action Christ will bring about.

The merit in question is, of course, the work of Christ. Here the assumption
is that Christ's work constitutes a merit that is of sufficient value to bring about
the election of some number of fallen humanity. This in turn, depends upon a
basically Anselmian insight: Christ, being the perfect God-Man, does not need
to merit salvation; and he is not required to perform the act of atonement he
does. Yet his voluntary work of incarnation and atonement generates a merit of
infinite worth, since it is a work of *God* Incarnate. The merit generated by this
supererogatory act may be used for the salvation of some number of fallen
humanity in order to off-set the demerit of original sin possessed by such
humans, thereby bringing about reconciliation with the Father. And it is this
work of Christ that is in view. His meritorious work is the foundation of election, causing some number of fallen humanity to be saved according to the
divine decree. (Whether the merits of Christ are a sufficient cause of this
election is another matter, and one which some of Turretin's opponents would
have contested. For Arminians, Christ's merit is not sufficient for salvation
because human beings must appropriate Christ's benefits by an act of their
own libertarian free will, and the state of grace that this confers upon the

believer is contingent upon the believer's perseverance in faith. But we can leave this to one side for present purposes.) Next:

4. This foreseen merit is a necessary condition of election, but not necessarily a sufficient condition.

For instance, it might be that the combination of the divine decree to elect and Christ's foreseen merit are both necessary, and only conjointly sufficient for election, a matter to which we shall return. But, at any rate, what is important for present purposes is that on this way of thinking the foreseen merit of Christ is a necessary condition for election. There can be no election without this foreseen merit being factored into the economy of the divine decrees. To return to the main reasoning:

5. This foreseen merit is the work of Christ in Incarnation and Atonement.
6. But Scripture teaches that the ground of election is 'the good pleasure of [God's] will' (Eph. 1.5).
7. So, the foreseen merit of Christ cannot be the ground of election.

As Turretin sees things, the right ordering of the divine decrees with respect to election is like this:

8. If Christ is neither the ground of election, nor one of several grounds of election, there is some other ground of election.
9. The ground of election given in Scripture is the good pleasure of God's will.
10. This is a necessary and sufficient ground of election.
11. The merit of Christ is the primary means by which election is executed, but this means is dependent upon the logically prior decree of election according to the good pleasure of God alone.

Now, it might be thought that Turretin's objection boils down to a dispute between those in the Reformed tradition who stood with the Orthodox in the post-Reformation period, and those who aligned themselves with the Remonstrants, that is, the followers of James Arminius.[18] But, as should be apparent from the first section of this chapter, matters are hardly that straightforward. Quite apart from the fact that the Reformed confessions do not appear to speak with one voice on this matter, there are other ecclesial communities

---

18. For an interesting recent account of Arminius' doctrine of the election of Christ, see F. Stuart Clarke *The Ground of Election, Jacobus Arminius' Doctrine of the Work and Person of Christ* (Milton Keynes: Paternoster, 2006) particularly, pp. 134–135.

that think Christ's merit is the ground of election. For instance, Lutherans have traditionally thought that Christ's foreseen work is a meritorious cause of election, as the *Formula of Concord* makes clear when it rejects the idea that 'the mercy of God and the most holy merit of Christ is not the sole cause of the divine election'.[19] In a similar fashion, the twentieth-century Lutheran theologian Francis Pieper maintains that 'the merit of Christ . . . [is] part and parcel of the eternal act of choosing itself' along with the sanctification of the Holy Spirit and the bestowal of faith, 'and do[es] not merely, as the Calvinists teach, enter into the execution of the decree of election'.[20]

But, as we have already established, it is the Salmurians, and those amongst the Reformed whose theological sympathies lay with Salmurian theology on this matter, that most troubled Turretin because they remained within the Reformed fold whilst holding to views on the cause of election not dissimilar in certain important respects to that of the Arminians, Lutherans and Roman Catholics. As Turretin concedes, 'with them [i.e., with the Arminians, Lutherans and Roman Catholics] some of our divines who defend universal grace also agree'. Although there were Reformed divines other than card-carrying Salmurians that this could include (Martinius, Davenant) it certainly does include them. Later in his response to the same topic, Turretin elaborates on this point as follows:

> Although by some orthodox theologians, the election of Christ is maintained to be prior to the election of men, they are not therefore to be considered as favouring the innovators [i.e., the Arminians, et. al.]. First, because this is so understood by them as to be a priority only of order, not of causality (as the Arminians hold). Again, the election of Christ as Mediator should not be extended more widely than the election of men who are to be saved, so that he was not destined and sent for more than the elect (the contrary of which the patrons of universal grace hold). (Inst. IV. X, pp. 354–355)

This brings us to the matter of what it was about the Salmurian position that Turretin found so distasteful. We can summarize the Salmurian view like this. God ordains an initial universal election of all human beings that is conditional upon each human being responding to the divine call by faith and appropriating the means of salvation. However, foreseeing that this decree would fail, on account of the fact that not all fallen human beings will respond to the universal call to salvation, God subsequently decrees the salvation of some particular number of fallen humans whom he effectually calls through the work of the Holy Spirit. This latter decree is unconditional and effectual.

---

19. *Formula of Concord, Article XI. Negativa IV,* in Schaff, *Creeds of Christendom, Vol. III,* p. 172.

20. Francis Pieper, *Christian Dogmatics, Vol. III* (Saint Louis, MO: Concordia Publishing, 1953) p. 476.

Thus, there is a first conditional and unfulfilled decree to elect, the scope of which is universal (encompassing all humanity) and a consequent, unconditional and effectual decree, the scope of which is limited to some number of humanity less than the total number. Grace is universal and the atonement is, in one sense, unlimited in scope – according to the first conditional decree. But it is effectual only for the elect. The benefit of this view is that it enabled the Salmurians to hold together biblical passages that speak of God's desire that all humans be saved, together with those biblical passages that speak of only a particular number less than the whole mass of humanity being saved. Due to the way in which this scheme conceives of a two-stage decree of election, the first ineffectual, the latter effectual, and given that the first decree is universal in scope (offered to all humanity), this position is usually termed *hypothetical universalism*.[21]

The election of Christ has a particular place in this Salmurian way of thinking. Christ's election is the foundation of election in the sense that his work is the means by which God is able to offer a first hypothetically universal decree of election, prior to the particular decree to redeem only some. If we ask why all of humanity is initially elect, according to Salmurian theology, the answer is that the foreseen merit of Christ's work is sufficient to bring about the salvation of all humanity, and God elects all humanity on this basis, according to a first decree of election. But this decree is ineffectual because, though sufficient to save all humanity, the foreseen merit of Christ's work does not bring about the salvation of all humanity. It is not effectual in this respect, because there must be a response of faith on the part of the human beings concerned, and not all such human beings will respond with faith in the absence of divine enabling grace. So, though God desires the salvation of all humanity (in one respect) and provides the means by which all human beings might be saved (the foreseen meritorious work of Christ), and although God elects all humanity to eternal life on the basis of the foreseen merit of Christ's work, yet not all are saved because not all will appropriate this work by faith, without the aid of divine prevenient grace. So the Salmurians thought that the election of Christ was, as Turretin put it, 'the foundation and meritorious cause, not of salvation *a posteriori*, but of election *a priori*; not on the part of the effect in man, but of the act of willing in God.' They denied that the initial, but ineffectual decree to elect was absolute, 'not as to the means, but as to the antecedent cause'. They also appear to have thought that there was no theological obstacle to maintaining that God hypothetically elects all humanity, even when he knows that not

---

21. But as Moore points out, there are different strains of hypothetical universalism in Post-Reformation Reformed thought. The English version of the doctrine that predates the Salmurian theology, particularly as set forth by John Preston, does not require the sort of change to the ordering of the divine decrees that the Salmurian position did. See *English Hypothetical Universalism*, pp. 217–219.

all (in fact, presumably, not any) of the mass of humanity thereby elected will avail themselves of this saving work in the absence of divine enabling grace.[22]

Still, we might want to ask how it is that Christ's work is the cause of election on the Salmurian way of thinking. The answer is that the merit that Christ's work generates, and which satisfies divine retributive justice, thereby atoning for human sin, is part of the cause of the first, conditional decree of universal election. The cause of this election is the divine good pleasure and will, which, we might say, is motivated by the foreseen merit of Christ's work. So Christ's work is something like a necessary but insufficient causal factor in an unnecessary but sufficient divine decree to conditionally elect all humanity, the other causal factor being the divine will and good pleasure (derived from Paul's words in Ephesians).[23] In this way, Christ's election has to do with the foundation of election; it is not merely that Christ is elected to carry out the work of salvation as a consequence of the divine decree to ordain the salvation of some number of humanity.[24]

From this it should be clear that Turretin's objections to the idea that Christ is the ground of election were aimed at the Salmurians (and perhaps, by extension, the Lutherans and even the Roman Catholics), whose doctrine of election included Christ's work as, in an important sense, the meritorious cause and foundation of the election of fallen human beings.

3. *The Moderate Reformed Position on the Election of Christ*

Having sketched the historical background to the dispute about Christ's election in Post-Reformation theology, and having seen what Turretin's objection to Christ being the foundation and cause of election were in light of the Salmurian position, we are now in a position to offer an alternative account of the election of Christ. For want of a better term, I shall designate this view the *Moderate Reformed Position* (or MRP). In fact, this account is not so much an alternative to the position espoused by Post-Reformation theologians like

---

22. Without a great deal more explanation, this makes God seem insincere in his desire to save all humanity, and elect them – even hypothetically. The Salmurians wanted to say that not all humans (perhaps no humans) *will* avail themselves of Christ's work on this first conditional decree. But their own commitment to a doctrine of the total depravity of human nature meant that no human *could* avail him- or herself of Christ's saving work without divine enabling grace. So there appears to be a sleight of hand in the way the Salmurians presented the decree of hypothetical universalism. For the logic of their position precludes all (indeed, any) of the mass of humanity from appropriating the means of salvation offered in this decree.

23. Here I have borrowed from J. L. Mackie's notion of an INUS causal condition.

24. This is not the only possibility open to the Salmurian. One could argue that the first ineffectual, conditional decree of election depends only on the divine will and good pleasure, whereas the second, effectual decree depends upon the divine will and good pleasure along with the foreseen merit of Christ's work. Then Christ's work is part of the foundation of the effectual decree, but not of the ineffectual one. I thank Paul Helm for pointing this out to me.

Turretin, as a more careful extrapolation of the doctrine that stays within the bounds of the Reformed Confessions and discussions of this matter, mentioned earlier. The Moderate account of the election of Christ I have in mind maintains that Christ is the ground of election in one important sense, which includes the idea that he is the meritorious cause of election (with certain careful qualifications). In this respect, this more carefully formulated doctrine may form the basis for some rapprochement between those contemporary theologians who favour something like the CRP, and those modern Reformed thinkers who are more persuaded by the Salmurian position instead – or, at least, something more like the Salmurian position. Nevertheless, the MRP version of the doctrine insists that Christ's election is subject to the divine will, as per the view of those aligned with Turretin. For the sake of clarity, brevity and simplicity I shall set out the substance of this mediating position in numbered propositions, in the following way:

1. God decrees the election of some number of humanity.
2. The cause of this decree is the good pleasure of the divine will (Eph. 1.5).
3. There are two aspects to this decree that are logically, but not temporally, distinct. These are (a) the decree to elect Christ, and (b) the decree to elect a particular number of fallen humanity.
4. These two parts of the decree are necessary but (taken singly) insufficient – though jointly sufficient – conditions of an unnecessary but sufficient decree to elect.
5. The second aspect of this decree is consequent on the first. That is, God's election of Christ as Mediator and, thereby, the means by which salvation is effected, is logically prior to the election of a particular number of fallen humanity, though these are two aspects of one decree.[25]

No fallen human being can be elected without the logically prior election of some means by which the election of such fallen human beings can be vouchsafed. Any planned outcome is dependent for its successful execution upon the means by which that outcome is to be achieved. In this way, we might say that any planned outcome is dependent upon the means by which this outcome is to be achieved being in place (logically) prior to the setting out what the outcome envisaged is to be. This is true even though the means by which an outcome is brought about normally occurs later in time than the moment at which that outcome is instigated. Thus, if I plan to take a holiday in a particular resort, the successful prosecution of that goal requires that I have in place the means to achieve that end – the money to pay for the holiday – without which I will be

---

25. This is true on an infralapsarian scheme. It may be true on a supralapsarian scheme as well. I am not concerned here to enter into discussion of the infra- versus supralapsarianism that is an important aspect of Post-Reformation (and modern) discussion of the divine decrees.

unable to attain my goal. I must have the financial wherewithal to pay for the holiday in place (or at least promised) prior to planning it, although paying for the holiday usually occurs at some point in time later than the actual planning of the holiday. This, of course, is one instance of the notion that 'what is first in divine intention is last in execution' – an idea familiar in Post-Reformation theology.

In this sense the decree to elect Christ as the means of salvation (the Mediator) must be logically prior in the decree to elect, than the election of a particular number of fallen humans. We proceed as follows:

6. Strictly speaking, Christ is not the cause of this decree; God is.
7. But Christ is one (subordinate) end of the decree.

In other words, God decrees election, and he decrees that Christ be one of the ends of this decree, one of the goals to which election aims.

Now, so far this reasoning is in keeping with at least one reading of the Reformed Confessions. But there is a problem here. How can Christ be said to be merely the means of election and not its meritorious cause if he is God Incarnate? All orthodox Reformed theologians want to affirm the notion that the external works of the Triune God are in indivisible (*opera trinitatis ad extra sunt indivisa*): each of the external works of God involves each of the three divine persons, even if one of the divine persons is the principal agent involved in bringing about the action concerned, for example, the agency of the Son in becoming Incarnate. But if this principle of catholic theology obtains, it cannot be set aside when it comes to the ordering of the divine decrees, since the divine decrees are divine works. Yet the ordering that seems to underpin the sort of reasoning offered by supporters of the CRP does appear to violate this principle, even if unwittingly. For if Christ is merely the means by which election is realized, he is not a cause of the decree to elect. But this cannot be right if Christ is the Second Person of the Trinity Incarnate. There must be some important sense in which the Second Person of the Trinity is involved in ordaining the decree of election, including within that the decree to elect Christ as the means of salvation. For if this is not the case, then the *opera ad extra* principle does not obtain with regard to this crucial aspect of the external works of God.

But there is another related problem in the neighbourhood of this first one. Many Reformed theologians have been at pains to explain how it is that the Son compacts with the Father to become the means by which election is made effectual in salvation. The Son volunteers to become the Mediator of divine grace to fallen humanity in what is usually called the *pactum salutis* (covenant of redemption). But where in the logical ordering of the divine decrees does this come? If it is logically dependent upon the decree to elect, then the Son's 'choice' to become the Mediator occurs subsequent to the Father decreeing to elect some number of humanity according to his good pleasure and will. But this seems to imply an unwarranted subordination of the Son to the

Father in the ordering of the divine decrees that jeopardizes the *opera ad extra* principle once again, although for different reasons. For, on this way of thinking, it appears that the Father decrees to elect some number of fallen humanity, and this decree has, as a consequent, the decree to elect Christ as Mediator, which, we might say, is the means by which the prior decree is brought into effect. But it is only at the logical 'moment' of this consequent decree that the *pactum salutis* obtains. All of which raises the following problem: whether the Son is 'involved' in the decree to elect or not, or whether he is only involved in volunteering to provide the means by which this election is brought about in time, logically subsequent to the decree of election.[26]

This might be thought to be a problem for the ordering of the decrees *per se*, in which case, it is a difficulty that belongs to a rather different discussion, having to do with whether God decrees election logically prior to the decree to create and permit the fall, or logically after. This, of course, would be to touch upon the much broader issue of the relation between supra- and infralapsarianism. And this is another argument. But a few moments' reflection on this problem is sufficient to show that the question of where in the order of the divine decrees one places the *pactum salutis* is intimately connected to our question of the placing of the election of Christ in the divine decrees, via the *opera ad extra* principle. For if the Son volunteers to become the Mediator at some logical 'moment' in the sequence of divine decrees later than the decree (by the Father?) to elect, then it is natural to think that Christ's election is subsequent to the decree to elect, being an outcome of the Son's willingness to be elected, which is itself dependent upon the logically prior decree to elect. But if the *opera ad extra* principle has currency with respect to all God's works *ad extra*, then the Son is also in some important sense involved in the decree to elect: this decree, as with all the other decrees of God, is a Triune work, involving Father, Son and Holy Spirit.

Now, assume that this is the case. Then, a rather different picture of the ordering of divine decrees emerges. God ordains election – but, as with all the external works of God, this is a Triune work (given the *opera ad extra*

---

26. Covenant theologians in the Post-Reformation period had thought about this problem, of course. For instance, Hermann Witsius says this:

> For, as that engagement was nothing but the most glorious act of the divine will of the Son, doing what none but God could do, it implies therefore no manner of subjection: it only imports, that there should be a time, when that divine person, on assuming flesh would appear in the form of a servant. (*Economy of the Covenants Between God and Man in Two Volumes, Vol. I.* trans. William Cruickshank (Escondido, CA: The Den Dulk Christian Foundation, 1990 [London, 1822]) p. 180). And, 'If the Son be considered as God, the whole of this covenant was of his own most free will and pleasure. . . .' ibid., p. 184.

My main point is that the development of covenant theology with respect to the particular point at issue here (viz., the election of Christ) does not lend itself readily to answering questions about the ordering of the divine decrees.

principle). Hence, the Triune God ordains election. From this we can map out the following reasoning:

8. The Triune God decrees that there be an election (of some number of human beings to eternal life).
9. The cause of this decree is the good pleasure of the triune divine will (extrapolation of Eph. 1.5 given the *opera ad extra* principle).
10. There are two aspects to this triune decree that are logically, but not temporally, distinct. These are (a) the election of Christ, and (b) the election of a particular number of fallen humanity.[27]
11. These two parts of the decree are necessary but (taken singly) insufficient – though jointly sufficient – conditions of an unnecessary but sufficient decree to elect.
12. The second aspect of this decree is consequent on the first. That is, God's election of Christ as Mediator and, thereby, the means by which salvation is effected, is logically prior to the election of a particular number of fallen humanity, though these are two aspects of one decree.

But now it should be clear that our previous thinking set forth in propositions (1)–(7) was skewed, if the relationship between election and mediation is a triune one. For then the Son is party to the decree to elect as well as offering himself as the Mediator of election. This is an important point acknowledged in Post-Reformation Reformed thought, where a distinction was made between the Son as the *fundamentum electionis* (ground of election) and Christ's theanthropic office as Mediator of election (*fundamentum salutis electorum*). According to Richard Muller,[28] the Post-Reformation Reformed Orthodox argued as follows. The external works of God are divided into two sorts, the works that are in some sense independent of the actual act of creation (*opus Dei essentialis ad intra*), such as the divine decrees; and the works that result in the creation or conservation of the cosmos (*opus Dei essentialis ad extra*). The paradigmatic examples of this latter sort of divine work are creation and providence, the *opus naturae*. All the external works of God are works of the Trinity. But some of these works terminate upon a particular divine person, with whom the work in question is associated, and whose agency is particularly important in the work. The paradigmatic example of this is the Incarnation, which terminates on the person of the Son, as the God-Man.

---

27. Those Reformed theologians who dislike the idea of a particular redemption will have to make the relevant adjustments to what follows. I am assuming redemption is particular.

28. I have drawn on Richard A. Muller's *Dictionary of Latin and Greek Theological Terms, Drawn Principally from Protestant Scholastic Theology* (Grand Rapids, MI: Baker, 1985) in what follows.

By applying these theological distinctions common in much Post-Reformation Reformed thought to our concern about the election of Christ, we arrive at the conclusion that Christ's election must be intimately connected with the divine decree to elect. Moreover, the Son, as party to the decree to elect, is the one who volunteers to become the Mediator of the election of some number of fallen humanity. To put it bluntly, the Father and the Son together with the Holy Spirit compact together to elect the Son who, *qua* God Incarnate, is the one through whom the election of fallen humanity obtains. But then, there is one important sense in which Christ *is* the ground of election, contrary to the reasoning of (1)–(7) above. It would be consistent with this line of approach to say that the divine decree is the efficient cause of election, and this is ordained by the divine Godhead. But the work of Christ is the instrumental cause of election, which triune work terminates upon the Second Person of the Trinity Incarnate.

This may seem like a rather subtle – even casuistical – distinction. What, if anything, of theological importance follows from this 'correction' to a CRP approach to this question of Christ's election? Several things:

First, it makes clear what some of the Reformed Orthodox (including Turretin) did not, namely, that the Second Person of the Trinity is intimately involved in the cause and foundation of election, and is also involved as the Mediator of this decree to elect, as God Incarnate. Turretin and his modern Reformed epigone have not always made this as obvious as they might.[29]

Second, it makes clear that the Salmurians and Lutherans were right to stress that, in one important respect, Christ is the cause and foundation of election, and that his causal role is a necessary condition for the decree to elect, as a divine person of the Godhead. They were also right to point out that Christ's role as the Mediator of the covenant of redemption has an intimate connection with the decree to elect. For the one electing (in the person of the Son) and the one elected as Mediator of that covenant (in the person of the God-Man) is one and the same.

Of course, the crucial issue is whether the Salmurians and Lutherans (and Roman Catholics) were right to suggest that Christ's work is a meritorious cause of election: does God elect some number of humanity *because* of Christ's work? Here recourse to some distinctions concerning divine knowledge will help to make the MRP position with respect to this issue more transparent.

Let us say that there are two metaphysically distinct 'moments' to God's knowledge. The first is usually called God's natural knowledge. It consists of all necessary truths that are independent of God's free will, such as that $1 + 1 = 2$, or that if something is false in all possible worlds, then it is necessarily false.

29. Compare Heinrich Heppe, *Reformed Dogmatics* (London: Wakeman Trust, n.d. [1950]) pp. 166–172.

Then, there is God's free knowledge. This consists of thing contingent upon the divine free will. So, if God chooses to actualize a particular world that contains you and me, he knows how you and I will act in that world in all the circumstances we will be placed in by him, because all these states of affairs are dependent on him bringing them about.

Now, although the divine decrees are works of God a*d extra*, they are, in some sense 'internal' to God because they are not works that take place once the cosmos is created, but are logically, though not, according to traditional Reformed theologians, temporally, prior to the first moment of creation (if God is atemporal). Still, one might think that God foresees the meritorious work of Christ and that this is in some sense included in the causal factors that give rise to his decree to elect. The problem here is that if God is atemporal, there is no such thing as divine 'foresight'. Only divine knowledge that is immutable. In decreeing to elect some number of humanity to eternal life God is making a decision; he is exercising his free knowledge – for the eternal decrees are, we might think, eternal but contingent upon the divine will. So at every step of the divine decrees God knows what the outcome of his decision will be. Nothing is hidden from his sight. I want to suggest that the cause of election is the divine will, as per Ephesians 1, and that it is a mistake to think that the meritorious work of Christ somehow enters into the causal factors in this decision. Christ's election is not the cause that motivates election in that way. Nevertheless, Christ's election is the first requirement of the decree to elect. In this sense, Christ is the foundation of election because he is the Elect One; it is he who is elected in the first instance, as the Mediator, in and through whom human beings may be reconciled to God. The particular number of humanity chosen for this reconciliation is the second aspect of this decree of election, which depends upon the election of Christ.

So I think that the Salmurians were mistaken in factoring the meritorious work of Christ into the cause of election as a motivation for election (if that is what they meant to imply). His work is not the efficient cause of election. But he is the instrumental cause of the election of human beings; and he is himself elect. In fact, he is himself the first of the elect, since he is the Elect One in and through whom all those who are included in salvation are elected.

This concludes my setting out of the MRP. In a final section, I shall consider whether this doctrine has any contemporary significance, by comparing it to the sort of view advocated by Karl Barth.

4. *The Moderate Reformed Position and 'Barthianism'*

The foregoing argument suggests a number of ways in which the MRP mirrors aspects of Barth's account of the election of Christ. For Barth, Christ is the *subject of election*: he is one of the three 'modes' of the Godhead that decrees to elect. But he is also the *object of election* in the person of Christ: as the God-Man he is literally the Elect One, who is chosen by the Triune God, 'in' whom fallen humanity are derivatively elected. All of this is consistent with the MRP. Accounts of Barth's doctrine are often less clear about whether the election of Christ has the connotation that Christ's work is a causal factor in the decree to elect.[30] I suggest that the MRP offers a description of Christ's election that is clear on this matter in addition to upholding a number of key concerns Barth raises (i.e., Christ being the object and subject of election).

But although the MRP does sound like a 'Barthian' account of election on the matters of Christ being, in some sense, the object and subject of election, it does not countenance the additional substantive changes to the traditional Reformed doctrine of election that Barth's refocusing of the doctrine on Christ as the sole object of election makes. The MRP is clear that Christ is the object of election in one limited sense, but not the sole object of election. His election is to the end that some number of humanity (other than his own human nature) will be elected. This is not strictly true on Barth's account. For it is Christ who is Elect and humanity that is derivatively elect 'in' him.

What is more, the MRP is consistent with a more traditional Reformed view of the scope and effectuality of election. Christ is not the Reprobate One on this view (at least, not as I have set out the MRP – although I concede one could take the doctrine in this direction). His work does not necessarily bring about the salvation of all humanity. It might, depending on what the scope of redemption is. But – and this is crucial – the MRP is consistent with a particular atonement: a certain number of humanity is effectually elected 'in' and 'through' Christ. It is not clear that this is Barth's position. He appears at times to endorse a doctrine of particular atonement alongside his commitment to all humanity being derivatively elect 'in' Christ. In which case, Barth's particular atonement doctrine is a species of universalism. The particular number of humanity saved is the whole of humanity. However, at other times he appears to withhold commitment to a particular redemption, opting instead for a conditional election whereby humans are elect-in-Christ until or unless they opt out of this elect status. And this does not appear consistent with a doctrine of particular redemption. The ambiguities of this aspect of Barth's account are avoided on the MRP.[31]

In setting out his own position against his forebears in the Reformed tradition (with whom he is frequently in constant and critical dialogue) Barth is clear

---

30. See, for example, Bruce McCormack, 'Grace and Being, The Role of God's Gracious Election in Karl Barth's Theological Ontology' in John Webster ed. *The Cambridge Companion to Karl Barth* (Cambridge: Cambridge University Press, 2000) p. 92–110; Joseph L. Mangina, *Karl Barth, Theologian of Christian Witness* (Aldershot: Ashgate, 2004) p. 72.

31. I have discussed the conflicting strands of Barth's account of election elsewhere and refer the interested reader to closer textual analysis of Barth's work there. See 'On Barth's Denial of Universalism' in *Themelios* 29 (2003): 18–29; 'On the *Letter* and *Spirit* of Karl Barth's doctrine of Election: A Reply to O'Neil' in *Evangelical Quarterly* LXXIX (2007): 53–67 and 'Barth and Jonathan Edwards on Reprobation (and Hell)' in David Gibson and Daniel Strange eds *Engaging with Barth: Contemporary Evangelical Critique* (Leicester: Apollos, 2008) pp. 300–322.

that the fundamental problem with the Augustinian and Calvinistic accounts of election is that they end up ossified into a set of axioms from which one simply derives certain theological principles – a matter that Barth regards as the death knell of truly vibrant, biblically informed theology. He is particularly scathing about Post-Reformation thought in this regard:

> It needed only the gradual disappearance of respect for the Word of God as such which characterized the age that followed [the period of the Reformation]; it needed only the increased prevalence of arbitrariness and systematisation, to transform the *utilitas* of Calvin into formally didactic and pedagogical axioms which as such claimed a permanent importance and the value of basic principles. Once that was done, it was these axioms which inevitably gave to the doctrine [of election] its shape and form. Already with Beza and Gomarus the glory of God had given rise to the concept of His comprehensive and exclusive action and efficacy.[32]

But, as we have already had cause to note, such a view of the Post-Reformation theology is, at the very least, questionable.[33] This is not the only factor relevant to Barth's reconceptualizing of the doctrine of election.[34] But it has been an important issue in much discussion of the matter in late twentieth-century theology that has taken Barth's view as a point of departure. This is unfortunate. The discussion in this chapter has been concerned to show that the post-Reformation discussion of the election of Christ was vibrant and varied and that it is possible to stay within the doctrinal parameters of this discussion, and yet offer an account of Christ's election that is theologically creative.[35]

For these reasons it seems to me that the MRP offers much that Barthians want to say about the nature of Christ's election, but without the problematic aspects of Barth's doctrine, or the implications it appears to have at some points in his development of it in *CD II/2*. It also offers an account of the election of Christ that is informed by the Post-Reformation discussions of this doctrine, and stands as a mediating position between the different schools of Reformed thinking on this matter.[36] The MRP may not solve all the problems the doctrine

---

32. Karl Barth, *CD II/2*, p. 37.

33. As previously mentioned, Richard Muller's work, especially *Christ and the Decree* and *Post Reformation Reformed Dogmatics* has led the way in correcting this misunderstanding.

34. Geoffrey W. Bromiley has a succinct explanation of the factors involved in Barth's rethinking of the doctrine in his *Introduction to the Theology of Karl Barth* (Edinburgh: T&T Clark, 1979) p. 85.

35. In this respect I hope I have fended off Barth's earlier criticism of theology that seeks merely to repeat Post-Reformation theological ideas parrot-fashion. I am sympathetic with Barth's criticism that such ways of thinking are really attempts to reify some particular way of thinking found in the history of dogma rather than attempts at constructive systematic theology. See *CD II/2*, p. 36.

36. This is not to suggest that Barth's account might not be read as an attempt to refocus discussion of this topic in the Reformed tradition. If anything, I want to affirm that there is a range of views on this matter, that Barth's position is one creative attempt at reformulating the doctrine

of Christ's election poses. But it goes a long way towards a careful, balanced construal of this doctrine that offers the prospect of fruitful dialogue with those amongst contemporary Reformed theologians who take a rather different view of the matter – whether Salmurian or Barthian.[37]

---

from *within* the Reformed tradition, and that the MRP is another such attempt, but one that may appeal to those in the Reformed tradition who find Barth's account problematic in various ways.

37.   John Calvin's account of the election of Christ in his Commentary on Ephesians 1.5 is like the MRP in several respects. He speaks of Christ as the material cause of election, the efficient cause being the good pleasure of the will of God, and the final cause, the praise of God's grace (*Commentary on Ephesians, Calvin's New Testament Commentaries Vol. 11,* trans. T. H. L. Parker, eds David W. Torrance and Thomas F. Torrance (Grand Rapids, MI: Eerdmans, 1965) p. 126). But I have argued for more than this here. Christ is not merely the *material* but the *instrumental* cause of election on the MRP. That is, he is not merely the *means* by which our election is secured; he is the one who, as one of the three persons of the Godhead, *ordains* that our election takes place, becoming the Elect One who makes that possible. For a fascinating discussion of this matter in Calvin's thought, see David Gibson's doctoral thesis, 'Reading the Decree: Exegesis, Election and Christology in Calvin and Barth' (University of Aberdeen, 2008), especially, pp. 77–89.

Chapter 3

THE PRE-EXISTENCE OF CHRIST

Scripture teaches us that Christ is the logos of God.

Jonathan Edwards, 'An Essay on the Trinity'[1]

Does Christ pre-exist the Incarnation? The simple traditional answer to this question is this: yes, if this means that Christ, who is the Son, the second person of the Trinity, pre-exists the Incarnation; but no, if this means that Christ pre-exists his conception in the womb of Mary *Theotokos* as a human being. The human Jesus of Nazareth cannot pre-exist the Virginal Conception. No human being pre-exists its conception as a human being.[2] (If the human 'part' of Christ has a first moment of existence like other human beings have a first moment of existence, then the human 'part' of Christ cannot pre-exist that first moment as a human being.[3]) It is the Word who exists in some sense 'prior' to the first moment of Incarnation and it is the Word who assumes human nature at the Incarnation. In so doing, the Word takes to himself the human nature of Christ and becomes a human being in addition to being a divine being. But prior to this event in time, no human called Christ existed, although the divine person who is Christ existed. (So, Christ is necessarily a divine being and only contingently a human being.) As H. R. Macintosh put it almost a century ago, 'Christ cannot after all be pre-existent in any sense except that in which God Himself is so relatively to the incarnation'. Who, then, is said to pre-exist the Incarnation? Macintosh responds,

> not the historic Jesus, exactly as he is known in the Gospels. The Church has never affirmed that the humanity of Christ was real prior to the birth in Bethlehem [sic]; and

---

1.   From Jonathan Edwards, *Treatise on Grace & Other Posthumously Published Writings,* ed. Paul Helm (London: James Clarke, 1971) p. 106.

2.   It might be that human nature can pre-exist the Incarnation, depending on whether or not one assumes the human nature of Christ is a property of the Word, or a concrete particular – body-soul composite – assumed by the Word. But on either of these views it is still the case that the human *being* Jesus of Nazareth, cannot pre-exist his own conception. And that is the point I am making here. On the question of these two views of Christ's human nature, see Crisp, *Divinity and Humanity,* ch. 2.

3.   It may 'pre-exist' as some property that the Word will assume at the first moment of Incarnation. But it may not pre-exist as a human being, a body-soul composite (assuming that humans are body-soul composites).

if, as must be admitted, certain apostolic statements . . . have the appearance of saying quite the opposite, it must be considered that this was inevitable in the case of men using the intensely concrete language of religion, not the coldly correct phraseology of the schools.[4]

The 'certain apostolic statements' he has in mind are almost certainly those of St Paul who says in several places that Christ pre-exists his incarnate life in some fashion. (e.g., 1 Cor. 8.6 and 10.4.) It seems to me that Macintosh is right about the way in which St Paul phrases these passages. Later Pauline or Deutero-Pauline statements, such as those found in Colossians 1.17 and Hebrews 1.2 are consistent with the idea that Pauline theology developed a more sophisticated account of the pre-existence of Christ than that present in 1 Corinthians. Whereas the early Paul says that it is Christ who pre-exists the Incarnation (in some way) the later Pauline corpus suggests that it is the Son who pre-exists, which is to say, the second person of the Trinity pre-exists the Incarnation. Of course, it could also be that the Pauline statements about Christ's pre-existence in 1 Corinthians are an instance of Paul speaking with the vulgar, whereas the later Paul (or Deutero-Paulines) 'correct' this by explaining that Paul is thinking with the learned. Then it is not strictly speaking Christ who pre-exists but the Son, although one could speak as if Christ pre-existed.

But there is a third way of thinking about this problem with the Pauline corpus that I will call *the traditional view.*[5] On this view we may speak of the pre-existence of Christ, since the Christ is just a phase of the life of the Word. In a similar way, when I speak of my wife aged twelve years old, I mean to refer to the earlier phase of the life of this individual who became my wife at a later moment in time. For, clearly, she was not my wife when she was twelve, although the girl of twelve would become my wife. So, being my wife is a certain phase in the life of the individual who is my wife; but the individual in question pre-exists that phase of her life. And perhaps this is all that the Pauline *corpus*, taken as a whole, seeks to express with regard to the person of Christ.

---

4. H. R. Macintosh, *The Doctrine of The Person of Jesus Christ, Second Edition* (Edinburgh: T&T Clark, 1913) p. 457. Macintosh's claim that Christ's humanity was not real prior to his birth in Bethlehem is surely a slip of the pen. He should have said something like 'Christ's human nature did not physically exist prior to the Virginal Conception'. For the Word had already assumed human nature prior to his being born of the Virgin! Compare Donald Bloesch 'The traditional view that the Word pre-existed but not the humanity of Jesus indubitably remains the dominant position in conservative Christianity.' *Jesus Christ. Savior and Lord* (Downers Grove, IL: Inter-Varsity Press, 1997) p. 137.

5. This seems to be the view that Macintosh, Bloesch and others identify as the traditional view. Some revisionist theologians, like John Robinson, have claimed that the biblical picture is commensurate with a far weaker claim about Christ's pre-existence, namely that Christ 'completely embodied what was from the beginning the meaning and purpose of God's self-expression'. But this is hardly the traditional view of the matter. See Robinson, *The Human Face of God* (Philadelphia, PA: Westminster Press, 1973) p. 179.

(This would also be consistent with the Johannine material on the pre-existence of the Word.) If the Word is the Christ, then it is true to say both that before the Incarnation the human Jesus of Nazareth did not exist, and that before the Incarnation Christ pre-existed. Both of these things can be the case because the Word is the Christ. True, the human Jesus of Nazareth does not exist before the Virginal Conception. But in an important sense, Christ does pre-exist the Incarnation – or at least the Word does and, since Christ is simply the Word Incarnate, we can say that Christ pre-exists the Incarnation as the Word of God. On this third way of thinking about the Pauline material we may, with Macintosh, continue to speak of the pre-existent Christ taken in this qualified way, or, as Macintosh has it, taken as the 'concrete language of religion', rather than the 'phraseology of the schools'.

But how would the story about Christ's pre-existence go according to the 'phraseology of the schools'? One approach to this question, in keeping with the mainstream of Christian tradition (at least, in the Latin west) depends upon the claim that God is outside time. If God is timeless, then there is a sense in which the Word is eternally God Incarnate. There is no time at which he becomes Incarnate on this view, because time has no application to an a-temporal being. So it is not the case, on this timelessness view of God that before the Incarnation the Word was non-Incarnate, but from the Incarnation onwards became incarnate. Rather, if the Word is timeless, he is timelessly God Incarnate, although the human Jesus of Nazareth begins to exist at a certain time (around 4–7 BC).[6] If this account of the Incarnation is true, then there is a sense in which the Word is eternally God Incarnate because he is a-temporally God Incarnate. Nevertheless, this does not mean that the human being, Jesus of Nazareth, is eternal, nor does it mean that Jesus of Nazareth had no beginning in time. (I presume, with the tradition and *contra* theologians like David Brown,[7] that Christ has no end in time, because the Incarnation is permanent: the Word is, after the first moment of Incarnation, forever after the Word Incarnate.) Let us call this a-temporal construal of the traditional account the *a-temporal traditional view* of Christ's pre-existence.

There are theological peculiarities that come with the a-temporal traditional view. Chief amongst these – at least, for the purposes of systematic theology – is the distinction between the so-called *logos ensarkos* (Word enfleshed) and *logos asarkos* (Word non-fleshed). These two terms have been the subject of some discussion in recent theology, where they are used in a technical, rather than trivial, sense.[8] As far as I can make out, those who affirm the former of

---

6. A recent and philosophically sophisticated defence of this view can be found in Brian Leftow's essay, 'A Timeless God Incarnate' in Stephen T. Davis, Daniel Kendall and Gerald O'Collins eds *The Incarnation* (Oxford: Oxford University Press, 2002).

7. See David Brown, *The Divine Trinity* (London: Duckworth, 1985).

8. It seems trivially true to say 'if Jesus of Nazareth is God Incarnate, then he is the Word enfleshed' since this looks like just another way of saying 'Jesus of Nazareth is God Incarnate'.

these mean to say that there must be some sense in which the Word of God is eternally enfleshed, that is, is eternally God Incarnate. Becoming Incarnate cannot, on this way of thinking, be a substantive change in the divine life; it is always, or eternally, the case that the Word is Incarnate. Those who affirm the latter, that the Word of God is (somehow) the Word without flesh, mean, I think, to preserve the contingent relation between the Word and the human nature he assumes. The Word of God voluntarily becomes the Mediator of human salvation, which includes his becoming Incarnate. So the Incarnation is a contingent, not a necessary, event in the divine life. Some think the *logos asarkos* claim implies some hidden God who decides to become God Incarnate, but whose essence is forever concealed behind that event in the divine life. As shall become clear in a moment, I do not think this is a strict implication of the *logos asarkos* view, when coupled with an a-temporal account of the divine life.

On the a-temporal view, the Word of God is eternally enfleshed as Jesus of Nazareth. That is, it is eternally true that the Word of God is Jesus of Nazareth, that the Word of God assumes the human nature of Jesus, and so forth. This means that the a-temporalist is committed to a strong view of the relationship between the Incarnation and the life of the Trinity. For if the Word is eternally God Incarnate, indeed, if he is eternally Jesus of Nazareth, then there is a very strong connection between the human Jesus and the divine person who is the subject of the Incarnation. In which case, an a-temporalist about the Incarnation can accommodate the *logos ensarkos* notion.

But is it also true to say that, in some sense, the Word of God is without flesh – that is, is the *logos asarkos*? Can this second aspect of the distinction be upheld by the a-temporal traditional view? There are several good Christological reasons for embracing the *logos asarkos* notion. The first of these has to do with the so-called *extra calvinisticum*. The Word of God penetrates all created things via Christological perichoresis.[9] But he also has a particular metaphysical ownership of the human nature he assumes. If this is right, then there must always be some sense in which the Word of God is *asarkos*, even during the Incarnation, on pain of denying the omnipresence of the Second Person of the Trinity.[10]

It might also be thought that if the Second Person of the Trinity exists in some sense prior to the generation of his human nature, then it is true to say that he exists without his flesh. This is a more contentious claim, of course, and does not appear to have an obvious, trivial sense in the way that the *logos ensarkos* claim does. One of the appealing aspects of the a-temporal traditional view is that it can make good (non-trivial) sense of both these Christological notions.

9. As I have argued in *Divinity and Humanity*, ch. 1. One need not hold to a traditional a-temporal view to embrace this deliverance of the *extra calvinisticum*, of course.

10. Note that this does not necessarily mean that the Word of God is located at every point in space. With a number of classical divines, I take it that God, being essentially immaterial, cannot be contained by any physical object and is not literally located in any physical object – including his human nature. This seems odd at first blush, but is an implication of those versions of substance dualism, according to which souls are literally nowhere: if my soul is essentially immaterial, then it can have no location, within or without my body.

But secondly, the advocate of the a-temporal view can say this: there is a sense in which the Word of God has a sort of metaphysical priority, such that we might speak in abstraction from the Incarnation, as it were, of the *logos asarkos*. This need not commit the theologian to the sort of dreaded *Deus Absconditus* (hidden God) that some contemporary theologians worry about, provided it is made clear that this affirmation of the *logos asarkos* is really a means by which we can distinguish between the Word of God in his economic function as that member of the Trinity who eternally assumes human nature, and his ontological function as that member of the Trinity who, as a member of the Trinity, assumes human nature.[11] The distinction is a fine one, to be sure. But I think it is also an important one, given the current theological climate. Such an affirmation of the *logos asarkos* could be taken in a direction that leads towards a rather apophatic account of the divine nature – perhaps even a sort of theological scepticism about what can be known of the divine essence. In the service of such theological scepticism about the divine essence, or at least strong apophaticism concerning what we can know of the divine life, the defender of the a-temporal traditional view of Christ's pre-existence may end up espousing a kind of divine 'hiddenness'. And this may well pose theological problems. But the affirmation of the *logos asarkos* notion by defenders of an a-temporal view of God need not be taken in this direction. One could hold to the following consistent set of beliefs: God is a-temporal; the Word of God is eternally God Incarnate; the Word of God is eternally Jesus of Nazareth; The Word of God is that member of the Trinity who, in the divine counsels of the Triune God, voluntarily takes it upon himself to become the Mediator of human salvation, and thereby, to become God Incarnate. Provided something like the MRP argument of the previous chapter is kept in mind here, I think the advocate of the a-temporal traditional view can affirm both the *logos ensarkos* and the *logos asarkos*, without necessarily embracing a 'God behind God', some hidden Deity standing behind Jesus of Nazareth. Yet, importantly, the a-temporalist can also affirm that the Second Person of the Trinity *voluntarily* took upon himself his work as Mediator of salvation. He chooses to take up human nature; he is not forced to do so. And in order to make sense of that claim one must be able to speak of a divine decision to act in this way – even if it is an eternal decision.

---

11.   Here I think of Bruce McCormack's essays 'The Actuality of God: Karl Barth in Conversation with Open Theism' in Bruce L. McCormack ed. *Engaging the Doctrine of God, Contemporary Protestant Perspectives* (Grand Rapids, MI: Baker Academic, 2008) pp. 185–244 and 'Grace and Being: The Role of God's Gracious Election in Karl Barth's Theological Ontology' in Bruce L. McCormack, *Orthodox and Modern, Studies in the Theology of Karl Barth* (Grand Rapids: Baker Academic, 2008) pp. 183–200. In his *Systematic* Theology Robert Jenson also follows Barth in his suspicion of the *logos asarkos* notion, as we shall see presently. Paul Helm offers a response to McCormack in his essay 'John Calvin and the Hiddenness of God' in Bruce L. McCormack ed.*Engaging the Doctrine of God, Contemporary Protestant Perspectives* (Grand Rapids, MI: Baker Academic, 2008) pp. 67–82.

By contrast, if one were to take the view that God is in time, then it seems that there is a time at which it is possible to say the Word was *asarkos* and another, later time, at which it is possible to say the Word is *ensarkos*. (Of course, one could also deny this and still affirm that God is temporal.) If God is in time, along with the created order, then one can surely speak of a time at which God was not Incarnate, and a time at which he became Incarnate. To begin with, he had no human nature; but at a certain point in time, he assumes one. Let us call this construal of the traditional account the *temporal traditional view* of Christ's pre-existence. Both the a-temporal and temporal traditional views are taken in the tradition. I shall not offer an argument for either of them here, although it seems to me that the view that God is timeless has a stronger claim to be called the dominant traditional view.[12] And I do not think that this is the result of the infection of good Hebraic theology by pagan Greek philosophy, the old, tired Harnackian thesis about the development of Christian doctrine that has recently been given a new lease of life in some quarters, for example, amongst Openness theologians. It certainly seems to me that the a-temporal traditional view is compatible with the teaching of Scripture.[13]

What I am calling the traditional account of the pre-existence of Christ (understood according to an a-temporal or temporal view of divine eternity), has recently been challenged by Robert Jenson in his *Systematic Theology*.[14] Or, more precisely, Jenson has attached a somewhat idiosyncratic view of Christ's pre-existence to an untraditional doctrine of divine eternity with some rather strange consequences.[15] In this chapter, I intend to show from a systematic theology perspective that Jenson's account is (a) incompatible with the traditional views I have just sketched and (b) deeply problematic as an account of what it means, to say Christ pre-exists his Incarnation. Jenson's *Systematic Theology* is undoubtedly one of the most rich and forthright statements of ecclesial theology that has been produced in recent years. But it seems to me

---

12. For recent discussion of the different views of God's relation to time see Gregory Ganssle ed. *God and Time: Four Views* (Downers Grove, IL: Inter-Varsity Press, 2001).

13. See, for example, Paul Helm's contribution to *God and Time: Four Views*. There he distinguishes two sorts of data in Scripture, that which fits best with a temporal view of God, and that which fits best with an a-temporal view. As he points out, much depends on which data set we allow to 'control' the other data set. If we think the temporal-sounding biblical passages should be understood in terms of the atemporal-sounding ones, then we are likely to end up with an a-temporal view of God, and vice versa. Like Helm, I think that Scripture is metaphysically underdetermined in this respect. That is, the data is compatible with more than one understanding of the eternity of God.

14. Jenson, *Systematic Theology, Volume 1*. Hereinafter cited as ST 1, followed by page reference. Reference to Jenson's *Systematic Theology, Volume 2, The Works of God* (New York: Oxford University Press, 1999) follows the same pattern.

15. Simon Gathercole has offered a similar critique of Jenson's argument from a more biblical–theological perspective in the recent literature. See Simon Gathercole, 'Pre-existence, and the Freedom of the Son in Creation and Redemption: An Exposition in Dialogue with Robert Jenson' in *International Journal of Systematic Theology* 7 (2005): 36–49.

that the mark of any important statement of theology, as Jenson himself points out early on in his work, is to have it subjected to the scrutiny of one's peers.[16] It is somewhat ironic that Jenson's discussion of this matter, offered up in a body of divinity that is explicitly ecumenical in outlook, advocates a doctrine of Christ's pre-existence that is not acceptable to the majority of voices in the tradition, and looks distinctly partisan.

1. *Outlining Jenson's View of Christ's Pre-Existence in ST1*

There are places where Jenson deals with the pre-existence of Christ, other than in his *Systematic Theology*. And there are interesting ways in which his thinking in this area has changed over the course of his career. But I do not intend to offer a critical account of the development of his thinking in Christology, not least because this has been done elsewhere (as Gathercole points out in his piece). But even if it had not, we shall restrict ourselves to the mature reflections found in the *Systematic Theology*. This seems to me to be a legitimate way of approaching a particular thinker's ruminations on a topic, and is a common enough feature of academic literature that I shall not pause to defend it further.

What then, is Jenson's account of the pre-existence of Christ in ST? What are its contours, and what its central and defining theses? Let us begin by laying out, in brief, a critical exposition of what Jenson says about the matter. Jenson begins his account of Christ's pre-existence with a traditional-sounding refrain:

> It is 'one and the same' who lives both of these communal stories. This one, the one that Christ is, is dogmatically specified to be the Logos. Christ's identification as one of the Trinity and his identification as one of us are not ontologically symmetrical. Christ's human history happens because his divine history happens, and not vice versa. . . . It means that as God the Son he must ontologically precede himself as Jesus the Son. In the tradition's language, he 'pre-exists' his human birth. What kind of 'pre-' can that be? (ST 1, p. 138)

He prefaces his answer to this question by explaining that the 'Aristotelian' notion of time as a linear sequence and the 'Platonic' notion of eternity as a-temporal will not suffice as the metaphysical underpinning of a Christian doctrine of Christ's pre-existence.

> Rightly to construe 'In the beginning was the Word,' we therefore need an accommodation for 'pre-existence' not suggested by the Greeks; here is a specific place in which theology must do its metaphysics in a predominantly negative relation to the culture. (ST 1, p. 139)

---

16. 'It is the fate of every theological system to be dismembered and have its fragments bandied about in an ongoing debate.' ST 1, p. 18.

This metaphysical effort is governed by three observations. They are: First, the biblical witness shows us both that the Word (or the Son) pre-exists and that Christ refers to himself as pre-existing. Thus it would be wrong, according to Jenson, to think that the New Testament refers only to a pre-existing divine entity that has yet to become the created person of Christ. Jenson cites two theologians who have followed up these biblical leads (as he puts it): Ireneaus of Lyons and Karl Barth. Irenaeus speaks of 'the Word of God who *is* Jesus'. This appears 'violently paradoxical' to Jenson, and yet seems to express an important truth about the identity of God Incarnate. In contrast, Jenson highlights Barth's articulation of the divine choice of the second person of the Trinity not just to become Christ, but to be identified with Christ (from whence Barth and Jenson seem to derive a measure of their distaste for the *Logos asarkos* notion). Jenson writes as follows:

> If we then ask *what* is chosen, in the act of choice that is the eternal being of God, Barth's answer is: he chose to unite himself, in the person of Christ, with humankind; he chose to be God only as one person with the man Jesus. But since God is his act of choice, God in making this actual choice not only chooses that he *will be* the man Jesus; as the event of the choice, *he is* the man Jesus. (ST 1, p. 140)

Second, Jenson denies that the Logos is ever *asarkos*. The Son is 'his own presupposition in God's eternity'; he appears in the Old Testament, not as unincarnate, but as the 'narrative pattern of Israel's created human story' before he may appear as a particular Israelite in that story. Thus,

> [w]hat in eternity precedes the Son's birth to Mary is not an unincarnate state of the Son, but a pattern of movement within the event of the Incarnation, the movement to incarnation, as itself a pattern of God's triune life. (ST 1, p. 141)

It seems that there is a 'pattern of movement' in the life of the Son, which, according to Jenson, can be traced through the history of Israel to the person of Jesus of Nazareth. In fact, the historic Israel of the Old Testament is, in some sense, the pre-existent Christ. So, Jenson says

> in the full narrative of Scripture, we see how the Son indeed preceded his human birth without being simply unincarnate: the Son appears as a narrative pattern of Israel's created human story before he can appear as an individual Israelite within that story. (ST 1, p. 141)

Gathercole explains this rather sibylline utterance in the following way:

> Israel is (and still today, is) thus the pre-existent Son, a point which is explained in particular through Jenson's fine exegesis of Isaiah 53. The Patristic *totus Christus* in which Christ and his church are bound together in one body finds its mirror in the Old Testament in the conception of the Suffering Servant, 'a figure by which now Israel,

now someone within Israel is picked out'. [ST 1, p. 80] Thus, the historic, concrete, temporal entity of Israel is the dominant aspect of the Son's pre-existence in Jenson's work.[17]

So, for Jenson it is really the case that the pre-existent Christ is identified with the historic Israel of the Old Testament. This could be taken to mean that, prior to his Incarnation, Christ *was* the people of Israel; the people of Israel were a prior stage or phase of the life of Christ. But it could mean something weaker than this, such as, that Christ is especially present with his people Israel prior to his Incarnation. We will return to this matter presently.

Third, Jenson says that there is an eschatological dimension to Christ's pre-existence often overlooked by traditional formulations of this *theologoumenon*. Citing Romans 1.3-4, he explains that there is an important parallel in this passage between Jesus who is born of the seed of David according to the flesh and declared to be the Son of God through the action of the Holy Spirit in his resurrection. It is not that Jesus only becomes the Son in being resurrected. It is rather, that Christ's sonship comes 'from' his resurrection, that is, from the eschatological life of God of which Christ's resurrection is the first fruit in Pauline theology. With this in mind, Jenson asks, 'How does Christ's birth from God precede his birth from the seed of David?' The answer is, 'Led by this sort of logic in the New Testament, we must answer: Christ's birth from God precedes his birth from the seed of David in that in God's eternal life Christ's birth from God is the divine *future* of his birth from the seed of David.' Jenson goes on to explain as follows:

> Nor is this paradoxical unless we again forget that God's eternity is the infinity of a life. For what obtains in *life* always comes from a future; the difference between God and us is that he, as the Spirit, is his own future and so is *unboundedly* lively. (ST 1, p. 143)

It should be clear from this brief recapitulation of Jenson's three observations about the pre-existence of Christ that Jenson qualifies his initially traditional sounding doctrine of Christ's pre-existence in significant ways. Jenson offers an important amplification of several issues in his doctrine of Christ's pre-existence later in chapter thirteen of ST 1, where he discusses divine eternity. But before turning to this section of Jenson's work, we need to touch upon his understanding of the relation between philosophy and theology, since it has an important bearing on what he says about divine eternity and its application to

---

17. Gathercole, 'Pre-existence and the Freedom of the Son', p. 43. Compare Jenson, ST II, p. 173:

> The Father . . . is the 'pre-' of all being. He is this as the one who speaks the Word that grants purpose and so being to others than himself; using language leading to our point here, as he determines their destiny. That to which he directs all things is the *totus Christus*.

Christ's pre-existence – and is a theme pertinent to the analytic theological approach of the present volume.

2. *Against 'Greek' Metaphysics*

Jenson's line on divine eternity is partly to do with a repudiation of metaphysics inspired by what he calls, 'the Greeks' (i.e., Hellenistic philosophers and their intellectual heirs). In the prolegomenal section to ST 1, Jenson claims that classical philosophy is just secularised theology, or theology under the name of philosophy. Indeed, he seems to think that philosophy is not a different academic discipline some of whose content overlaps with theology; it is a rival theological account of the nature of things that is to be resisted:

> We usually refer to the work of Greece's theologians with their name for it, 'philosophy'. We have thereupon been led to think this must be a different kind of intellectual activity than theology, to which theology may perhaps appeal for foundational purposes or against which theology must perhaps defend itself. But this is a historical illusion; Greek philosophy was simply the theology of the historically particular Olympian-Parmenidean religion, later shared with the wider Mediterranean cultic world. (ST 1, pp. 9–10)

For this reason, Jenson opposes any attempt to find the 'right' metaphysics with which to pursue the theological enterprise. Indeed, he appears to believe that any attempt to utilize the metaphysical tools on offer in the work of 'officially designated philosophers' is bound to end in a Bablyonian captivity for theology, as evidenced in the work of Process theologians, and Bultmannians, dependent on the metaphysics of Martin Heidegger, to name two particular recent theological cases (ST 1, p. 21). This construal of the relationship between philosophy and theology is important for Jenson's metaphysical commitments in several ways. First, it explains his antipathy towards what he calls the 'Aristotelian' understanding of time as linear, and the 'Platonic' notion of eternity as timeless, in his discussion of Christ's pre-existence. Second, it motivates his attempt to rethink the doctrine of pre-existence without these categories, preferring instead to present a version of the doctrine indebted to a certain eschatological perspective on these matters. Let us turn to a consideration of what he has to say on the matter in chapter thirteen of ST 1.

3. *Adding ST 1 Chapter Thirteen into the Mix*

What does chapter thirteen of ST 1 add to Jenson's discussion of Christ's pre-existence in chapter eight? The answer is that it makes explicit some of the claims touched upon in the earlier chapter. Chapter thirteen sets forth Jenson's understanding of the metaphysical issues in his doctrine of God, and in the course of this discussion he returns to the topic of divine eternity in the context of explaining Gregory of Nyssa's doctrine of the divine nature. According to

Jenson, Gregory, unlike the Greek philosophers, did not think of divine infinity on analogy with space (infinitely extended) but on analogy with time: God is temporally infinite (like an infinite temporal series, one presumes). 'The infinity that according to Gregory is God's deity is *temporal* infinity' (ST 1, p. 216). Gregory's reflection on the doctrine of God was expressed in conscious opposition to the Greek-inspired theology of the Arians, whose God was outside of time and incapable of involving himself in time, which is why Christ is, on Arian theology, a creature rather than the creator. This is also a notion that Jenson finds in Barth. 'He [Barth] describes the particular "eternity of the triune God" as "pure duration [*reine Dauer*]"' (ST 1, p. 217). Yet, paradoxically, this divine duration does not admit of events receding into the past, or coming into reach from the future. God transcends the personal limitations, goals and beginnings that pertain to created beings, although he too is subject to time. 'What [God] transcends is any limit on what he can be by what he has been, except the limit of his personal self-identity, and any limit imposed on his action by the availability of time. The true God is not eternal because he lacks time, but because he takes time' (ST 1, p. 217). Thus far, Jenson is largely following Barth's lead. But he adds an important element that we encountered earlier in his discussion of pre-existence in chapter eight of ST 1. This is the eschatological element to divine eternity: [God] is temporally infinite because 'source' and 'goal' are present and asymmetrical in him, because he is primarily future to himself and only thereupon past and present to himself. (ST 1, p. 217)

But what are we to make of a deity whose infinity is temporal, to whom nothing is past or future, who is future to himself and thereupon past and present to himself, as Jenson contends? What manner of duration are we speaking of here, that is sequential (one presumes) but has no past, no present, no future? At this point Jenson is clearly struggling to make sense of the matter. He asks as follows:

> Can we speak of God's own 'time'? The life of God is constituted in a structure of relations, whose own referents are narrative. This narrative structure is constrained by a difference between whence and whither that one cannot finally refrain from calling 'past' and 'future', and that is congruent with the distinction between the Father and the Spirit. This difference is not relative and therefore not measurable; nothing in God recedes into the past or approaches from the future. But the difference is also absolute: the arrow of God's eternity, like the arrow of causal time, does not reverse itself. Whence and whither in God are not like right and left, or up and down on a map, but are like before and after in a narrative. (ST 1, p. 218)

4. *Critiquing Jenson's Account*

Jenson's attempt to make sense of Christ's pre-existence requires him to say something about the nature of divine eternity and divine infinity. His antipathy towards traditional metaphysics means this has to be done, in the footsteps of Barth, by holding what we might call *philosophical* metaphysics at arms length in order to construct a *theological* metaphysics.[18] This means developing a metaphysical framework that is not, in his view, dependent on prior philosophical notions imported into theology. It is to Jenson's credit that he does not fall into the trap some contemporary theologians have, of claiming they are not doing metaphysics when it is patently obvious that that is precisely what they are engaged in. There is a curious theological *positivism* in certain quarters, where theology is regarded as meaningful and philosophical notions are thought of as, if not meaningless, at least irrelevant or even poisonous to the theological task, and certainly to be resisted. Despite Jenson's dislike of metaphysical notions culled from the philosophers, he is clear that what his work amounts to is metaphysics of a sort. Being is, as he concedes at one point 'incurably theological', meaning, I think, that it is a concept common to both the Christian and Hellenistic-philosophical 'theologies' (ST 1, p. 208).

However, the metaphysics Jenson underpins his doctrine of Christ's pre-existence with (and his doctrine of God too), is difficult to make sense of. Perhaps this is due to the nature of the task: How *can* we even begin to fathom the interior life of God? But if this is the reason, it is not given prominence in Jenson's account. In any case, my concern is not with any purported mystery in the neighbourhood (although, the nature of God is mysterious). My concern is rather that Jenson's theologizing is somewhat unclear, and perhaps downright inconsistent. Despite the fact that Jenson writes with wit and style (and something close to an addiction to the pithy aphorism), on close examination of the metaphysical notions he deploys in his doctrine of God, it seems that what he has to say about divine eternity is rather murky.

Consider Jenson's conception of divine infinity: God is temporally infinite. This sounds like the view that God endures through time (the temporal traditional view), in which case, like all other things in time, it would seem that God has a past, a present and a future (at least, this is the traditional way of thinking about this matter. I am not concerned here with whether or not it is logically possible to think of other ways in which God might exist in time). Some things are in his past and appear to be irreversible. Some things are in the future and are yet to come. But Jenson denies this 'Aristotelian' picture of divine temporality. What does he replace it with? A notion that God is temporally infinite, but has no past or future and is past and present to himself because he is somehow future to himself. It is rather as if God exists through time by projecting himself backwards in time from his future to his past and present. But what

---

18. This will sound anachronistic to some readers. I am merely attempting to make sense of Jenson's ambivalence towards the western philosophical tradition and his own 'reconstruction', so to speak, of metaphysical notions using only theological data. This should not be taken to indicate my agreement with Jenson in this matter.

could that possibly *mean*? Despite valiant efforts, Jenson is unable to explain.[19] He suggests that the temporal referents of God are not like the cartographical referents used in orienteering: we cannot go backwards, forwards, up or down, to discover what this temporal infinity means. God's infinity, according to Jenson, is like the before and after of a narrative. And, like the arrow of time, God's eternity does not reverse itself. But this only makes matters more muddled. How can God's infinity be like the sequence of the narrative in a story when he has no past, and no future? Perhaps, like a narrative, there is a sequence of events that are temporal, but are not past, present or future to God. From other things that Jenson says in ST, it seems this is one way he could be understood. So, in his discussion of creation in ST II, Jenson recapitulates what he has said in ST I and extends it:

> The life of God is constituted in a structure of relations, whose referents are narrative. This narrative structure is enabled by a difference between whence and whither which one cannot finally refrain from calling 'past' and 'future' and which is identical with the distinction between the Father and the Spirit. This difference is not measurable; nothing in God *recedes* into the past or *approaches* from the future. But the difference is also absolute: there are whence and whither in God that are not like right and left, or up and down, that do not reverse with the point of view. . . . It indeed better suits the gospel's God to speak of 'God's time' and 'created time', taking 'time' as an analogous concept, than to think of God as not having time and then resort to such circumlocutions as Barth's 'sheer duration'. (ST II, p. 35)

Taken at face value, this adds the following to our understanding of Jenson's doctrine of God: God has a narrative-like life that is temporal, and which we may speak of in terms of past, present and future. However, God's past is identical with the Father (who creates?) and his future is identical with the Spirit. Moreover, time, as applied to God, is an analogous concept. In which case, we should take care not to think of past and future as literally true of God – or, at least, this seems to be what Jenson is getting at. But this is very strange indeed. Why should we think that God's past is identical with the Father, or his future with the Spirit? What does that mean, exactly? In what sense is one person of the Trinity identical with a particular time in the life of God? Surely if all the persons of the Trinity are co-eternal (and necessarily so) it is meaningless to speak of the Father as identical with the past and the Spirit with the future. It may be that co-opting a doctrine of analogy with respect to divine eternity is

---

19.   I mean this seriously: Jenson does not offer an *explanation* of what this means. If John says to Jane 'explain how this green plant photosynthesises' and Jane responds, 'well, a green plant needs sunlight to live. It also needs water and a certain amount of carbon dioxide in the atmosphere', she has not offered an explanation of photosynthesis. She has described some of the conditions necessary for a green plant to continue to live. But she has not *explained* to John how these conditions factor into the process of photosynthesis. It seems to me that this is just what Jenson does in ST 1, ch. 13.

helpful – after all, God's life is so unlike ours how are we to comprehend it? – but this does not help Jenson a great deal because it is difficult to see what divine eternity is analogous *to* on his doctrine of divine eternity.

Even if we concede that he can make sense of divine temporal eternity without duration, there are other problems lurking in the neighbourhood. For instance, how can it be the case that God's infinity does not reverse itself, and yet moves in sequence both from past to future and from future to past at one and the same time? Jenson offers no explanation of this matter. It is clear from the whole thrust of his systematic theology that, like Pannenberg (although for different reasons), Jenson's desire to emphasize talk of God's future has to do with what he sees as an important biblical theme: the hope of what is to come, and what is promised by God. (See, e.g., what he says about the Gospel as God's 'promise' that opens up, and even 'impels' history in ST 1, p. 15.) But it is one thing to make eschatology an important constituent of one's view of history from a God's-eye perspective. It is quite another to claim that God's future somehow constitutes or brings about his past and present. As it is, what Jenson gives us is a picture that makes very little sense of divine infinity and appears, in the absence of further clarification, to be incoherent.

5. *Trying to Marry Divine Eternity to Christ's Pre-Existence*

This makes the task of understanding what he says about the relationship between divine eternity and Christ's pre-existence extremely difficult. Jenson is happy to reiterate much of the tradition in what he says about who it is that pre-exists (although, as we have already noted, he goes well beyond the tradition in his three observations about Christ's pre-existence).[20] But how Christ pre-exists is much less clear. Recall that, in explaining the third of his observations governing his doctrine of Christ's pre-existence, Jenson says, 'God's eternity is the infinity of a life. For what obtains in *life* always comes from a future; the difference between God and us is that he, as the Spirit, is his own future and so is *unboundedly* lively' (ST 1, p. 143). This fits with what he

---

20.   An important constituent of Jenson's account of Christ's pre-existence has to do with his commitment to a basically Lutheran account of the *communicatio idiomatum* (communication of attributes) in the Incarnation. Jenson refuses to separate out aspects of the human and divine in Christ in order to avoid certain perceived Nestorian tendencies in christologies that do make such a move. Jenson's discussion of the real (corporeal) presence of Christ in the Eucharist in ST 1, pp. 204–206 makes this point, as does what he says in ST 1, pp. 144–145, where he offers this:

> once it is clear that there truly is only one individual person who is the Christ, who lives as one of the Trinity and one of us, and that he is personal precisely as one of us, then to say that he as creature is our savior – or that he as creature exercises any divine power – is simply to say he plays his role in the triune life and does not need to abstract from his human actuality to do so.

It is perhaps worth pointing out that this Lutheran factor is playing a part in Jenson's emphasis on the pre-existence of Christ, even though he takes the doctrine in directions that are rather unusual.

says in chapter thirteen about the infinity of God. But it is contentious. Jenson says Christ's life comes 'from the future' because the life of the Godhead comes from the future in some fashion. However, even if some sense can be made of this notion,[21] why is it preferable to traditional ways of thinking about the divine life? Part of the answer seems to be that Jenson thinks it is inappropriate to incorporate metaphysical concepts from philosophy in Christian theology because philosophy presents a rival theological account of the world. On this view, any understanding of the divine life that relies upon philosophical notions imported into theology is tainted. Jenson's point is not that his understanding of the divine life is preferable to some other view. His point is that the *biblical picture* should govern what we say about the divine life, not some prior metaphysical commitments. This is an important theological insight. But I know of no orthodox theologian who would deny it. Indeed, one test of whether or not a theologian is orthodox is often thought to be whether or not they make a procrustean bed for Scripture out of their prior metaphysical commitments.[22] And if this is true, then the dialectical force of Jenson's point is considerably blunted. Obviously, Jenson is not claiming that all metaphysical notions that have been incorporated into Christian theology have to be expunged. For then, we would need to eliminate all talk of the doctrine of the Trinity or of Chalcedonian Christology from our theology. It seems that what he is committed to is the rather weaker claim that the 'Greek' theological (i.e., philosophical) account of metaphysics is false, and a Christian account is true. (Even this is too strong. What he needs to say is that much of Greek metaphysics is false, although some of it has been usefully appropriated in Christian theology, in such doctrines as the Trinity and Incarnation, since he would agree that these two classical doctrines have their place in a systematic theology.) But it is not clear which thinkers he has in mind when he makes this sort of claim. For instance, does this include all philosophers that have ever written on metaphysics, or just the non-Christian philosophers who have written on the subject? A charitable reading might include only the latter. In which case, his point would be something like this: metaphysics done in a purely philosophical way, without reference to Christian theology, if appropriated uncritically by theologians, is likely to end up distorting one's theology, rather than enhancing it. This might be true (I am not committing myself to this view, merely conceding the point for the sake of the argument). But, one would also have to say,

---

21. I cannot make sense of what Jenson says, as it stands, in anything other than a trivial way. My life 'comes from the future' in this respect: the future moments of my life lie ahead of me in the future and become my present experience as they occur. But Jenson's comments about the divine life require something stronger than this.

22. Compare, for example, the way in which Openness theists have been accused by other evangelical theologians of revising their concept of God – and, specifically, their understanding of God given in Scripture – in light of certain philosophical concerns with the dilemma of divine foreknowledge and creaturely freedom.

in all fairness, that classical theologians relied to a considerable extent, on prior philosophical training in their theologizing and were happy to use the tools of philosophy for theological ends (even where they apparently repudiate much of their philosophical training, as with Calvin or Luther).[23] It seems to me that it could be argued – I think persuasively – that classical theologians who rely on such a method are not, for the most part, guilty of subordinating theology to philosophy as Jenson seems to think they are.[24] (And, to be fair to Jenson, at one point in his discussion in ST 1, p. 21, he does allow that St Thomas' metaphysics are derived from dialogue with Aristotle, not through an uncritical and osmotic absorption of Aristotle's thinking).

So, if we accept Jenson at his word, it seems that his view amounts to a preference for his own metaphysical commitments over other, possible ways of thinking about the metaphysics of divine eternity, rather than a rejection of metaphysics *per se* (whether he wants to call his metaphysics 'theological' as opposed to 'philosophical' is largely irrelevant to the issue, in as much as it is *metaphysics* he is engaged in). Furthermore, the advantage of traditional ways of articulating this doctrine over Jenson's account is that they are both compatible with Scripture *and* have the *imprimatur* of the vast majority of the tradition, something conspicuously absent in Jenson's account.

6. Jenson's Doctrine of Christ's Pre-Existence

We come to the question of Jenson's doctrine of Christ's pre-existence. Earlier, I said that Jenson's account appears to be fairly traditional at first glance. Certainly, his initial observation about what should govern our theologizing about this doctrine sounds traditional – it fits with at least one of the traditional accounts (or versions of a traditional account) I gave at the beginning of this chapter. Christ pre-exists as the Word; the human nature of Christ does not pre-exist the Incarnation. Moreover, somehow the pre-existent Word is eternally the Christ (which is what a defender of the a-temporal traditional view of Christ's pre-existence could say – although Jenson is no friend to this traditional view). But his second and third claims are much more contentious. Let us

---

23.   See, for example Paul Helm, *John Calvin's Ideas* (Oxford: Oxford University Press, 2004), Richard Muller, *After Calvin, Studies in The Development of a Theological Tradition* (Oxford: Oxford University Press, 2003) and David Steinmetz, *Luther in Context, Second Edition* (Grand Rapids, MI: Baker Books, 2002).

24.   I am not saying there are not instances where this may have happened (Faustus Socinus comes to mind). My point is simply that, for the most part, classical theologians did not think they were guilty of subordinating theology to philosophy. In fact, recent historical scholarship has shown that in the case of some Protestant Orthodox theologians in the post-Reformation period, this was certainly true. For instance, Sebastian Rehman argues that John Owen, the paradigmatic English scholastic theologian, has a surprisingly ambivalent attitude towards the theological use of philosophy, despite his reputation as a school theologian. See *Divine Discourse: The Theological Methodology of John Owen* (Grand Rapids, MI: Baker, 2002).

examine each of them in turn, bearing in mind what we have said about Jenson's doctrine of divine eternity as we do so.

Jenson's second observation was that the Son is never 'without flesh'. Christ pre-exists his Incarnation in Israel as a 'pattern of movement' in the life of Israel. There are several problems here. The first of these, mentioned earlier, is that it is unclear what it means to say that Christ pre-exists as Israel or as a pattern of movement in the life of Israel. Perhaps this means something like the following: Christ exists 'within' the life of Israel in some fashion, prior to his Incarnation rather like the Holy Spirit is said to exist 'within' the lives of Christians. Even if this is true, it is hardly sufficient to claim that Christ cannot be 'without flesh' in this pre-existent state; in fact, it does not seem to mean anything more than that the second person of the Trinity was present with his people Israel prior to his Incarnation in some special or particular way (distinct from his general work of upholding and conserving his creation), which Paul alludes to in 1 Corinthians 10.

The second thing to say is that it is not the case that Old Testament Israel *is* the pre-existent Christ. At times, what Jenson says sounds as if he means it *is* the case that Israel is identical to Christ. Thus: 'the Son indeed precedes his human birth without being simply unincarnate: the Son appears as a narrative pattern in the history of Israel'. But also: 'What in eternity precedes the Son's birth to Mary is not an unincarnate *state* of the Son, but a pattern of movement within the event of the Incarnation, the movement to Incarnation, as itself a pattern of God's triune life' (ST 1, p. 141). Taken together, these two excerpts from the same passage could mean the pre-existence of Christ is not an unin-carnate state but part of the Incarnation, a stage of Christ's life lived as a pattern in the history of Israel. But at other times in the same passage he seems to want to say something much less controversial. For instance, 'There must be in God's eternity . . . a way in which the one Jesus Christ as God precedes him-self as man, in the very triune life in which he lives eternally as the God-man' (ST 1, p. 141). I am minded to take this latter view of Jenson's claim here, not least because if Jenson is claiming that Christ's pre-existence *ensarkos* means Christ is identical with the Old Testament nation of Israel, then this seems bizarre. However, there are other places in ST 1 where Jenson seems to ally himself with the stronger of these two views. In ST, chapter three, on the iden-tification of God he remarks as follows:

> At several places in this chapter and before, a conceptual move has been made from the biblical God's self-identification *by* events in time to his identification *with* those events; moreover, it will by now be apparent that the whole argument of the work depends on this move. (ST 1, p. 59)

If we apply this reasoning to what Jenson says about the pre-existence of Christ, then it seems that the pre-existent Christ can be identified *with* the history of Old Testament Israel (he is not just identified *by* these events as the divine actor whose presence is demonstrated through the unfolding events of the history of Israel). But if we take this seriously, Jenson is committed to some very strange notions. To be identified with a particular thing is, I take it, to be the same as that thing, whereas, to be identified by a certain thing does not have this implication. Jenson is identified with the Lutheran theologian who wrote this particular two-volume systematic theology. He just *is* that person. But, by contrast, identifying Jenson by reference to his two-volume systematic theology does not mean Jenson is identical with his systematic theology. We could say, 'when I speak of the Lutheran author of this systematic theology, I mean by this to refer to Jenson'. Then we have identified Jenson *by* reference to his work, but have not identified him *with* his work. This seems to be the sort of distinction Jenson has in mind in the passage just cited. But if we apply this to his doctrine of the pre-existence of Christ, identifying Christ *with* Israel, then strange things follow. For this means all those individuals who made up the people of Israel prior to the Incarnation were physical parts of Christ prior to his Incarnation. On one construal of this sort of claim the pre-existent Christ would be a four-dimensional entity that exists across time for hundreds of years, made up of aggregated parts that are themselves distinct entities in some sense (being individual human beings). What is more, if Old Testament Israel is the pre-existent Christ, then it looks like Christ is identical with all the people who make up Old Testament Israel. And this raises all sorts of theological problems. For instance, it would mean that Abraham, Jacob, Moses, David and Malachi are all God Incarnate. Such a claim is so theologically exotic that it would be fantastic to think Jenson embraces it. So, I shall assume that Jenson means something more like the claim that Christ's pre-existent state in Israel involves his special presence with his people, although his language is sometimes a little extravagant and may lead some unwary readers to read more into what he is saying that he intends.[25]

Let us assume this is what Jenson means. Then, how is it that Christ is never 'unfleshed' (*asarkos*)? If Jenson were defending an a-temporal traditional view of Christ's pre-existence, we might be able to say that there is no time at which the Word is *asarkos*, although *qua* human he is *ensarkos* at a particular time. But, as we have already seen, Jenson denies this in what he says about divine eternity, despite what we have just seen he says about the existence of Christ in the Trinity prior to the Incarnation. Jenson is clear in chapter thirteen of ST 1 that God is temporal in some sense. But then, how is Christ never unfleshed? It is not clear. I suggest that Jenson's commitment to a temporal doctrine of God demands that he say Christ *is* unfleshed before the conception of Jesus

---

25. In making this move, I am assuming that Jenson's comments in chapter three of ST regarding the identification of God with, not by, the events of Israel's history should not be taken seriously with respect to the pre-existence of Christ for the reasons I have just given. If Jenson expects us to identify the pre-existent Christ with Israel, then he is committed to a view that has unorthodox consequences.

of Nazareth. If the second person of the Trinity is in time, then there is a time at which he was not Incarnate. This would require Jenson to retract what he seems to think is a mistaken theological commitment, namely the *asarkos* notion. But it would be more in keeping with what he says elsewhere about divine eternity and its relation to the Incarnation.

We come to Jenson's third observation about pre-existence. This depends on one of his central metaphysical claims about divine eternity:

> Led by this sort of logic in the New Testament, we must answer: Christ's birth from God precedes his birth from the seed of David in that in God's eternal life Christ's birth from God is the divine *future* of his birth from the seed of David. (ST 1, p. 143)

There are several things to be said here. First, as Gathercole has pointed out, Jenson moves between the second observation, where there is some sense in which Christ pre-exists his Incarnation, and this third statement where he appears to deny that this means there is any substantive way in which Christ actually pre-exists the Incarnation. Gathercole comments, 'this "pre-" in pre-existence is very much a pre-" in scare-quotes, as is often the case in Jenson's discussions.'[26] But then, if we ignore the second observation and embrace the third, Jenson's view amounts to a denial of any substantive meaning to the doctrine of Christ's pre-existence. And this seems inconsistent with other, more traditional-sounding things we have seen he does say in ST 1.[27]

To make this clearer, consider once again what Jenson says about divine eternity. God is 'temporally infinite because "source" and "goal" are present and asymmetrical in him, because he is primarily future to himself and only thereupon past and present to himself.' (ST 1, p. 217) Crucial to what Jenson says here is that God is future to himself and only thereupon past and present. Similarly, in the Incarnation it is the futurity of the Son that is somehow 'prior' to the Incarnation and it is in this futurity that the Son is eternally begotten by the Father. But it is very difficult indeed to know what to make of this. How can God's futurity, taken as Jenson says it must be, as a temporal futurity, constitute God here and now? And how can God's future life constitute what takes place in the present or the past (in the case of the Incarnation)? It seems that Jenson would have us believe that God exists in the future somehow, despite the fact that his existence is, in some attenuated sense, temporal and sequential, moving along a temporal sequence from past to present and, one presumes, future, as all things in time do (see ST 1, p. 218). But what can this mean?

---

26. Gathercole, 'Pre-existence, and the Freedom of the Son', p. 44.

27. Is the second observation consistent with the third? Could we say Christ is pre-existent within Israel in some sense and yet not pre-existent, but actually future to his Incarnation in some sense? Well, it certainly *looks* like this is contradictory. And if it is, this would be a serious problem for Jenson's account. But I shall assume that Jenson can tell a story in which both of these claims could be shown to be consistent with each other.

Admittedly, the metaphysics of time is a very tricky area and thinking about time in relation to God is harder still. Yet, it seems intuitive to think that if something exists in time it has a past, a present, and, one presumes, a future. It has duration.[28] But Jenson's God does not. According to Jenson, God has infinite temporal extension across time, but no past, present or future that are past, present or future to God himself. It also seems intuitive to think that if something is temporal it moves through time from the past to the future via the present (however that is construed). However, Jenson's God does not. Or at least, Jenson's God does not have a present in which certain things are past and other things are future to him because in Jenson's way of thinking nothing recedes into the past or comes to God from the future. Finally, it seems intuitive to think that no being that is temporal can constitute its own past and present from its future. And yet Jenson would have us believe this is how God exists, and that this offers an important insight into the way in which Christ 'pre-exists' his Incarnation. It is, I think, very difficult to see what this means. The upshot of all this is that when we put Jenson's account of divine eternity side-by-side with what he says about the pre-existence of Christ, we end up with a view of God, time and Incarnation that is simply incoherent.

7. Conclusion

In a recent symposium on his work, Jenson advises us that his *Systematic Theology* is 'in one aspect an effort of revisionary metaphysics, aimed at allowing one to say things about God that scripture seems to require but that inherited metaphysics inhibits'.[29] This certainly seems to be borne out by the foregoing examination of his doctrine of Christ's pre-existence. But where he has revised the tradition, what he has produced does not appear to be an improvement upon the work of his forbears. If anything, it is a departure from the tradition

---

28. Actually, this needs some qualification. Current metaphysics offers accounts of temporal duration in which this is not the case, but, since Jenson has explicitly repudiated all such metaphysics, I shall not pursue this in detail in this essay. Nevertheless, here is a short account of how it could be that God is temporal but without absolute past, present or future. One could claim that God exists omnipresently through time and that there is no 'God's eye' view from which we can say a particular moment is objectively past, present or future. Then, we could say that God is past, with reference to a particular circumstance, but that there is no past for God, objectively speaking. On such a way of thinking God does not, in one sense, have an objective past, present, or future without reference to particular circumstances, such as 'God created the world some time *before* this afternoon'. But even if one is willing to accept this view, it will not help Jenson because it does not entail that God's future *constitutes* his past and present. I thank Michael Rea for making this clear to me. For more on recent metaphysical arguments in this area, see Thomas M. Crisp, 'Presentism' and Michael C. Rea 'Four Dimensionalism' both in *The Oxford Handbook of Metaphysics*, eds. Michael J. Loux and Dean W. Zimmerman (Oxford: Oxford University Press, 2003).

29. Jenson, 'Response to Watson and Hunsinger', *Scottish Journal of Theology* 55 (2002): 230.

in several important respects that is at times very difficult to make sense of (if sense can be made of parts of it such as his account of divine eternity). It is unfortunate, given what Jenson says about the advantages of revising our view of Christ's pre-existence, that his treatment of this doctrine actually ends up demonstrating (albeit inadvertently) the perils attending revisionist metaphysical explanations of the person and work of Christ.

Chapter 4

The 'Fittingness' of the Virgin Birth

> *This is the month, and this the happy morn,*
> *Wherein the Son of heaven's eternal king,*
> *Of wedded Maid and Virgin mother born,*
> *Our great redemption from above did bring.*
>
> John Milton[1]

At the end of his recent treatment of the metaphysics of the Incarnation in medieval philosophical theology, Richard Cross concludes, '[o]ne final consequence of all this is that the doctrine of the Virgin Birth is wholly extrinsic to the doctrine of the Incarnation. It seems to me that this is the case whichever model of Chalcedonian Christology we accept'.[2] I think Cross is right about this. Strictly speaking, neither the Virgin Birth nor the Virginal Conception is necessary for the Incarnation (and he is not the first person to have noticed this). Christ could have been born through natural generation, rather than via the miraculous working of the Holy Spirit. And this is perfectly compatible with a Christology, which, in other respects is entirely in keeping with the catholic faith. Consequently, defences of the Virgin Birth that claim that it is somehow a *requirement* for a doctrine of Incarnation, are, in my view, mistaken. However, I do think that there is a good argument to be made for the fittingness of the Virgin Birth as the means by which the second person of the Trinity became incarnate. One of the aims of this chapter is to set out one such argument, in the spirit of Anselm's discussion of this matter in his treatises, *Why God Became Man* and *On the Virgin Conception and Original Sin*.[3]

---

1. From *Ode on the Morning of Christ's Nativity*, composed in 1629, reprinted in *The Faber Book of Religious Verse*, ed. Helen Gardner (London: Faber & Faber, 1972).

2. Richard Cross, *The Metaphysics of the Incarnation, Thomas Aquinas to Duns Scotus* (Oxford: Oxford University Press, 2002), p. 324. Cf. p. 21. Other theologians have expressed similar sentiments, including Karl Barth, Keith Ward and David Brown. For discussion of this point, see Brian Hebblethwaite, *Philosophical Theology and Christian Doctrine* (Oxford: Blackwell, 2005), 67–68.

3. See *Anselm of Canterbury, The Major Works* eds. Brian Davies and Gillian Evans (Oxford: Oxford University Press, 1998).

The argument proceeds in several stages. First, an account of the Virgin Birth is given that is compatible with classical Christology. This is followed by an outline of a robust doctrine of the Incarnation *without* the Virgin Birth. Call this version of a doctrine of the Incarnation, a *No Virgin Birth version* of the Incarnation, or NVB version for short. The Virgin Birth is clearly taught in Holy Scripture and is a constituent of the ecumenical creeds of the Church. I take it that if a doctrine is set out in canonical Scripture and is clearly endorsed by the ecumenical creeds of the Church, it is theologically orthodox. There is no good theological reason I can think of for rejecting a doctrine clearly taught by both of these sources of authority (despite what a number of modern theologians have said to the contrary)[4]. However, it might still be thought that the Virgin Birth is somehow an inappropriate way for the Word of God to assume human nature. In the last section of the chapter, I argue that, although there are several insufficient theological–philosophical reasons often given for the traditional doctrine of the Virgin Birth, the Virgin Birth is, nevertheless, a fitting mode of Incarnation – and that arguments can be found that support this conclusion.

1. *The Default Creationist Account of the Virgin Birth*

The doctrine of the Virgin Birth comprises the Virginal Conception, gestation and Virgin Birth of Christ. We shall treat each of these aspects of the traditional doctrine in turn. However, before turning to consider these dogmatic questions, a word about the metaphysics that underpins them seems to be in order. In what follows (not merely this chapter, but the several other places in succeeding chapters where this point is taken up) we shall assume a particular approach to the relationship between Christ's human nature and human personhood. Put briefly, this is that all human beings, Christ included, possess a human nature,

---

4.   Some modern theologians have asserted that the birth narratives of Matthew and Luke are legendary accretions that should be treated with caution, if not excised from contemporary theology. (The two sets of birth narratives are no longer regarded as late additions to the Gospels in which they appear.) For two twentieth-century treatments of the Virgin Birth that make these sorts of claims (although, for different reasons), see Emil Brunner, *The Christian Doctrine of Creation and Redemption, Dogmatics Vol. II*, trans. Olive Wyon (London: Lutterworth Press, 1952) pp. 350–357 and Pannenberg, *Jesus – God and Man*, pp. 141–150. For criticism of this sort of view, see Bloesch, *Jesus Christ, Savior and Lord*, Raymond E. Brown *The Virginal Conception and Bodily Resurrection of Jesus* (London: Geoffrey Chapman, 1973), Robert W. Jenson, 'For Us . . . He Was Made Man' in Christopher R. Seitz ed. *Nicene Christianity, The Future for a New Ecumenism* (Grand Rapids, MI: Brazos Press, 2001), Gerald O'Collins, *Christology, A Biblical, Historical and Systematic Study of Jesus* (Oxford: Oxford University Press, 1995) and John Wilkinson, 'Apologetic Aspects of The Virgin Birth of Jesus Christ' in *Scottish Journal of Theology* 17 (1964): 159–181. Perhaps the most influential modern defence of the Virgin Birth is that of Karl Barth. See his *Dogmatics in Outline,* trans. G. T. Thomson (London: SCM Press, 1949) p. 100 and *Church Dogmatics I/2* eds. G. W. Bromiley and T. F. Torrance (Edinburgh: T&T Clark, 1956).

comprising a human body and soul that are distinct substances (the former material, the latter immaterial). Normally, possession of a human body and soul is sufficient for a human person to exist. If an entity has a human body and soul, so this theory goes, then the entity in question has a human nature. And, if such an entity possesses a human nature, then normally this means the entity in question is a human person. Yet according to some classical theologians, this is not the case with Christ. He has a human nature like other human beings. That is, he has a human body and soul. But, unlike other human beings, in the case of Christ, the presence of a human body and soul does not constitute a human person distinct from the Word. The reason is this: Christ is a divine person with a human nature, not a human person with a divine nature, nor a human person and a divine person subsisting together – a view that is unorthodox.[5] Although he is fully human, possessing a complete human nature, this human nature does not form a human person independently of the Word of God. Rather, the Word 'assumes' this human nature into his person at the Incarnation. (As theologians put it, Christ's human nature is 'enhypostatic'.)

This is not the only view of the relationship between Christ's divine nature and his human nature, or between divine and human personhood, that can be found in the literature. Some philosophical theologians maintain that Christ's human nature is a property possessed by the Word of God, rather than a body-soul composite assumed by the Word at the Incarnation. Although there are aspects of such an approach to the Incarnation that are appealing, in what follows we shall suppose that Christ's human nature is a body-soul composite assumed by the Word. In the very act of assuming this body-soul composite, the Word 'personalizes' this human nature, making it his own. Thus, Christ's human nature is the human nature of the person of the Word of God.[6]

1.1 *Virginal Conception*

With this in mind, we come to the doctrine of the Virgin Birth. The Virginal Conception of Christ refers to the miraculous asexual action of the Holy Spirit in generating the human nature of Christ in the womb of the Virgin Mary, using an ovum from the womb of the Virgin and supplying the missing genetic material (specifically the Y chromosomes) necessary for the production of

---

5. In fact, this view is Nestorian. Nestorianism is the heresy that Christ is composed of two persons, one human and one divine. This was condemned by the Council of Chalcedon in AD 451.

6. I have fleshed much of this out in *Divinity and Humanity*, chs 2 and 3 and refer the interested reader there for further discussion. For an admirably clear account of the same sort of approach to these matters, see Thomas P. Flint 'Risky Business: Open Theism and the Incarnation' in *Philosophia Christi* 6 (2004): 213–233. See also Cross, *The Metaphysics of the Incarnation*, passim.

a human male.[7] The moment at which the embryonic human nature of Christ is complete – and therefore the moment at which the Incarnation takes place – is a matter of dispute amongst theologians. Some have held a delayed ensoulment view, according to which the human embryo must reach a certain stage of maturation before it can sustain a soul. In the tradition, a number of theologians have argued that this maturation stage is reached at around forty days after conception for a human male, and that only then can the embryo sustain a soul.[8] This would mean that only at that point in embryonic development is a complete human nature present. Others have believed that ensoulment takes place at conception. Few have thought ensoulment takes place later than forty days after conception. I know of no orthodox classical theologian that claims human beings are without souls. There are contemporary theologians who espouse some version of materialism about human beings, but detailed discussion of such views will have to wait until Chapter 7.[9] Of those who believe ensoulment takes place at conception, some theologians take the creationist view, according to which the soul of each individual is created by divine fiat, *ex nihilo*. Others take the traducianist view, according to which souls are (somehow) passed down the generations from parents to children, just as genetic material is passed down from one generation to the next. There are still other views that are refinements of these positions, where creationists and traducians also hold to some notion of delayed ensoulment. But I shall not go into such matters here, although we shall return to them in subsequent chapters. For present purposes it is sufficient to see that there are a number of competing views on the moment of ensoulment, and therefore the moment at which a complete human nature is present in the life of a human embryo. This debate has important implications for the doctrine of the Virginal Conception of Christ, a point that has not gone unnoticed in the tradition.

For the sake of the argument, I shall assume the view taken by many, although by no means all, Christian theologians on this matter. This is a version of the

---

7.   There are examples of natural parthenogenesis. However, as Arthur Peacocke points out, it will not do to reason from such examples to the idea that the Incarnation is a case of 'natural' rather than supernatural, parthenogenesis for this reason: natural parthenogenesis cannot produce a male, since Y chromosomes must be supplied by the male spermatozoon. See Peacocke, 'DNA of our DNA' in George J. Brooke ed. *The Birth of Jesus, Biblical and Theological Reflections* (Edinburgh: T&T Clark, 2000) p. 63. For an interesting discussion of parthenogenesis in humans and other mammals as it bears upon the Incarnation, see R. J. Berry, 'The Virgin Birth of Christ' in *Science and Christian Belief* 8 (1996): 101–110.

8.   This medieval view of the soul's development can be found in the work of Thomas Aquinas, amongst others. It was subsequently taken up in much Roman Catholic theology. Although the forty-day threshold has fallen out of favour in contemporary Roman Catholic theology (ensoulment for female humans was thought to take place later than forty days!), there are still theologians who advocate delayed ensoulment of human foetuses after conception. See, for example Norman M. Ford, *When Did I Begin?* (Cambridge: Cambridge University Press, 1988) and Joseph Donceel, 'Immediate Animation and Delayed Homization' in *Theological Studies* 31 (1970): 76–105.

9.   By a materialist understanding of human beings I mean that family of views according to which human beings are material beings that have no immaterial soul, as Chapter 7 makes clear.

creationist account.[10] The version of creationism I am interested in stipulates that God creates each new soul *ex nihilo*, or out of nothing at the moment of conception and, at that very moment, 'attaches', or integrates it into the body of the individual in question. (As I have already said, there are creationists who do not think ensoulment is co-terminus with conception, but we shall not deal with this sort of creationist view.) On the creationist view we are concerned with – call it, *the default creationist view* – human nature is composed of two substances, a human body and soul, and both of these substances begin to exist at the moment of conception. The human body is generated from the matter of its parents, whereas God creates the soul out of nothing. And I shall suppose, again, in keeping with a number of classical theologians that the same process applies to the conception of Christ's human nature as applies to the conception of other human beings, who are generated through a normal act of procreation – aside from the matter of the Virginal Conception. That is, the Virginal Conception, like the conception of other human beings, must begin with the fertilization of a human ovum with a certain combination of human genetic material, in order to generate a human male. Thomas Aquinas, amongst other medieval theologians, believed that Christ was not generated in this way, but conceived as a fully formed embryo, capable of sustaining a soul. This meant that, according to Thomas, Christ's conception was unlike the conception of other human beings in significant respects. But, on the sort of creationist view I am concerned with, this is not the case. The conception of Christ's human nature begins with a fertilized human egg – a zygote – that is ensouled from the first moment of conception, as are all other humans.[11]

Moreover, at the moment of Virginal Conception, the Holy Spirit somehow miraculously generates the human body of Christ using only the raw material supplied by Mary's ovum. Thus, Christ is a human being because he shares with the rest of humanity a certain amount of genetic material, which is sufficient for Christ's humanity to be the same as the humanity of Mary, such that he might be properly called a 'son of Adam' (according to his human nature).[12]

10.   There is no consensus on which view of the origin of the soul is correct. Augustine famously wavered on the matter and refrained from unqualified commitment to either view. By contrast Jerome and, later, Thomas, came down in favour of creationism as Catholic. But no ecumenical council has pronounced on this matter. In the Reformation debate, Luther took the traducianist view, and most Lutherans (although not Melanchthon) followed him in this. But Calvin took the creationist position, and this has shaped most Reformed theology (with notable exceptions like William Shedd and Augustus Strong in the nineteenth century). For a good overview of these issues, see David Albert Jones, *The Soul of The Embryo: An Enquiry into the Status of the Human Embryo in the Christian Tradition* (London: Continuum, 2004) chs 7–10.

11.   Thomas Aquinas' view on the conception of Christ is discussed in more detail below.

12.   This problem has a long history in the tradition. Anselm was aware of it and incorporated discussion of it in his *Why God Became Man*, Bk. II, ch. 8. Thomas also mentions it in *Summa Contra Gentiles* IV. 45. 6. However, some modern theologians, unhappy with the traditional doctrine, claim that Incarnation via a Virgin Birth suggests Christ is not truly a 'son of Adam'. Consider the comments of Dietrich Bonhoeffer: 'The doctrine of the Virgin Birth is meant to express the

Here is one way this could be cashed out in a doctrine of the Virginal Conception of Christ that ensures Christ is a member of humanity, not merely a facsimile of humanity, or merely partly, rather than fully, human. (I do not claim this is the truth of the matter, merely that it is one way in which God could have ensured Christ was truly, and fully, human.) Perhaps there is a certain threshold of genetic material all human beings share that an individual must possess in order to be counted a member of the natural kind, 'human being'. Assume that this threshold amount of genetic material can be found in an unfertilized human ovum. Then, Christ has this minimum amount of genetic material, and belongs to the kind, human. The genetic material that would normally be supplied by a human spermatazoon, particularly, for a human male, the Y chromosomes are miraculously supplied by the Holy Spirit. Although this miraculously supplied genetic material appears, to all intents and purposes, to be identical to the missing genetic material that would normally be supplied by a human male through a normal act of human procreation, it is not in fact, strictly speaking, human. It is a divine duplicate of the required human genetic material that is supplied by the miraculous act of the Holy Spirit.

This sort of reasoning presumes that, in order to be counted as a member of a particular natural kind, like the kind human being, or the kind horse, or dog, or whatever, a particular entity must share a certain amount of genetic material with other members of that kind.[13] If, say, the genetic material of a particular human being were gradually replaced by Martian genetic material over some period of time, then eventually that person would cease to be a human being. They would no longer have sufficient human genes to be counted a member of humanity. It may be that when this point is reached is difficult to stipulate – perhaps it is inherently *vague*, in which case, a version of Sorites' paradox may apply.[14] Nevertheless the point at which the human being becomes a Martian will be reached, if we continue to replace the genes of the particular human with the genes of a Martian, which, at least at face value, seems metaphysically

---

incarnation of God and not just the fact of the Incarnate One. But does it not miss the decisive point of the incarnation by implying that Jesus has *not* become man wholly as we are?' in *Christology*, trans. John Bowden (London: Harper Collins, 1966) p. 109. Bonhoeffer does not spell out what he means here. But the sentiment he expresses lies behind the problem we are discussing. See also John Macquarrie, *Jesus Christ in Modern Thought* (London: SCM Press, 1990) p. 393 for a similar view.

13. This seems to be what is behind Peacocke's reasoning, although he does not set his argument up in terms of natural kinds. See 'DNA of our DNA'.

14. Sorites' paradoxes have to do with the problem of vagueness. One classic formulation of the paradox is this: when is a heap of sand no longer a heap? When one grain of sand is removed, or ten, or a hundred, or ten thousand? It is difficult to know, although intuitively one wants to say there must be some point at which the heap is no more, and we are left with just a few grains of sand. Problems with vagueness have been subjected to sophisticated philosophical analysis in recent years. And this sort of paradox is in view here.

possible (depending, of course, on the compatibility of Martian with human physiology and the sophistication of Martian medical technology).

In the case of the Incarnation, no Martian genes are involved. But the Holy Spirit does create genes, including Y chromosomes that are indistinguishable from human Y chromosomes, yet are not generated by a human being. It might be thought that this poses a problem for Christ's status as a fully human being, if this threatens his status as a member of the natural kind, human. For, like the case of the Martian genes, it might be thought that introducing miraculously generated human chromosomes into a human ovum thereby fertilizing that ovum does not necessarily constitute the generation of a *human* life, even if, to all intents and purposes it seems *like* a human life.

This sort of objection to the Incarnation based on an argument from natural kinds relies, of course, on a certain view of natural kinds where belonging to a kind involves (amongst other things) sharing in a common genetic heritage that is passed down from one generation to another. If a miraculously generated part of that genetic heritage is introduced into a kind, it might be thought this is rather like the introduction of an alien body into a living organism that is able to mimic, or simulate, the characteristics of the living organism, passing itself off as a part of that living organism. Or, to change simile, it may be rather like the difference between pounds sterling issued by the Bank of England and counterfeit pound notes made by a band of unscrupulous criminals. Even if the counterfeits are of such quality that they are indistinguishable from the real money, they are nevertheless counterfeit and would not count as 'real' money if they were in circulation. At least part of the reason for this is that legitimate sterling has to be produced by the Bank of England. The counterfeit currency does not have the same origin. We might say, in a rather loose way, that the counterfeit notes are not of the same 'kind' as the genuine notes, although they look, to all intents and purposes, like the real notes. Even if, in fact, the counterfeit money is indistinguishable from legitimate currency in all particulars apart from the fact that it is manufactured illegally, the illegal currency made by the criminals concerned might still be thought counterfeit.

The same sort of reasoning is in view with respect to the natural kinds argument against the Incarnation. However, if the threshold for belonging to the kind, human, can be met by the genetic material present in the Virgin's ovum, the other genetic material being miraculously created by the Holy Spirit, then this objection may be met. For then, Christ would have enough genetic material from the kind in question – the threshold amount, supplied by Mary's ovum – to be counted a member of that kind. In which case, Christ's status as a member of the kind human, and so, his full humanity, may not be threatened at all by this argument from natural kinds. And, crucially, unlike the case of the counterfeit bank notes, in the Incarnation, the ultimate (although, not the proximate) origin of the miraculously generated genetic material supplied by the Holy Spirit, is the same as that given by Mary's ovum. The Holy Spirit creates the miraculously generated genetic material required for the Virginal

Conception immediately, and the genetic material of Mary's ovum mediately. For, presumably, God creates the first human genes and then ensures that these genes are successfully passed on down the generations.[15]

But even if this reasoning is sound, it might still be thought that, in miraculously supplying new Y chromosomes in the Incarnation, God has not created a new member of the human race that originated with Adam. He has created a new type of human, perhaps, but not one that can clearly be called a 'son of Adam'. And this might be a problem if it is important to salvation that Christ is 'like us in *every* way, sin excepted' (Heb. 4.15 – emphasis added). But, this problem does not obtain if, in order to be a member of Adam's race, so to speak, all that is required is the threshold amount of genetic material, supplied by the Virgin's ovum. I shall presume that this is so. As I said at the beginning of this excursus, I am not suggesting this is the truth of the matter. I am merely offering one plausible way by which the Virginal Conception could be reconciled with the problem posed for this doctrine by membership of the natural kind, human.[16]

But this sort of reasoning has been disputed. Arthur Peacocke, in a recent essay on this particular aspect of the traditional doctrine of Christ's Virginal Conception, has this to say: 'In light of our biological knowledge it is then impossible to see how Jesus could be said to share our human nature, if he came into existence by a virginal conception of the kind traditionally proposed.'[17] He also claims that the biological considerations to do with whether Christ has sufficient human genetic material to be counted a human being show how the traditional doctrine has docetic implications. In other words, if the traditional

---

15. Alternatively, perhaps God creates the initial matter of the universe out of nothing, and then ensures, through his providential control of the universe, that some of the matter he has created becomes, through a complex series of evolutionary changes, the genetic material of human beings.

16. Another argument to substantially the same conclusion: assume all that distinguishes the Spirit-generated DNA and the Virgin-generated DNA in the Virginal Conception of Christ is the issue of the origin of that DNA. In every other respect the genetic material is indistinguishable. Then, for every act of cell-mitosis subsequent to the act of syngamy that generates the Christ-zygote, the new mitosis-generated cell is produced via a normal biological process. Such mitosis-generated cells would count as 'human' cells because they occur (i.e., originate) through normal biological processes. The question of their provenance does not arise as it does for the genetic material supplied by the Holy Spirit in the moment of syngamy. This means that, in the case of the Christ-zygote, for every act of cell-mitosis after syngamy, the resulting cell thereby generated is a human cell. Although the 'non-human' (i.e., Spirit-generated) biological material involved in the original zygotic cell would remain, all later cells would be human cells because they are produced by mitosis – that is, they originate through a normal biological process. Eventually the biological material of the original cell would degrade and be replaced through normal cell-wastage. From that point on, no part of Christ's human nature originates outside of normal biological processes. I am grateful to Jonathan Chan for suggesting this argument to me, though it may still have to overcome concerns about temporary docetism, if the initial Spirit-generated DNA is not human, strictly speaking.

17. Peacocke, 'DNA of our DNA', p. 65.

view means Christ only *appears* to be truly human, but in fact cannot be truly human because the biological facts preclude this, then the traditional view is docetic. It denies the true humanity of Christ; his humanity is only *ostensible*.[18] But what biological fact precludes the traditional view? Peacocke objects that the traditional doctrine postulates 'an extraordinary, almost magical, divine act of suddenly bringing into existence a complex biological entity.'[19] But, surely, this is precisely the point of the traditional doctrine. Christ's birth is a miracle. Peacocke cannot be opposed to the idea that God is able to perform miracles, if he believes that God created the world, or that God raised Christ from the dead.[20] There is not really another reason given for the 'biological' objection in Peacocke's essay. So it is difficult to see what the 'biological' objection amounts to, apart from the fact that Christ's birth is, indeed, a special birth.[21] As to the charge of docetism, this only obtains if something like the story I have told regarding the threshold amount of DNA required to belong to humankind, fails – which is to say the traditional view is only docetic if Christ is not fully a human being, the very point at issue. Nothing Peacocke says *shows* that the deliverances of current biological knowledge of human reproduction precludes the sort of story I have set forth. Consequently, there is no reason to think Peacocke has given us a biological reason for rejecting the traditional doctrine of the Virgin Birth.[22]

So, on the default creationist account, the Holy Spirit miraculously generates the human body of Christ. His body is truly human (assuming the foregoing

---

18.   Ibid, p. 66.

19.   Ibid., p. 65. This is somewhat curious, given his earlier concession that miracles can mean a 'wonder' or a 'sign'.

20.   Of course, these things might be denied (Peacocke does not deny that God creates the world – I do not know what he says about the resurrection). But if one denies that God creates the world, one can hardly be called a theist. And if one denies God raised Christ from the grave, one can hardly call oneself an orthodox Christian.

21.   Furthermore, his (frankly unorthodox) insinuation that the traditional doctrine means the Holy Spirit, by supplying the sperm that fertilizes Mary's ovum, *impregnates* Mary betrays a failure to understand the traditional position. See 'DNA of our DNA', p. 63. For example, the Reformed Orthodox were quite clear that the Holy Spirit is the efficient but not material cause of the Virginal Conception in order to rebut the Socinian allegation that the Holy Spirit was the father of Christ's human nature. Thus Wollebius, ' "for since the title of Father requires generation from the substance of Him who generates and the generation of a nature like itself and neither occurs here, it is evident that the H. Spirit cannot be called the Father of Christ." ' Heppe, *Reformed Dogmatics*, p. 424. Thomas makes a similar point in *Summa Contra Gentiles* 1V.

22.   It might be objected that the universe is a causally closed system, precluding any interference by an agent outside this system, were there any such agent. But, although he mentions this in passing, Peacocke does not make much use of this notion. In any case, classical theology has the resources to respond to this sort of argument. The idea that the universe is 'causally closed' depends on a certain way of thinking about causal relations, physical laws and induction that are certainly not beyond dispute. For recent discussion of this, see Alvin Plantinga, 'Can God Break the Laws?' in Andrew Dole and Andrew Chignell, eds *God and The Ethics of Belief: New Essays in Philosophy of Religion* (Cambridge: Cambridge University Press, 2005) pp. 31–58.

reasoning, or something like it that can overcome the problem posed by natural kinds). The Holy Spirit also creates the soul of Christ that he attaches to, or integrates into, the body of Christ. Thus a complete human nature (body + soul) is generated in the Virginal Conception. However, although, on this view, in the normal procreation of human beings the presence of a human body and soul – a complete human nature – coincides with the formation of a new human person, this is not the case in the Incarnation (at least, not on the default creationist account of Virginal Conception in view here). The body and soul of Christ do not form a human person in abstraction from the Word of God. In fact, the Word of God assumes this complete human nature, and at that moment the human nature formed by the Holy Spirit becomes the human nature of the second person of the Trinity, and is, as it were, 'personalized' by him. Hence the Word is essentially divine, but only accidentally, or contingently, human. In other words, the Word would have existed without the Incarnation, because he is the second person of the Trinity. But as a matter of fact, the Virginal Conception teaches us that, at a certain moment in time, the Word becomes incarnate. So the human nature he assumes at the Virginal Conception, he assumes 'into' his person (what in dogmatic theology is usually called the doctrine of the *enhypostatos phusis*, or 'personalized (human) nature' of Christ). And, of course, all of this happens at one-and-the-same-time, according to most orthodox accounts of the Incarnation. By that I mean there is no time lapse between the generation of the human body in the womb of the Virgin by the Holy Spirit, the creation and 'attachment'/integration of the soul to the body, and the assumption and 'personalization' of this complete human nature (the body + soul composite) by the Word of God. All these events take place simultaneously at the Virginal Conception. If there were any delay between these different conceptual 'moments' of the Virginal Conception and Incarnation, the result, I suggest, would be something other than an orthodox account of the Incarnation. For suppose it turns out that under normal circumstances a human body is first formed in the womb at the moment of syngamy, that is, the moment the gametes are fused, and then, at some later time, ensouled. And suppose that the development of the embryonic Christ is the same as other human beings in this respect (*pace* Thomas). Could it not be that the Word assumes a human body at the Virginal Conception, and then assumes a soul that is 'attached' to, or integrated with, the body already possessed by the Word of God, at the later time at which a soul is normally generated for a human body? The Reformed Orthodox theologian Francis Turretin, thought this was possible. He says it is not important to 'inquire curiously' about the time at which the Christ's soul was united to his body, or the Word to his flesh. It is sufficient to believe that, from the moment of its first existence, the human nature of Christ never existed apart from the Word. He goes on to say,

> if the soul could not be poured into the body unless already organized and completely formed (a point on which physicians are not agreed among themselves [sic]), it does

not follow that the *Logos (Logon)* could not at once unite the flesh to himself, since his work could not be constrained either with the soul present or absent. Nor is it more absurd for the body of Christ (not as yet animated) to be united to the *Logos (Logô)*, than for the same (when lifeless in the sepulchre) to remain conjoined with the same (as theologians acknowledge was done in the death of Christ).[23]

But Turretin is mistaken about this. His view would mean that, possibly, the Incarnation was an event that occurred in stages. The first stage would be the assumption by the Word of a human body, at the moment of Virginal Conception. The second would be the ensoulment of the human body that the Word has assumed, which, on this view, would take place at some time during the gestation of Christ's human body, later than conception. The problem with this is that it means at the Virginal Conception the Word does not assume human nature as such, just a human body. But then, for the period between conception and ensoulment, Apollinarianism obtains! (Apollinarianism is the heresy that Christ did not have a 'rational' soul – its place being taken by the Word of God.) So Turretin is incorrect to suggest that inquiring into when the soul is united to the body of Christ, or when the Word is united to his human nature, is unimportant. It is of crucial importance in foreclosing the possibility of Apollinarianism obtaining for some period at the beginning of the Incarnation, between conception and ensoulment. If ensoulment normally takes place at some time later than conception for human beings other than Christ, then it cannot take place in the same way for Christ precisely because this opens the door to temporary Apollinarianism (between conception and ensoulment).[24]

1.2 The Gestation of Christ

This brings us to the other aspects of a traditional doctrine of the Virgin Birth. The gestation of Christ is not usually discussed at length in theological expositions of the traditional doctrine of the Virgin Birth. It is simply assumed. However, in medieval theology there was some discussion of this matter relevant to the question of the time of ensoulment. As has already been mentioned,

---

23.   Turretin, *Institutes of Elenctic Theology, Vol. II*, Topic 13, Q. XI, § XIII, p. 343.

24.   This raises two interrelated issues. First, even if Christ is ensouled from conception, is he conscious *qua* human? Clearly not: he has no brain at this stage of development. But then, for some period he is ensouled in a human body and not conscious as a human. I think this is perfectly feasible. I presume I am ensouled when unconscious – my soul does not depart when I am asleep. In any case, I take it that a soul is literally nowhere. Its relation to a particular physical organ when 'attached' to a particular body, even if that organ is the brain, is not a physical relation. So there can be no physical dependence of the soul upon the brain, or some other physical organ, for example the pineal gland. In fact, I think that the soul is not dependent on the body for its continued existence in any way. The attachment of soul to body is a contingent relation. (It may be that the soul has some relation to the physical matter of the developing zygote from conception which becomes a particular relation to, say, the brain, as the body develops.) Consequently, Turretin cannot mean that Christ may be incapable of being ensouled until such time as he develops a brain.

Thomas Aquinas maintained that, unlike the development of other human beings, Christ was formed as a complete embryo that could sustain a soul from conception.[25] Christ did not, Thomas maintained, develop in the same way as other embryos. Rather,

> [t]he body's very formation [i.e. Christ's body] in which conception principally consists, was instantaneous, for two reasons. First, because of the infinite power of the agent, viz. the Holy Ghost, by whom Christ's body was formed. . . . Secondly, on the part of the Person of the Son, whose body was being formed. For it was unbecoming that He should take to Himself a body as yet unformed. . . . Therefore in the first instant in which the various parts of the matter were united together in the place of generation, Christ's body was both perfectly formed and assumed. (*Summa Theologica* IIIa. Q. 33. art. 1)

Moreover, 'Spiritual perfection was becoming to the human nature which Christ took, which perfection he attained not by making progress but by receiving it from the very first' (*Summa Theologica* IIIa. Q. 34. art. 2).[26]

But this need not be a requirement of a creationist view, and we shall exclude it from the default creationist account of Virginal Conception.[27] (Although note that Thomas, unlike Turretin, sees the problem temporary Apollinarianism poses for a two-stage Incarnation, and is careful to avoid it.) On the default account, Christ develops in the womb as other human beings do, and becomes a fully formed embryo during gestation, rather than from the moment of conception. Nevertheless – *pace* Turretin – the foetal Christ sustains a soul from the moment of conception.[28]

Secondly, does my objection to Turretin imply that any orthodox version of the Incarnation is at least *logically* Apollinarian because ensoulment requires the 'prior' presence of a human body? (Not temporally, but conceptually prior.) Well, perhaps. I do not think that the logical priority of a human body over a human soul in this sense is theologically damaging. The damage is done when Christ is said to be embodied but not also ensouled at a given moment in time.

25.   Recall that Thomas held to a two-stage view of normal human development. He believed other (male) human beings were conceived and then ensouled forty days afterwards.

26.   Thomas' views on this matter are complicated. He thought that only when it is fully developed can an embryo sustain a soul, which gives form or organisation to the body. This means that Christ's body must be a fully formed embryo, if it is to sustain his soul from the moment of conception. And yet he still gestates for a full nine months! For more on this, see Jones, *The Soul of The Embryo*, ch. 8 and Donceel, 'Immediate Animation and Delayed Hominization', p. 83.

27.   Turretin says '[m]omentous formation of the entire body of Christ and its conjunction with the soul is feigned without Scripture (in which no trace is found of such a miraculous formation)', *Institutes*, Topic 13, Q. XI, § XIII, 343. I think that, on this particular matter, Turretin is right. There is no good Scriptural reason to believe Christ's human nature was formed in a different way from other human natures. Indeed, Luke 2.40 suggests that Christ developed normally after birth – why believe his foetal development was any different?

28.   This means that the default creationist account is incompatible with certain sorts of hylomorphist accounts of substance dualism, such as the version advocated by Thomas. But it is not necessarily incommensurate with all versions of hylomorphism.

1.3 *The Virgin Birth*

Like the matter of Christ's gestation, the Virgin Birth (meaning here, that aspect of the complete doctrine of the Virgin Birth that refers to the nativity) is not usually discussed at length in theological accounts of the doctrine of the Virgin Birth. The dogmatic problems in the doctrine of the Virgin Birth are mostly focussed on the issue of the Virginal Conception of Christ, not his gestation or birth, despite the fact that it is the doctrine of the Virgin *Birth*. However, there are exceptions to this. One such is the Swiss theologian Emil Brunner who asserts that the birth narratives in Matthew and Luke's Gospels 'do not refer to the Incarnation of the Eternal Son'. Instead, they deal 'with the origin of the Person of Jesus Christ'.[29] Later in the same chapter he says:

> The great, unthinkable, unimaginable miracle of the Incarnation which the Apostles
> proclaim, is not that the Eternal Son of God was born as the son of a virgin, but that the
> Eternal Son of God, who from all eternity was in the bosom of the Father, uncreated,
> Himself proceeding from the Bring of God Himself, became Man.[30]

Brunner seems to think there are several things that tell against the traditional account of the Virgin Birth of Christ, as given in the birth narratives of Matthew and Luke. First, the accounts of Christ's human origin in the New Testament do not explain to us that Jesus Christ is the Eternal Son of God. Secondly, the doctrine of the Incarnation (the passage in which the above comments are made suggest the suffix, 'as given in the New Testament, apart from the birth narratives of Matthew and Luke') is not about a Virgin Birth, but about the Eternal Word of God becoming man. The suggestion seems to be that the New Testament apart from the birth narratives (which he thinks historically suspect)[31] tells us about the Incarnation, but without mention of a Virgin Birth.[32]

---

29.   Brunner is not the only influential twentieth-century theologian who has taken this sort of view. However, his argument is interesting because, unlike liberal theologians who have rejected the Virgin Birth, he wishes to retain a robust doctrine of the Incarnation without the Virgin Birth. Hence, his view on this matter is particularly pertinent to the present essay.

30.   Brunner, *The Christian Doctrine of Creation and Redemption,* pp. 352 and 356 respectively. Cf. Emil Brunner, *The Mediator, A Study of The Central Doctrine of The Christian Faith,* trans. Olive Wyon (London: Lutterworth Press, 1934), p. 322.

31.   At one point in his discussion of the Virgin Birth in *The Mediator,* Brunner says, 'everything goes to prove that this doctrine arose rather late, thus that it arose for dogmatic reasons and not out of historical knowledge', p. 324.

32.   Thus, Brunner says:

> The doctrine of the Incarnation of the Eternal Son of God in Paul and John, and
> the doctrine of the conception of Jesus through the Holy Spirit, in the womb of the
> Virgin Mary, are two independent parallel attempts to interpret the mystery of
> Jesus. Whether they can be combined with one another, is at least an open question.
> (Ibid., p. 352)

But of course, this is not an open question according to classical theology.

So, if the historicity of the birth narratives is in question, perhaps we can have a doctrine of the Incarnation without the Virgin Birth that they teach.[33]

In response to this, several things can be said. It is true that the canonical birth narratives do not explicitly refer to the Eternal Son of God. Their concern is to explain the origin of the human Jesus of Nazareth. It is also true to say that there is no other *explicit* reference to the doctrine of the Virgin Birth in the rest of the New Testament. (That said, there may be other *implicit* references to the Virgin Birth – for instance, Jn 1.14, 2 Cor. 8.9, Gal. 4.4, Phil. 2.6.) I suppose one could argue on this basis that no one New Testament document explicitly teaches *both* the origin of Jesus of Nazareth *and* that the origin of Jesus is the moment of the Incarnation of the Eternal Son of God. But this is everywhere assumed in the New Testament, just as in Franz Kafka's suffocating novel, *The Trial,* we never know why the protagonist is being tried – but the fact that he is being tried *unjustly* is presupposed on almost every page. If the reader were to miss this crucial point, he or she would fail to understand what Kafka is trying to convey. And if one takes passages like John's Prologue and the birth narratives of Matthew and Luke together, as telling different aspects of one particular story – the story of the Incarnation and Virgin Birth of the Word of God – then, not unnaturally, one will end up with the idea that, taken as a whole, in the New Testament the question of the origin of Jesus Christ is at-one-and-the-same-time a question about the Incarnation of the Eternal Son of God. In fact, the reader of the New Testament who misses this arguably fails to understand the story these documents tell. (This is certainly the traditional Christian view of the matter, whether or not Brunner agrees with this view.) Brunner seems to think that the birth narratives in the New Testament *only* teach about the origin of Jesus of Nazareth and remain silent on whether or not the Virgin Birth of Jesus is also the Incarnation of the Eternal Son of God. By contrast, other passages of the New Testament, such as John's Prologue, tell a different story of Incarnation without Virgin Birth (in fact he thinks that John's Prologue may be written *against* the birth narratives of Matthew and Luke, to give an alternative view of the Incarnation). But this presumes a certain way of reading the documents of the New Testament which will not appeal to those already

---

33.   Brunner again:

> Of course, as the theology of the Church has done for centuries, we can interpret the narratives of Matthew and Luke in such a way that their statement can be brought into harmony with that of the Gospel of John; but apart from this re-interpretation there is a clear contradiction. It is therefore not wholly improbable that the Johannine Prologue was deliberately placed where it is, in opposition to the doctrine of the Virgin Birth. (Ibid., p. 353)

Sadly, he does not explain how the birth narratives and John's Prologue are contradictory, nor why the placing of the Prologue is likely to be in direct opposition to the doctrine of the Virgin Birth. We are left with unsubstantiated assertion. Wolfhart Pannenberg expresses similar sentiments. See *Jesus – God and Man*, p. 143.

convinced (on other grounds or for other reasons, such as the internal testimony of the Holy Spirit) that, when taken together, the texts of the New Testament teach a consistent story according to which the Virgin Birth of Christ is intimately connected with the Incarnation.[34] Brunner is right to say that the New Testament without the birth narratives could be read as endorsing a doctrine of Incarnation without Virgin Birth. And we shall see presently that an NVB version of the Incarnation seems plausible, given certain assumptions about the New Testament documents and the nature of the Incarnation. But unless one is already convinced by, say, the findings of certain historical biblical critics that the birth narratives are historically suspect, one is unlikely to find Brunner's argument convincing.[35] And the fact is, the birth narratives are canonical Scripture. This means that there is a very good theological reason for trusting them: they are divine revelation.[36] But what reason is there to trust Brunner's reconstructed account of the Incarnation? Only his assertion that there are two parallel accounts of the Incarnation in the New Testament that contradict one another, namely the Matthean-Lukan birth narratives and the Johannine Prologue, coupled with his underlying assumption that the birth narratives are historically dubious (for which he offers no argument). On this basis I am inclined to think that the objections Brunner raises against the historicity of the birth narratives are really not as damaging as he thinks they are, and are certainly not sufficient to undermine their trustworthiness as scriptural accounts of how the Incarnation took place. Nevertheless, Brunner's (it has to be said, somewhat incidental) insight into the fact that the Virgin Birth is not necessary for a doctrine of the Incarnation has theological mileage, and may prove useful. It is to this issue that we now turn.

2. The No Virgin Birth (NVB) Version of the Incarnation

In this section we shall be concerned to set out a strong doctrine of the Incarnation without a doctrine of the Virgin Birth. The NVB version of the Incarnation I shall outline here depends on several assumptions. To begin with, we shall assume a Christology entirely in keeping with the canons of Chalcedonian, apart from the doctrine of the Virgin Birth. All that is at issue here is the *means by which* the Word became Incarnate, not the fact that the Word became

---

34. Thomas Torrance makes a good case for the claim that Paul and other New Testament authors do allude to the Virgin Birth although they do not mention it explicitly. See Thomas F. Torrance, 'The Doctrine of the Virgin Birth' in *Scottish Bulletin of Evangelical Theology* 12 (1994): 8–15.

35. Of course, it is also unconvincing on other grounds: it is an argument from silence.

36. If, in keeping with what was said in the first chapter about 'high' views of Scripture, one took a more 'Barthian' view of the nature of revelation, things would be somewhat different. But even with a 'Barthian' view, one could argue that the New Testament birth narratives are records that witness to divine revelation, and that may become the means by which such revelation occurs now.

Incarnate, or what the Incarnation involves, apart from the doctrine of the Virgin Birth. On this particular issue, the NVB account and Brunner's view converge. And to this extent, Brunner shares Richard Cross' conviction, and the conviction of a number of other theologians, that the Virgin Birth is not a matter that is essential to the Incarnation.

Second, and also in keeping with Brunner, we shall assume that the birth narratives of Matthew and Luke are historically *misleading* accounts of the means by which the Incarnation took place. Perhaps these birth narratives are legendary, as a number of theological opponents of the doctrine have asserted. That is, they may preserve an essential (historical) truth, that Christ's human nature has a beginning in time. So, with respect to his human nature, Christ was born of a woman. This does not mean that the Word has a beginning in time. He is the eternally begotten Son of God. So, with the Council of Chalcedon, this NVB doctrine affirms the *double generation* of Christ. He is eternally begotten according to his divine nature, and begotten of (a man and) woman by normal generation according to his human nature. Hence, on this NVB doctrine, something like Brunner's criticism of the traditional doctrine of the Virgin Birth obtains. I say something like it obtains, because Brunner is not always as precise about what his doctrine entails as we might wish him to be. (It should be clear that this assumption is stronger than the mere *possibility* that God might have brought about the Incarnation without a Virgin Birth, by normal human generation. All orthodox theologians can agree to this. Brunner, and other revisionist Christologists are asserting that the Incarnation *actually* took place without a Virgin Birth. This calls the historicity of the birth narratives into question.)

A third assumption is a version of the default creationist view of the origin of Christ's soul, outlined earlier. This account of the origin of Christ's soul has the advantage of representing a large section of the western Christian tradition, although I also believe it is the right way of thinking about the origin of Christ's human soul. Of course, the default creationist view is not a requirement of an NVB account. One could take another view of the generation of Christ's soul as some theologians have. Provided the alternative is theologically orthodox, this does not affect the overall point we are driving at, in setting out an NVB account of the Incarnation.

How might an NVB explanation of the Incarnation go? Well, here is an alternative account of the Incarnation, which includes the assumptions just mentioned, and is an NVB version of the doctrine that makes clear what Brunner's view suggests about the Incarnation – without the need for a Virgin Birth.

Jesus was born to Mary and Joseph through a normal act of human procreation. There was no miraculous generation of Y chromosomes or fertilization of Mary's ovum involved in this act. Assume Joseph was the natural father of Christ (according to his human nature). At the moment of conception, as Joseph's sperm fertilized Mary's ovum, God created a human soul out of nothing, which he 'attached' to, or integrated into the fertilized ovum. Yet at the self-same moment of conception, the Holy Spirit intervened in this miraculous respect: he ensured that the soul of Christ was without original sin.[37] However, this action of the Holy Spirit in ensuring Christ's human nature has no original sin is the only way in which Christ's human nature differs from the natures of other human beings. The way it is generated is otherwise the same as the process that applies in the case of all other normal human conceptions. At the same moment in which God creates the human nature of Christ in the womb of Mary, the Word of God assumes it. There is no temporal lag between the generation of the human body of Christ, the creation out of nothing of the soul of this body (which is created without original sin), the immediate ensoulment of this body with the soul created by divine fiat for this purpose, and the Incarnation. All these different events occur simultaneously. Finally, after a successful gestation, Mary gives birth to the Christ child.

But this NVB account is not without problems. First, there are problems pertaining to the orthodoxy of this argument (apart from the denial of the Virgin Birth). One such objection is this: can Christ have two fathers, one human and one divine? This seems more serious at first glance than it may in fact be. The objection cannot be that a human being is involved in the generation of Christ's human nature, because this is also true of the traditional view, where the human Mary bears Christ's human nature. But, it might be argued, the problem is not that a human being is involved in this account of the Incarnation, but that *only* human beings are involved. On this NVB account, the generation of Christ's human nature is entirely a matter of human procreation, not immediate divine creation. However, once we see that it is only the human body of Christ that is humanly procreated, much of the force of this objection dissipates. The Holy Spirit is still miraculously involved, ensuring that the soul belonging to this particular human body is without original sin. In one sense Christ does have two fathers, if this account is granted. But not in a way any more damaging than the claim that Mary is the Mother of God or the *Theotokos* (God-Bearer), where this means, 'Mary is the Mother/Bearer of the human nature of the Second Person of the Trinity'. Could not Joseph be the Father of God in a similar way? That is, could he not be said to be 'the Father of the human nature of the Second Person of the Trinity'?

---

37. An aside: I presume, with classical theologians, that original sin is a property of the soul, not a property of the body, although original sin has physical effects, such as fatigue, illness and so on. However, if original sin is also somehow a property of the body, then the Holy Spirit ensured that those aspects of original sin that would have polluted Christ's body – apart from the effects of sin, such as fatigue, sadness and so on – did not pollute Christ's body at the moment it was generated. For an extended treatment of these aspects of original sin, see my *Divinity and Humanity*, ch. 4.

A second objection is that this NVB account implies Christ was born out of wedlock.[38] But if we concede the assumption that the birth narratives of Matthew and Luke are legendary, this may not be so damaging. The notion that Mary is a virgin fits with the idea of a Virgin Birth. But if there was no Virgin Birth, (if the birth narratives are legendary, or false) then there is little reason to believe that Christ was conceived out of wedlock, apart from the desire to cast aspersions on the circumstances involved in the conception of Christ. I suppose that if Christ were born to an unmarried woman, this would have been scandalous as well as sinful, although there is no reason to think that Christ could not have been preserved from sinfulness despite the circumstances surrounding this sort of conception. But surely God would not have ordained that the Incarnation occurred through a disordered, or immoral sexual act. That would, I suggest, be an entirely unfitting mode of Incarnation. On our NVB account, we shall assume that Christ was born to the married Mary and Joseph.[39]

A third potential objection is that the NVB account looks Nestorian. But this is easily dealt with. It is only Nestorian if the Word of God assumes an existing person. But this need not be the case on an NVB account if what is formed with the fusion of gametes (and ensoulment) in the case of Christ is a human nature not a human person that is, *at the very moment of syngamy*, assumed by the Second Person of the Trinity, whose human nature it becomes. Provided the defender of an NVB is careful enough to ensure that there is no time at which that which is formed by the fusion of gametes and immediate ensoulment is not also the human nature of the Second Person of the Trinity, it is not Nestorian.

A fourth objection has to do with the implications such an NVB account may or may not have. In the first half of the twentieth century, Gresham Machen maintained that denial of the Virgin Birth inevitably leads to one of two outcomes: the evasion of a biblical doctrine of sin or evasion of the biblical presentation of Christ's supernatural person.[40] But I do not see why this needs be so. Christ could be both sinless, through the work of the Holy Spirit at the moment of conception, and possessed of two natures, as per Chalcedonian orthodoxy, on an NVB account, as I have tried to suggest. Machen also asserts that, 'even if the belief in the virgin birth is not necessary to every Christian',

---

38.   Wilkinson notes that this is the traditional Talmudic view of Christ's conception. See 'Apologetic Aspects of The Virgin Birth of Jesus Christ', pp. 159 and 165. See also Berry, 'The Virgin Birth of Christ', p. 104.

39.   But, it might be said, there is nothing in the New Testament that suggests Christ was born to Mary and Joseph once they had married. But this is no more speculative than the idea that Christ was born out of wedlock or to Mary and a Roman centurian (another aspersion), or some other explanation other than the one that is given in the New Testament, namely his Virginal Conception and Birth. If the birth narratives are discounted as unreliable or legendary, what is there to prevent us assuming some other state of affairs obtained than the one traditionally thought to have done so?

40.   J. Gresham Machen, *The Virgin Birth of Christ* (London: Marshall, Morgan and Scott, 1930), p. 395.

because some are ignorant of it, or find themselves unable to believe it for some reason, 'it is certainly necessary to Christianity'.[41] In one sense, this is perfectly true. The Virgin Birth is a constituent of the theology of Scripture and the Creeds, without which we would have a mutilated, or at least depleted, account of the Incarnation as it has been traditionally understood. But God could have brought about the Incarnation without a Virgin Birth. As John Wilkinson has put it, the Incarnation is a central affirmation of the faith. But the *mode* of Incarnation is not.[42] Nevertheless the Virgin Birth *is* how God brought about the Incarnation (according to Scripture and tradition). And if God decreed the Virgin Birth, it follows that, once God had decreed how the Incarnation would take place, the Virgin Birth was a necessary constituent of an orthodox doctrine of the Incarnation. So Machen is right, if the necessity he has in mind is conditional upon God's ordaining that the Incarnation takes place by virgin birth. But it is not the case that the Virgin Birth is a necessary mode of Incarnation, in the sense that it was the only *metaphysically possible* way for the Incarnation to take place. God could have ordained matters otherwise.

I suggest that the NVB account given here is compatible with a two-natures doctrine of the Incarnation and a default creationist view of the origin of Christ's soul. The Reformed Orthodox distinguished between the formation of Christ's human nature by the Holy Spirit, his sanctification of that human nature and its assumption by the person of the Word of God (all three being conceptual, not temporal distinctions).[43] This NVB account preserves the second and third aspect of the traditional account whilst amending the first. The claim is that the human nature of Christ is generated through normal procreation, rather than divine intervention. Therefore, it offers a robust Christology, aside from the crucial fact that it does not teach a Virgin Birth.[44] However, this fact alone is, I suggest, sufficient to make an NVB account of the Incarnation theologically unacceptable (quite apart from the problem it raises for the authority of the biblical birth narratives).

3. *Insufficient Reasons for the Virgin Birth*

This brings us to the matter of theological reasons for the Virgin Birth (as traditionally understood). As has already been indicated, I do not think there are sufficient reasons to reject the doctrine of the Virgin Birth because it is clearly set forth in Scripture and is taught in the ecumenical creeds of the Church.

---

41. Ibid., p. 396.

42. Wilkinson, 'Apologetic Aspects of The Virgin Birth of Jesus Christ', p. 159.

43. See Heppe, *Reformed Dogmatics*, p. 424.

44. This NVB version of the Incarnation also has the benefit of being more transparent than some of the alternatives on offer. For instance, Pannenberg claims that the Virgin Birth is merely a legend, but that it may be retained as one aspect of the 'liturgical confession' of the Church because

However, it might still be thought that Incarnation via Virginal Conception, gestation and Birth, as taught in the tradition and Scripture, is somehow an *unfitting* means for the Incarnation of the Son of God. This sort of objection goes back at least to Tertullian's treatise *On the Flesh of Christ* (*De Carne Christi*), where Tertullian accuses Marcion of excising the birth narratives from his collection of the Gospels because, amongst other things, Marcion 'arraigned' the Virgin Birth 'as undignified'.[45] The same sort of accusation against the Virgin Birth can be found later in the tradition. For instance, in Odo of Tournai's *Disputation With the Jew, Leo, Concerning the Advent of Christ, the Son of God*, Odo has Leo, his Jewish interlocutor, say this:

> In one thing especially we [Jews] laugh at you [Christians] and think that you are crazy. You say that God was conceived within his mothers' womb, surrounded by a vile fluid [sic.], and suffered enclosure within this foul prison for nine months when finally, in the tenth month, he emerged from her private parts (who is not embarrassed by such a scene!). Thus you attribute to God what is most unbecoming, which we would not do without great embarrassment.[46]

There are several responses to this sort of thinking that can be found in the theological literature that are, to my mind, insufficient to the purpose of show-ing that the Virgin Birth is a 'fitting' means by which the Son of God becomes Incarnate. It is worth clearing these insufficient reasons out of the way before considering the argument given by Anselm, which is, I shall argue, a more satisfactory way of responding to this objection.

---

it safeguards two important theological notions. These are, that from his conception, Christ is the Word of God (he calls this an 'antiadoptionist thought'), and secondly, that Christ was truly human (an 'antidocetic point'). He concludes,

> because the intention of the creed's formulations is to be sought precisely in their antidocetic and antiadoptionist function, the creed, even with the formulation 'conceived by the Holy Spirit, born of the Virgin Mary', can be confessed in worship without abandoning truthfulness. . . . Whoever joins in the confession of the church confesses the unity of Christianity through time by placing himself in the context of the intentions expressed in the formulations, even where the mode of expression must be perceived as inappropriate. (*Jesus – God and Man*, p. 150)

But, aside from the fact that Pannenberg's two theological safeguards can be expressed without dissemblance in an NVB account of the Incarnation, his rationale for retaining a liturgical use for the creedal affirmation of the Virgin Birth seems more than a little disingenuous. Better to come clean and give clear biblical and theological reasons for rejecting the doctrine than retain the pretence of confessing a doctrine that one no longer believes to be true.

45.   Tertullian, *Treatise on The Incarnation,* ed. and trans. Ernest Evans (London: SPCK, 1956), chs 4, 13.

46.   In Odo of Tournai, *On Original Sin and A Disputation With the Jew, Leo, Concerning the Advent of Christ, the Son of God, Two Theological Treatises,* trans. Irven M. Resnick (Philadelphia, PA: University of Pennsylvania Press, 1994) p. 95.

The first of these insufficient reasons is what we shall call an anti-docetic thesis. As we have already had cause to note, docetism denotes the unorthodox view that Christ only appeared to be human. He was not truly human. In a similar way, an angel might appear to be human (as in Gen. 18, perhaps), but not be truly human. So an anti-docetic thesis in favour of a Virgin Birth would be something like this: *the traditional doctrine of the Virginal Conception and Birth of Christ preserves his true and complete humanity.* But, as we have seen, this is not obvious. If anything, an Incarnation without a Virgin Birth would be a better way of ensuring the true, full humanity of Christ, because it would not raise problems such as those raised by the natural kinds argument.[47]

A second insufficient reason for the Virgin Birth is what we shall call an anti-adoptionist thesis. Recall that adoptionism is, roughly, the view that the Word of God 'possessed' an existing human being.[48] So an anti-adoptionist thesis in defence of the Virgin Birth might be this: *the traditional doctrine of the Virginal Conception and Birth of Christ forecloses the possibility of divine 'possession' of an existing entity (or an existing human being) in the particular case of the Incarnation.*[49] But once again, this seems wholly inadequate as a reason for the Virgin Birth. For here, as before, this thesis could be satisfied according to an NVB doctrine of the Incarnation. In fact, the means by which the Incarnation takes place is entirely beside the point for an anti-adoptionist thesis. All that is in view in such a thesis is the moment of Incarnation (when in the process of human generation the Incarnation takes place), not how this comes to be (whether by a Virginal Conception and Birth, or by normal human procreation). So this sort of reasoning can hardly be used to justify the Virgin Birth as the most fitting means by which the Incarnation takes place.

A third insufficient reason for the Virgin Birth has to do with Christ's sinlessness. By this I mean, the sinlessness of his human nature. I presume, with a number of orthodox theologians in the tradition, that Christ was incapable of sinning according to his divine nature, because God cannot sin. He is impeccable. But his human nature is not, in abstraction from the Incarnation, as it were,

---

47. Or, indeed, other arguments similar to this, such as Bishop John Robinson's contention that the traditional doctrine sets up a *cordon sanitaire* between Christ's humanity and ours that seems inconsistent with Hebrew 4.15. See John A. T. Robinson, *The Human Face of God*, pp. 47–56.

48. Adoptionism might be thought of as one aspect of Nestorianism. Both views claim Christ is composed of two persons, one divine the other human. But I suppose Adoptionism might be broader than Nestorianism in this respect: the Word might 'adopt' or take possession of, an existing entity other than an existing human person.

49. The use of 'forecloses' here should not be taken to mean 'makes metaphysically impossible'. It is metaphysically possible that God possess an existing entity, even in worlds where an Incarnation takes place. God could, after all, take possession of some entity in addition to becoming Incarnate – a matter to which we shall return in the final chapter of this volume. The point here is just that, in the case of the traditional doctrine of the Incarnation, it is not true to say the human nature of Christ is an existing entity that is then 'possessed' by the Word. The traditional doctrine forecloses *that* possibility.

impeccable in this way. It is, we might say, constitutionally sinless, but not constitutionally impeccable, although its assumption by the Word in the Incarnation renders the human nature of Christ, for all practical purposes, incapable of sinning.[50]

Here is a sinlessness thesis in defence of the Virgin Birth: *only the traditional doctrine of the Virginal Conception and Birth of Christ ensures Christ's human nature is without sin from the first moment of conception.* The problem with this is twofold. First, as before, this is simply not to the point. What is in view in the doctrine of Christ's sinlessness is not the Virgin Birth, but that Christ is without sin from conception. But as we have seen on the NVB account of the Incarnation, it is possible for the sinlessness of Christ's human nature to be safeguarded from conception onwards, on an NVB account. This brings us to the second point. Given a default creationist account of the Virginal Conception, the preservation of the Christ foetus from conception to birth (and thereafter) in a sinless state is a matter for the hypostatic union, not the Virgin Birth. More specifically, on one influential way of thinking about this matter, the sinlessness of Christ's human nature from conception onwards is due to the preservation of the human nature by the divine nature of Christ. But this means that the question of the sinlessness of the human nature of Christ from conception onwards has nothing to do with the question of the Virgin Birth and everything to do with the doctrine of the hypostatic union.[51]

4. *The Fittingness of the Virgin Birth*

However, there is another reason often given for the Virgin Birth (aside from the fact that it is canonical and is supported by the creeds) that seems more promising. This has to do with the 'fittingness' of the Virgin Birth as the means by which the Incarnation is brought about. This notion of the 'fittingness' of the Incarnation has a long theological pedigree.[52] One theologian in particular who favoured it is Anselm. His discussion of this issue has several different strands and I do not intend to enter into a detailed exposition of all he says on this matter here. Some of his discussion in *Cur Deus Homo* II: 8 overlaps with what has already been said concerning the natural kinds objection to the Incarnation. He also spends time in the same passage showing why it is fitting

---

50. Detailed argument for this claim can be found in Chapter 6.

51. This point has not always been understood. Some Doctors of the Church believed that the Virgin Birth was necessary to ensure Christ was conceived and remained, sinless in the womb. This is a mistake. One could hold both Christ's sinlessness on an NVB account, and a traditional doctrine of sin. See Raymond E. Brown, *The Virginal Conception,* pp. 40–41 for discussion of this.

52. J. K. Mozley observes that 'the fittingness of the Virgin Birth in connection with the person of Christ has been widely felt within the Christian Church', in *The Doctrine of the Incarnation* (London: The Unicorn Press, 1936) p. 55. It can be found in the work of Anselm and Thomas, amongst others. See, for example, *Cur Deus Homo,* II. 8 and 16, *De Conceptu Virginali* § 8 and 18 and Thomas, *Summa Contra Gentiles* 4. 42.

that the Incarnation take place according to a Virginal Conception and not, as might have been the case, via normal human procreation, through no human agency at all (as was the case with Adam's creation) or through the agency of a human father without a mother, as was the case in the biblical story of Eve's creation. There are four specific reasons he gives for the fittingness of the Virginal Conception in this section of *Cur Deus Homo*. The first of these is that God had yet to create a human via virginal conception (he had previously used the three other logically possible methods). Second, it is appropriate that as the curse originated with a woman (Eve), so salvation begins with a woman (Mary). Third, the inclusion of Mary in salvation history is the occasion by which God is able to rebuild the hope of women, which might have been crushed by the action of Eve in bringing about original sin. Fourth, as Eve was created from the 'virgin' Adam without a woman, it is fitting that Christ's human nature is created from a virgin, Mary, without a man.

Elsewhere, Anselm notes that the Son chooses Mary to be the bearer of his human nature (*De Conceptu Virginali,* § 18) and that in order to bring about this Incarnation Mary is cleansed from original sin by faith before the conception of Christ (*Cur Deus Homo* II: 16 and *De Conceptu Virginali* § 18). He seems to think this is also the means by which the sinlessness of Christ's human nature is ensured.

There are several things worth noting in Anselm's account. First, as we have seen, Anselm is right when he implies that the Virginal Conception was not the only means by which the Incarnation could have taken place. He is also correct to suggest that Christ's true humanity has to be guarded in an orthodox account of the Virgin Birth. Moreover, it seems plausible to think that the second person of the Trinity chooses Mary to be the bearer of his human nature. Anselm is also right to emphasize the need to preserve the sinlessness of Christ's human nature (although his claim that this is done by ensuring Mary is without sin is only one way this might be achieved, and not one that is part of the default creationist account I have defended). His claim that God chose Incarnation via a virgin, because he had not yet used this method of creating human beings is rather curious – and may, for all I know, be true – but it is hardly a strong reason for the Virgin Birth. However, his inferences from Eve to Mary are less persuasive today than they might have been for medieval theologians. It is not clear to me that the curse originates with Eve's action alone, as Anselm suggests. Nor do I think that there is any good theological reason for thinking that the inclusion of Mary in the Incarnation somehow rebuilds the hope of women, as if women in particular should be ashamed of the actions of our first parents. After all, Eve was not the only human person who sinned in the primeval garden!

So, as it stands, Anselm's attempt to supply reasons for the fittingness of the Virginal Conception of Christ is not, I suggest, an unqualified success, despite several insightful observations. (But, to be fair to Anselm, part of the reason for this may be that the criteria for 'fittingness' are not all that clear.) However, there are other reasons that may be used in an Anselmian spirit, to make the same sort of point. This latter-day Anselmian reasoning also has the benefit of responding to at least one objection to the traditional doctrine of the Virgin Birth in the recent literature.

The reasoning I am thinking of was suggested to me by reading through Raymond Brown's little book, *The Virginal Conception and Bodily Resurrection of Jesus*. One problem that several modern theologians have raised with the doctrine of the Virgin Birth is that it conflicts with the doctrine of Christ's pre-existence. Thus, Wolfhart Pannenberg says as follows:

> In its content, the legend of Jesus' virgin birth [sic.] stands in an irreconcilable contradiction to the Christology of the incarnation of the pre-existent Son of God found in Paul and John. For, according to this legend, Jesus first *became* God's Son through Mary's conception. According to Paul and John, on the contrary, the Son of God was already pre-existent and then as a pre-existent being had bound himself to the man Jesus.[53]

However, it seems to me that the opposite is the case. If the Word pre-exists his Incarnation (which, of course, is the orthodox view of the matter), then NVB accounts of the Incarnation face a problem that the traditional Virgin Birth doctrine does not. The problem is this: on the traditional way of thinking, the Incarnation involves the assumption of human nature by a pre-existing divine being, the Word of God. Although the Word could have become incarnate in some other fashion – as we have already seen and as Anselm and others suggest – the biblical account shows that he actually becomes Incarnate via a Virginal Conception and Birth. Indeed, the traditional way of thinking seems to be that this is more *fitting* than the alternative modes of incarnation available (as Anselm points out). A special birth signals the fact that it is a divine person taking on human nature, not the beginning of the life of a new individual, as a normal process of human generation from two human parents might suggest. It is Pannenberg and other revisionist Christologists like him, who have to address themselves to the compatibility of the pre-existence of Christ with an NVB account of the Incarnation, not those who adopt a traditional view of the Virgin Birth.

This does not mean that the logic of an NVB account precludes the notion of Christ's pre-existence. I have suggested that an NVB account can accommodate a robustly Chalcedonian Christology *sans* the doctrine of Virgin Birth. This might include a doctrine of Christ's pre-existence as well as other components of Chalcedonian Christology (apart from the Virgin Birth). To this extent, objectors to the traditional doctrine of the Virgin Birth like Pannenberg are correct. But, if anything, the traditional doctrine of the Virgin Birth is a better

---

53.   Pannenberg, *Jesus – God and Man*, p. 143, author's emphasis. See also p. 150. There he deals in more detail with his understanding of Christ's pre-existence.

'fit' with Christ's pre-existence than an NVB account is. What the traditional doctrine provides that an NVB account does not, is a signal, or marker for the Incarnation that preserves the uniqueness of this event, without explaining it (it is, after all, a divine mystery). On the one hand it ensures there is no ambiguity about the conception and birth of Christ. He was not born as a result of an indiscreet liaison out of wedlock, nor did he begin to exist at the moment of his conception only to be 'co-opted' or 'adopted' by the Second Person of the Trinity. Although neither of these things need apply to a careful NVB account, they are objections to the Incarnation that are harder to overcome in the absence of the Virgin Birth. On the other hand, the traditional doctrine of the Virgin Birth points to the fact that Jesus of Nazareth is the second person of the Trinity. It is the pre-existing person of the Word of God who assumes human nature in addition to his divine nature at the Incarnation. And this unique event is marked by the mode of his conception and birth.

To sum up: the manner in which the Incarnation takes place is not essential to the doctrine of the Incarnation, as the NVB account shows. Yet it is fitting that the Incarnation takes place according to the traditional doctrine of the Virgin Birth. And, contrary to what Pannenberg maintains, there is certainly no contradiction between Christ's pre-existence and Virgin Birth. In fact, I suggest that it offers a better 'fit' with the Incarnation of the pre-existing Word of God than an NVB account does. This is by no means a decisive point. The theological case for the Virgin Birth does not rest on its 'fittingness'. But, I submit, this reasoning does mean that a certain sort of objection against the compatibility of the traditional doctrine with Christ's pre-existence can be met.

5. *Conclusion*

In a recent essay on the Virgin Birth Robert Jenson observes, rather dryly:

> Mary became pregnant, gestated, and gave birth and the one whom she gestated and gave birth to was the sole and solitary person of the Son of God. She gave birth to one hypostasis of the Trinity. You may contrast that with what is preached and taught in the mainline churches, which can plausibly be described as a sustained effort to evade this scandal.[54]

In my judgment, Jenson is entirely correct. Although, as we have shown, it is possible to set forth a robust two-natures doctrine of the Incarnation that conforms to Chalcedonian Christology in all other particulars apart from its denial of the Virgin Birth, such a doctrine does not reflect the teaching of Scripture or the tradition. Consequently, such an NVB argument is wholly inadequate, indeed, is an unorthodox statement of how the Incarnation took place. (This is

54. Robert Jenson, 'For Us . . . He Was Made Man', p. 83.

so overwhelmingly obvious that it is almost embarrassing to have to state is so baldly.) And, although there are insufficient reasons often given for the traditional doctrine, I have argued that an Anselmian approach to the 'how' question of the Incarnation (viz., 'How did the Incarnation come about?') offers a fruitful way of showing that the Virgin Birth is a most fitting way for the Son of God to become man. In fact, it is more fitting than the NVB alternative that can be found in some revisionist accounts of the Incarnation.

Chapter 5

CHRIST AND THE EMBRYO

If we should wish to charge our own generation with crimes against humanity because of the practice of this experimental research [on human embryos], I would suggest that the crime should not be the old-fashioned crime of killing babies, but the new and subtle crime of making babies to be ambiguously human, of presenting to us members of our own species who are doubtfully proper objects of compassion and love.

Oliver O'Donovan, Begotten or Made?[1]

This chapter follows closely on the heels of the previous one. It is, in some respects, an *excursus*, in as much as I offer a specifically Christological argument for thinking that humans are normally persons from conception, rather than focusing on a set of purely dogmatic issues raised by a particular aspect of the doctrine of the Incarnation. We might call this an exercise in *applied Christology*. Thus there is some conceptual overlap between this and the previous chapter. This is inevitable given the subject matter under discussion. But I think it is warranted, not just because this reasoning has important contemporary bioethical implications, but also because it offers an illustration of one way in which analytic theology (and, indeed, systematic theology more generally) can speak to pressing concerns of a more practical nature – in this case, concerns about whether embryos are human persons or not, and what that might mean for how we treat human embryos in biological research.

1. *Preamble*

There is much discussion in contemporary bioethics about when in the development of a human embryo a human person begins to exist. The reason for this is not difficult to discern: an answer to this problem has important ethical implications. For example, if a human embryo is a person from conception, this has important consequences for the way we think about bioethical issues like early abortion, in vitro fertilisation (IVF), stem-cell research and human cloning. A constituent of most standard defences of these particular bioethical technologies is that embryos at the early stages of development are not human

---

1. From Oliver O'Donovan, *Begotten or Made?* (Oxford: Oxford University Press, 1984) p. 65.

persons and can, as a result of this, be treated differently from human persons.[2] (They can, for example, be destroyed, or used for research purposes.) So the conclusion one reaches about the relationship between human development in the womb and the beginning of human personhood is not merely an abstruse philosophical, theological or ethical matter.[3]

In this chapter I want to offer a *theological* argument for preferring one view before the others on this matter. I suggest that if one begins with certain Christological considerations about human nature, human being and human personhood, this has important implications for the relationship between the human embryo and human personhood. It seems to me that a properly Christian theological account of these matters cannot ignore this Christological dimension to the discussion. In fact, if this dimension is left out of consideration, or factored in at the end of otherwise philosophical considerations (that do not take into account the specifically Christological basis of my contention), this may well result in a misconceived view of the relationship between the development of human embryos and human personhood and skew theological judgement on several important matters in contemporary bioethics.

To date insufficient attention has been paid to the Christological dimension to the question of when the embryo becomes a human person. There has been some recent discussion of this, which is important.[4] But, for the most part, where the relationship between the embryo and personhood is raised, the Christological dimension to this issue is ignored. This is strange for two reasons: the Virginal Conception of Christ has direct bearing upon the relationship between the development of human embryos and human personhood – a matter adverted to in the previous chapter. And, Christ's humanity is often said

---

2.   Note, I claim only that this is a constituent of most standard defences of these technologies, not that it is a *requirement* of such defences. I suppose someone could defend, say, IVF, without committing him- or herself to one particular view on those embryos that are not used in the process of fertilization, fail to implant, or are destroyed in the pre-implantation process of screening for inherited diseases. Such people may, like the *Warnock Report* of 1984 commissioned by the UK government, go straight to the question of *how it is right to treat an embryo,* and ignore the question of *when in the process of development the embryo becomes a human person.* See the *Report of the Committee of Inquiry into Human Fertilization and Embryology* (London: HMSO, 1984) para. 11.9. But, as David Jones points out, it is not clear that the Warnock Report remains true to this intention, and it may be difficult not to come to some judgement about these matters, if one is concerned to defend these new bio-technologies. See Jones, *The Soul of the Embryo,* p. 219.

3.   The question of when a human embryo is a human person (if at all) is a moral and theological issue, not a merely biological question. The biological considerations involved in the development of a human embryo will not determine when that embryo is a person, as I hope to show. This point has been noted elsewhere. See, for example, Robert Song, *Human Genetics, Fabricating the Future* (London: Darton, Longman and Todd, 2002) p. 34.

4.   Readers are directed to Jones, *The Soul of the Embryo,* ch. 9, and John Saward, *Redeemer in the Womb* (San Francisco: Ignatius Press, 1993), as two important recent treatments of these matters. Saward in particular offers detailed comment on the historical-theological background to the issues pursued in this chapter, which repays careful study.

to be the means by which we understand what it is to be truly human. If this includes what it means to be a truly human embryo – that is, if the manner of Christ's development in the womb is a blueprint for, or has important parallels with, normal human development *in utero* – then this has significant implications for the human embryo/human personhood issue. I will argue, contrary to some theologians in the tradition,[5] that this is indeed the case. Although, as was noted in the previous chapter, the mode of Christ's conception is different from other human beings, the manner of Christ's development from conception onwards is the same as other human beings. This offers an important theological insight on the basis of which we shall argue for the view that human conception is also the moment at which human personhood begins.

The chapter proceeds in four stages. First, we shall examine the Christological considerations relevant to the issue. This will mean dealing with human nature and its relation to human personhood. Secondly, we shall expound two arguments that reason from the ensoulment of Christ at conception, to the conclusion that all human embryos are human persons from conception, because, like Christ, all human embryos are ensouled from conception. In a third section, we deal with four objections to these Christological arguments. Finally, a concluding section raises some questions concerning the implications this reasoning might have for several bioethical issues that involve the early development of human embryos in relevant ways, including abortion, stem-cell research, human cloning and IVF.

2. *Christological Considerations*

To begin with, let us consider the distinction between a human nature, being and person. I shall take one influential view of the human nature of Christ that we shall call the concrete-nature view.[6] On this sort of view (for there is more than one way of cashing it out) human nature, and Christ's human nature as an instance of this nature common to all humans, is composed of two substances, a human body and a soul. At the Incarnation, so this view goes, the Word of God assumes human nature, which means he assumes a particular body-soul composite. The main competitor or family of competitors to this view, what we shall call the abstract-nature view, states that human nature is a property possessed by a particular entity. On the abstract-nature view, at the Incarnation the Word of God takes on the (conjunctive) property of human nature in addition to having a divine nature. And this property is often thought to have the

---

5. Chiefly, St Thomas Aquinas and his supporters.

6. I have dealt with this in more detail in *Divinity and Humanity*, ch. 2. Cf. Marilyn McCord Adams, *What Sort of Human Nature?* (Milwaukee, WI: Marquette University Press, 1999), Richard Cross, *The Metaphysics of the Incarnation*, Thomas P. Flint 'Risky Business: Open Theism and the Incarnation', Brian Leftow, 'A Timeless God Incarnate' and Alvin Plantinga, 'On Heresy, Mind and Truth' in *Faith and Philosophy* 16 (1999): 182–193.

conjuncts *being a human soul* (in addition to being a divine being) and *having a human body.*[7] I shall not deal with this alternative view here. Instead, I shall assume that human nature is a body-soul composite of some kind (whether of a Cartesian, hylomorphic, emergent or other variety, I shall leave open for now).[8] Those who defend this concrete-nature view about Christ's humanity claim that this body-soul composite human nature is necessary for being a human individual. We might say that a given human being, or individual is the referent of a particular human nature. Every human nature of every human being consists in a human body and soul (rightly related one presumes – however that is cashed out).[9] But this raises a question: If, as Scripture and the Creeds maintain, Christ is fully human, does this mean that in addition to having a human *nature*, he is also a human *person*? This is a difficult question and there have been a number of answers offered in response to it in the tradition. I presume that any theologically orthodox Christology has to affirm that Christ is fully human (compare Jn 1.14 and Heb. 4.15). This means that, on the concrete-nature view, Christ has a complete human nature (body-soul composite). But it cannot mean that Christ is a human person, because this is Nestorian. Christ is a divine person who has a human nature. He is not both a divine and human person at one-and-the-same-time. Nor, according to orthodox Christology, is he a human person with a divine nature.[10]

This way of thinking about the human nature of Christ may have certain advantages. But it also has peculiar consequences. One of these is that Christ is both fully human and yet not a human person, strictly speaking. He is a human being, that is, he is the referent of a human nature. But he is a divine, not a human, person. So, according to this way of thinking, human personhood

---

7.   This is not the only way the abstract-nature view could be cashed out, as I argue in *Divinity and Humanity,* ch. 2.

8.   A Cartesian view of the soul-body relation is roughly this: a human is essentially a soul that (normally, but contingently) possesses, or is related to, a particular human body. Hylomorphism states that the soul of a human is the form of his or her body. This means that the soul organises and gives structure to the body into which it is integrated, unlike Cartesian substance dualism. Christian hylomorphists also maintain that, although the soul may survive the death of the body, without a body it can only exist in an attenuated and diminished state. Emergent substance dualism (to be distinguished from property dualism, or double-aspect theory, according to which the body has certain immaterial aspects such as a mind) is, roughly, the idea that the body gives rise to a soul as it develops. The soul is, on this view, radically dependent on the body for its continued existence, in a way that it is not (or is not necessarily) on the other two views. All these views might be described as versions of substance dualism because all three suppose humans are (normally) composed of two substances: a body and a soul.

9.   I suppose one could have a body that has a soul that is not properly 'connected' to it. For instance, it might be that souls can become 'detached' from their bodies. But I shall ignore such considerations here.

10.   This would be to deny Christ's full divinity. It also suggests that Christ is essentially human but only contingently divine, which, if God is a necessary being, would appear to be metaphysically impossible.

is not necessary to being fully human.[11] I accept this consequence of this particular construal of Chalcedonian Christology with one crucial qualification: only in the case of the Incarnation do we have a human being who is not also a human person. All other human beings have a complete human nature and are human persons. What, then, is the difference between being human and being a human person? Following a suggestion by Brian Leftow (who himself is updating a medieval insight on this matter), I suggest that a human person is someone who has a human nature that is not assumed by the Word of God.[12] Perhaps, says Leftow, all human beings are created with something like a built-in 'God-shaped' port that the Word can 'upload' himself into (so to speak) at the moment of conception (rather like present-day computers have USB ports into which one can plug certain 'peripherals', or pieces of hardware that may then interface with one's computer). The Incarnation tells us that the Word did this in the case of Christ's human nature. Where this divine 'upload' takes place, assumption by the Word prevents the human nature in question from becoming a human person distinct from the Word, which is why the computer-port analogy breaks down: if it were parallel to the Incarnation, then the Incarnation would be Nestorian, whereas this medieval view is not Nestorian because the Word does not assume an existing human *person* – he assumes a complete human nature at the moment of its conception, before it becomes a distinct human person. And, as a number of theologians have maintained, at the Incarnation the human nature in question becomes the human nature of the Word of God. Where this divine 'upload' does not occur (in other words, where there is no Incarnation) the human nature formed at conception becomes a human person.

This is not to suggest (or so I think) that there is some sort of temporal lag between normal human conception and human personhood. Rather, at conception, a complete human nature is formed and, provided the Word does not assume it at that very moment of conception, it immediately forms a human person. It is important for Christology that the human nature assumed by the Word is complete; otherwise the Word is not fully human at the moment of Incarnation (given our previous point that a human being is an entity that possesses a complete human nature). An Incarnation that does not involve the

11. Not all contemporary Christian ethicists are as clear in their writings about the logic of Chalcedonian Christology as might be expected. For instance, Esther Reed maintains that Chalcedonian Christology 'affirms unambiguously that the Word of God did not assume human nature as a single lump, but, rather, full human personhood.' But this is unhelpful on two counts. First, it seems to include a rather fuzzy notion of Christ's human nature. Second, it is emphatically not a constituent of Chalcedonian Christology that Christ is a human person. As I have already pointed out, that would *entail* Nestorianism. But, to be fair to Reed, even St Thomas sometimes mistakenly slips into the language of 'human personhood' when speaking of Christ! See Esther D. Reed, *The Genesis of Ethics, On the Authority of God as the Origin of Christian Ethics* (London: Darton, Longman & Todd, 2000) p. 83.

12. See Leftow, 'A Timeless God Incarnate'.

assumption by the Word of a complete human nature is not theologically orthodox, according to the two-natures doctrine of the Council of Chalcedon of
AD 451. But it is also important for our purposes that possession of a complete
human nature is normally sufficient for human personhood *provided the Word
does not assume it at the moment of conception*.[13] If, *per impossibilis*, there
is a temporal lag between normal human conception (at which moment a complete human nature is granted the human zygote) and human personhood, and
if the conception of Christ also involves a temporal lag between conception
and personhood like the development of other human beings, then there was
no danger in the Incarnation of the Word of God assuming a human person.[14]
The Word could only have assumed a human zygote that would, at some later
time, have been ensouled, or developed a soul. But (as mentioned in passing in
the previous chapter) this entails Apollinarianism – or a version of *temporary*
Apollinarianism – from conception to ensoulment. And this is one of the unorthodox views of the Incarnation that the distinction between human nature and
human personhood given in the concrete-nature view, serves to guard against.
So, if at conception no human embryo (the Christ embryo included) can be
a human person because human personhood belongs to some later stage in
the embryo's development after conception when, say, it is ensouled (or
develops a soul) then the Incarnation *could not have* involved assumption of
a human person. Hence, this view avoids Nestorianism. But, given the logic
of Chalcedonian Christology, this is unacceptable because, in the case of the
Christ embryo, it entails Apollinarianism.

Of course, if one were to depart from these theological assumptions in one
way or another, a wedge could be driven between conception and human personhood.[15] But I suggest that all of the following are true: (a) Christ has a
complete human nature from conception (as per Chalcedonian Christology),

13.   I presume that the Word does not assume a human nature after conception because this
would fall within the parameters of Nestorianism – although it is metaphysically possible for God
to do so.

14.   This, it might be thought, is a big 'if'. Perhaps Christ's conception does not reflect normal
human conception in this respect (as in others). Perhaps Christ is conceived with a complete human
nature but other humans develop in two stages with a physical part first (the zygote), followed at
some later time by ensoulment. As we have already had cause to note, this is roughly the view
taken by St Thomas Aquinas, who tried to balance his commitment to hylomorphism with an
orthodox Christology. But, as I shall show presently, I think it is better to reject Thomas' view in
order to hold on to a more straightforward account of Christ's conception and development.

15.   One influential alternative that does just this is derived from the writings of John Locke.
He defines human personhood in these terms: 'a thinking intelligent being, that has reason and
reflection, and can consider itself as itself, the same thinking thing, in different times and different
places'. See Locke's *Essay Concerning Human Understanding*, ed. Peter Nidditch (Oxford:
Oxford University Press, 1975), Bk. II, ch. 26, para. 9. But the problems with this sort of definition
of human personhood are well known. It excludes certain groups that, I presume, a Christian theologian would want to include as human persons, such as the severely mentally handicapped and
infants.

(b) in this respect, Christ's conception is the same as that of other human beings, and (c) as a consequence, all human beings, like Christ, have a complete human nature from conception. Christ is not a human person, but other humans who possess a complete human nature are, because other human beings are unassumed by the Word and (immediately at conception) become human beings. In this way, I am suggesting that the question of human personhood depends in crucial respects upon Christological considerations. For, in this way of thinking about the relationship between the conception of a human embryo and human personhood, Christ is the template for what occurs in normal human conceptions. Like Christ, other human beings are conceived with a complete human nature. But unlike Christ, such individuals become human persons by virtue of remaining unassumed by the Word at the moment of conception. So it makes no sense to stipulate some temporal lag between normal human conception, the possession of a complete human nature, and human personhood, provided Christ's conception and development *in utero* is the same as that of other normal human beings. And, crucially, none of this calls into question the fact that the mode of Christ's conception is different from other human beings (viz., his Virginal Conception). It also offers a theologically orthodox account of the difference between Christ's personhood and that of other human beings who are not God Incarnate.

To sum up thus far, the version of the concrete-nature view of the Incarnation sketched here yields three important Christological insights into the relationship between human natures and human persons:

a. A complete human nature is a body-soul composite (of some sort).
b. A human being is the referent of a human nature.
c. A human person is a human being (that is, an entity with a complete human nature) unassumed by the Word at conception.

Before proceeding, a few words of explanation on the foregoing stipulations are in order. First, in this view, Christ is fully human on account of his satisfying the first two conditions, namely possession of a complete human nature and therefore being a human individual. But he is not a human person. Indeed, he cannot be a human person because, on the concrete-nature view offered here, a human person is an entity not assumed by the Word of God.

Second, (a) and (b) do not mean that disembodied souls are not human, although it does mean that disembodied souls are not human beings. We might put it like this: disembodied human souls are the souls of human beings, but, without the human body to which such a soul is normally 'attached', or into which it is integrated in some way; this human soul is in some way 'diminished'. It is not less than human, but it is not a complete human nature. It is, we might think, 'part' of a complete human nature, and therefore 'part' of what a complete human being consists in. But this does mean that human souls are not human persons, strictly speaking. And this would appear to exclude at least one form of substance dualism, namely, the Cartesian view. For according to the Cartesian view, human persons are identical with human souls. This is a minor problem, but it does conflict with my stated aim of not appealing to one over other views of substance dualism. The problem lies with (b) above. It could be rephrased so that it is acceptable to the Cartesian, like this:

(b') A human being is the referent of (the immaterial part of) a human nature.

But this will not be acceptable to other sorts of substance dualists. In what follows, I shall assume (b), although I think a Cartesian deploying (b') or something very like it could make the relevant mental adjustments to the argument that follows without too much effort.

Thirdly, I should also point out that condition (c) above is not intended to be a complete description or definition of human personhood. It is merely a sort of threshold requirement for human personhood. In other words, someone who is a human person must at the very least be an entity that is a human being (as per (a) and (b) above) unassumed by the Word at conception. It might be thought that any argument for the conclusion that human zygotes are human persons from conception (Christ excepted) would need to specify in some detail what the conditions of human personhood consist of. I think this is mistaken. What is required for the purpose of the present argument is that some stipulation is given that distinguishes human persons at the moment of conception from God Incarnate at the moment of conception. It seems to me that (c), or something like it, provides this distinction, given certain assumptions about what human natures consist of, coupled with a certain view of the Virginal Conception of Christ in relation to the conception of other human beings. It may be that the concept of human personhood includes more than (c) provides. But, in this way of thinking, to be a human person is at least to fulfil the requirement of (c) which all humans bar Christ do fulfil. And this, I think, is sufficient for the central argument of this chapter. It would not be sufficient if we were attempting to set out a complete account of human personhood. But that is not our concern here.

3. *Two Arguments from Christology to Human Personhood at Conception*

We are now in a position to explain how these Christological considerations are important for determining the relationship between the development of human embryos and human personhood.

Let us assume that the foregoing reasoning holds, and Christ's human nature is a body-soul composite that Christ has from the moment of conception onwards. Recall that it is imperative the Word assumes a complete human nature at the Incarnation, in order to avoid unorthodoxy. Assumption of a human body without a soul is Apollinarianism. Assumption of a human body and then a human soul at some later stage of embryonic development is a form of limited, or temporary Apollinarianism, because it means Christ has no human soul for some period between his conception (the moment of Incarnation) and ensoulment. There are no orthodox classical theologians I am aware of who claim Christ had no soul at any stage of his embryonic development because they all thought that this would be a departure from Chalcedonian Christology. Aside from these considerations, if Christ does not have a complete human nature from conception onwards, he is not a human being from conception onwards, given the version of the concrete-nature view outlined in the previous section. Possession of a complete human nature is, in this view, sufficient for an entity to be human. Christ has such a human nature from conception, so Christ is a human from conception. And apart from the miraculous mode of Christ's conception (viz., the Virginal Conception), there is no reason to think that Christ's embryonic development was abnormal (despite the fact that Thomas, amongst others, disagrees, a matter we shall attend to presently). So, there is no significant difference between Christ's human development in the womb, and any other normal human gestation. By 'significant' difference, I mean there is no difference of a relevant theological or metaphysical sort. There may be biological differences, as I presume there are from one pregnancy to another. Some of these may be significant (e.g., a congenital heart condition). But such differences are not relevant to the point being made here. If this is right, then, apart from the mode of conception, all other human beings are conceived with a complete human nature and are human beings from conception in the same manner as Christ.

Are all human beings that possess a complete human nature apart from Christ also human persons from conception onwards (unlike Christ)? Given the constituents of the version of the concrete-nature view I have opted for, the answer would be affirmative. All human beings apart from Christ that have a complete human nature are not assumed by the Word at their conception or thereafter, and, as a consequence, become human persons from that moment onwards. But this means that all human embryos, aside from Christ, that have a complete human nature at conception are human persons from conception. And, I presume that this accounts for the all of the rest of humanity, apart from Adam and Eve, both of whom have abnormal 'births' because they are the first humans created by God.[16] Christ is the only exception relevant here because, unlike other human beings, and as I have already explained, the Word does

---

16. If Adam was created from the dust, then he has a complete human nature from the moment God 'breathes' life into him. If Eve was created from Adam's rib, she has a complete human nature from the moment God finishes creating her. I suppose it is possible for God to permit human conceptions where the body generated does not receive a soul. If this were to happen, a human body would exist without a soul. But this is not a complete human nature and would not be sufficient to constitute a human person. Such an entity would be rather like a zombie. But there is no good theological reason for thinking that such entities actually exist.

assume a particular human nature at conception, preventing it from forming a person distinct from the Word from that moment onwards.

Not every classical theologian would concur with this reasoning. As we have seen in the previous chapter, St Thomas Aquinas claims that Christ has an abnormal human development. According to Thomas, in the Virginal Conception, Christ's human body is generated fully formed. Thomas was committed to a version of hylomorphism,[17] and believed that only a fully formed embryo could sustain a soul, which organizes or gives the 'form' to the body into which it is integrated. Thomas, following Aristotle, thought that normal human development occurred by stages. For instance, at one point Thomas states, '[w]e conclude therefore that the intellectual soul is created by God at the end of human generation, and this soul is at the same time sensitive and nutritive, the pre-existing forms being corrupted'.[18] First, according to Thomas, the human embryo is formed through procreation. Then it goes through a series of stages where a different soul is given to it, according to its state of material development. At each stage, the earlier soul (here read: Aristotelian form) is 'corrupted', giving rise to a more sophisticated soul. Then, at around forty days after conception (for males), the embryo is mature enough to be given a 'rational' soul. But, no doubt recognizing that this account of normal human embryonic development would entail temporary Apollinarianism if applied to the Incarnation, Thomas had to adapt his thinking to the demands of Chalcedonian Christology for his Christology to remain orthodox. The result is that Christ's embryonic development is quite different, on Thomas' account, from the development of other, human embryos.[19]

17.   Interpreters of Thomas are divided on what Thomas's version of hylomorphism committed him to. I shall not enter into specific exegesis of the nature of Thomas's hylomorphism. Interested readers might consult Eleonore Stump, 'Non-Cartesian Substance Dualism and Materialism without Reduction' in *Faith and Philosophy* 12 (1995): 505–531, and Brian Leftow, 'Souls Dipped in Dust' in Kevin Corcoran ed. *Soul, Body and Survival* (Ithaca, NY: Cornell University Press, 2001). These offer two interesting but different interpretations of Thomas.

18.   *Summa Theologica* 1a. 118. 2. ad. 2. Thomas defends an Aristotelean understanding of the development of souls, according to which a 'vegetative' soul is given at conception (roughly a soul like that of vegetation), which is supplanted by a 'sensitive' soul, and finally, the 'rational' soul, which is given by God when the forty day threshold is reached. At each stage, the previous soul is replaced by the next soul-stage, which includes within itself the properties of the previous soul-stage. But the new soul-stage supplants the previous one, which is corrupted. The process of development is therefore an interrupted one. One soul-stage does not develop into the next; it is corrupted and supplanted by the next.

19.   Not dissimilar reasoning could be developed along emergent substance dualist lines. Then, a human embryo begins with a nascent soul, or the dispositional propensity to generate a soul at a certain stage of development *in utero*. Once that stage is reached, a soul begins to develop 'in' the embryo. The problems that the Thomist faces with respect to the ensoulment of Christ would also apply, *mutatis mutandis*, to emergent substance dualists too. If Christ only assumes a human zygote with the disposition to generate a soul at the Incarnation, then for the period

There are some quaint aspects of Thomas's account. Most notably, the claim that an embryo is fully formed only forty or more days after conception, including an Aristotelian process of soul-development that occurs alongside that of the body. The idea that Christ's human nature is generated fully formed and still gestates for nine months is also rather difficult to swallow, given what we now know about the process of gestation in human beings. But there are contemporary moral theologians who think a modified Thomist account of human development is correct. Perhaps, they suggest, there is some delay between conception and ensoulment. Joseph Donceel has offered one such account:

> If form and matter are strictly complementary, as hylomorphism holds, there can be an actual human soul only in a body endowed with the organs required for the spiritual activities of man. We know that the brain, and especially the cortex, are the main organs of those highest sense activities without which no spiritual activity is possible.

Later in the same article, Donceel observes, 'since these organs are not ready during early pregnancy, I feel certain that there is no human person until several weeks have elapsed [after conception].'[20] The problem with this modern version of delayed ensoulment or 'hominization', as Donceel calls it is that, like Thomas, it would require a rather imaginative argument for it to apply in the case of Christ's embryonic development. For, as it stands, the case for delayed ensoulment in normal human development would mean temporary Apollinarianism if applied to the Incarnation. It seems to me to be much simpler to jettison hylomorphism (or at least, the version of it that Donceel seems committed to) in favour of a version of substance dualism that is able to accommodate the parallel between the embryonic development of Christ and the rest of humanity. It is only on this matter of hylomorphism (or the particular version of hylomorphism) that the Thomistic account, including Donceel's variation, and the version of the concrete-nature account offered here, differ. In all other respects they are almost indistinguishable. I suggest that if this

---

between conception and soul-emergence, Christ is without a 'rational' soul, and this is temporary Apollinarianism once more. If, on the other hand, Christ assumes a zygote with a nascent, or 'embryonic' soul from conception, then a version of emergentism could be consistent with the story being told here – a matter to which we shall return in due course. For an engaging account of emergent substance dualism, see the debate between Dean Zimmerman and Lynne Rudder Baker in *Contemporary Debates in Philosophy of Religion,* eds Michael L. Peterson and Raymond J. Vanarragon (Oxford: Blackwell, 2004). A more sophisticated account is given in William Hasker, *The Emergent Self* (Ithaca, NY: Cornell University Press, 1999).

20. Joseph Donceel, 'Immediate Animation and Delayed Hominization'. The citations are from p. 83 and p. 101 respectively. Cf. Norman Ford, *When Do I Begin?* who believes that ensoulment takes place once the so-called primitive streak occurs (that is, the beginnings of the central nervous system), at around two weeks gestation. See also Karl Rahner, *Theological Investigations Vol. IX,* trans. G. Harrison (London: Darton, Longman and Todd, 1972) pp. 226 and 236. Donceel derives his concept of hominization from Rahner.

hylomorphist account of substance dualism were exchanged for another version of substance dualism more in keeping with the version of the concrete-nature view expressed here, the gain would significantly outweigh the loss incurred. For one thing, it would not require the contortions Thomas gets himself into on the question of Christ's embryonic development. And this is a significant gain if it is thought important to ensure that Christ is 'like us in every way, sin excepted' (Heb. 4.15). On the Thomist account as it stands, there is a clear difference between the conception of Christ and the rest of humanity, quite apart from the miraculous mode of his conception. Although Christ's conception could be different from that of other human beings without this precluding his being fully human, there is no Scriptural warrant for believing this. In fact, it looks like Thomas is driven by purely metaphysical considerations to make adjustments to his Christology, in order to remain theologically orthodox. And this seems like unnecessary theological gerrymandering.

But a counterargument in favour of a broadly Thomist account occurs to me. And this brings us to the second argument for human personhood from conception – or perhaps, a variation on the same sort of argument. The Thomist could argue that the soul develops with the embryo from conception to maturity. As the soul becomes more sophisticated, so does the body of which it is the form. (This sounds somewhat like what Thomas does say about the *in utero* development of the soul through the different stages of an Aristotelian form.) Perhaps this is true of all human beings, Christ included. On this sort of view (whether it is compatible with hylomorphism or not, it is compatible with some version of substance dualism) Christ has a complete human nature from conception in this sense: he has both a human body (or the beginnings of one) and a human soul (or the beginnings of one). Then, the problem of temporary Apollinarianism is avoided. For in this view, Christ has a soul from conception. It is just that this soul, like the body to which it is attached, or integrated, develops whilst *in utero*. I think this is an appealing way of thinking that may avoid certain problems with the version of the concrete-nature view previously outlined. For instance, it would allow for the development of a soul with a body, something that may endear those bioethicists who think of human personhood in developmental terms, as something which has no clear beginning (as far as we know), but which emerges over time, during gestation. It also presumes an account of substance dualism, which, whilst perhaps not exactly the same as either Thomist hylomorphism, or emergent substance dualism, is similar to both in important respects. Finally, it also promises a theologically orthodox way of thinking about the Incarnation that is in keeping with much of the concrete-nature view I have defended here.[21] Indeed, for all I know this is how

---

21.   It could be objected that this modified Thomist account of human conception and personhood is not orthodox because it means Christ, and other human beings, do not have a 'rational' soul from conception onwards, and is therefore Apollinarian. There is some evidence that Apollinarians thought Christ had some lesser Aristotelian soul, but not the 'rational' soul or *nous*

human embryos develop, Christ's embryo included. So, in what follows, let us assume that one of these two views, the modified Thomist account or the version of the concrete-nature view I have defended here, are true. And let us designate them *the complete human nature version* and *the modified Thomist version* of the concrete-nature view, in order to distinguish them in the remainder of the chapter. In both cases, Christ has a complete human nature from conception (although in the case of the modified Thomist version, the soul as well as the body comprising a particular human nature develop *in utero*). And in both cases Christ's embryonic development, aside from the manner of his conception, may be parallel to that of other, normally procreated human beings. This means that, in both cases, human beings other than Christ may well be human persons from conception – which is the conclusion we wanted to reach.

4. *Objections to the Two Accounts*

We come to objections to the two arguments outlined in the previous section. Four such arguments will be considered. Although these are not the only objections that could be used against the two arguments of the previous section (hereinafter, 'the Two Arguments' for the sake of brevity) they are, it seems to me, the most problematic. These four objections, in no particular order of strength or priority, are as follows: The objection from monozygotic twins; the too many wasted embryos objection; the no clear moment of conception objection; and the objection from developmental accounts of human personhood. We shall consider each in turn.

First: the objection from monozygotic twins. Some twins are non-identical because they are formed from two different ova. Other twins are formed from the same zygote and are called identical or monozygotic twins. It is this latter group of twins that we are concerned with. The case of monozygotic twins raises the following problem for those who wish to defend the view that human personhood begins at conception. Unlike nonidentical twins, or other human

---

that corresponds to Thomas' final stage of the soul in normal human development. But theological orthodoxy does not, I suggest, require adherence to a particular metaphysical theory about a given theological matter, if, say, we have good reason to think the metaphysical theory in question is false and the theological issue is itself metaphysically underdetermined (i.e., compatible with more than one metaphysical 'story' about the matter in question). It may be that, although a soul develops from conception, it does not begin as something less than a 'rational' soul, in the sense of beginning as something less than the soul of a human being (a vegetative soul, say, as Thomas suggests). It may just be that the soul in question undergoes development as a human embryo does without any change of essence. We may have good (theological) reason to think the early stages of a human embryo are also the early stages of the life of a human being. The modified Thomist argument merely extends this sort of reasoning to the development of the soul of a human being. So I do not think that this view is necessarily Apollinarian, provided one thinks souls do not develop in stages from vegetative through to rational (human) souls.

embryos, one of the monozygotic twins (or, at least, its physical part) is generated not by the fusion of gametes as a result of sexual reproduction, but asexually, through the fission of an existing human zygote. But if a monozygotic twin is formed this way, then what shall we say about the generation of such human embryos, according to the Two Arguments? Is the twin generated in this fashion (call it, the second twin) without a complete human nature because it/he/she is without a soul? Does God grant a soul to the second zygote at the moment its physical part is asexually generated from the 'parent' zygote? Or does the second twin derive its (his/her) soul from the 'parent' zygote that it divides from (that is, from the 'first' twin)? Furthermore, does the 'parent' zygote of the first twin survive the moment of fission, or are two new zygotes thereby created, requiring two new human natures including two new souls? These are puzzling questions that have to do with the distinction between genetic and ontological identity.[22] Monozygotic twins are genetically identical as zygotes. But they are not necessarily ontologically identical. I take it most people have the intuition that after separation, the two monozygotic twin zygotes are ontologically distinct entities – although this could be disputed on philosophical grounds.[23] If they are not ontologically identical, they are two distinct entities. The question then becomes whether they are also two human persons.

Some have thought that the case of monozygotic twins tells against any argument for human personhood from conception, but I think this is overhasty. As the reader will have already worked out, there are several possible ways in which a defender of one of the Two Arguments can respond to this sort of objection. But before considering this, a word or two about what the advocate of one or other of the Two Arguments does not want to defend. First of all, given the logic of the Two Arguments, it would be theologically intolerable to think that the asexual generation of a human embryo through monozygotic fission generates a second zygote that is soul-less – even though it seems metaphysically possible. One reason why this is theologically unpalatable is that it means there are instances of human zygotes that are less than fully human beings – that are, in fact, zygotic 'zombies' (having a physical part, but no immaterial part). Although some theologians might allow this, few would welcome it.[24] Since adequate discussion of this would take us too far afield from the present concern, and since it raises grave theological and moral questions, I will simply

---

22. I owe this point to Norman Ford in *When Did I Begin?*

23. For example, one might argue that all monozygotic twin zygotes are two physical parts of one aggregated object that, after the moment of fission, occupy distinct, non-overlapping spaces.

24. For one thing, this position implies a host of moral and bioethical problems. Here are just two examples of these. A (potentially) theologically problematic metaphysical implication: God allows the generation of 'zombie' zygotes – that is zygotes that have no souls. A potentially problematic bioethical implication: these 'zombie' zygotes might be harvested for use in stem-cell research if they are not, or not at that stage of physical development, in possession of a human soul.

rule out any idea that the twin produced by division from the parent zygote is merely a physical human cell without a soul. Secondly, although the logic of the Two Arguments does not prevent the possibility that in the moment of fission the entity that is the 'parent' zygote ceases to exist and two new individual zygotes are created in its place, I think that most defenders of one of the Two Arguments would resist this sort of reasoning. For, quite apart from the fact that it involves a rather convoluted and controversial way of construing the metaphysics of monozygotic twinning (one individual perishing, to be replaced by two new individuals), it also seems unnecessarily wasteful: one individual being destroyed and replaced by two others. So I shall also pass over this possibility in silence.

The most appealing response to this sort of objection might be simply to argue that the second twin is granted a soul from the moment it divides from the 'parent' zygote, by divine fiat. Then, from the moment it begins to exist as an individual, the second twin has a complete human nature. In this case, a defender of one of the Two Arguments could simply concede that mono-zygotic twins present an interesting limit case to their account of human personhood. It need not undermine the claim that human persons, like Christ, begin from conception.

A similar story could be told by the defender of one of the Two Arguments who is also a traducian,[25] with this important difference: on the traducian account of the origin of the soul, the soul of the individual is generated from one or both of its parents, it is not created *ex nihilo* by God. Then, in the case of monozygotic twins, the soul of the second twin is generated from the soul of the parent zygote. At the moment of physical division between the two, there is also fission of soul-stuff, and, as with the version of the Two Arguments that is creationist, the second twin has a complete human nature from the first moment of fission. (In this context, creationism is the view that God creates the soul of each human being *ex nihilo*.) I think that these two responses to this objection are sufficient to the purpose, although I do not favour the tradu-cian alternative because I do not think souls are fissile, as physical things like bodies are.

What are we to make of the possibility that some monozygotic twins merge into one zygote before the primitive streak-stage of embryonic development? This presents a real metaphysical difficulty for the Two Arguments. I suppose one could argue that, in such cases (which, if they occur, are rare) one of two things takes place. Either, an individual is formed at the moment of fission, complete with human nature that is then lost when subsequent fusion takes place. This would be subject to the problem of wastage mentioned earlier, but perhaps it might be felt that this explanation, though not terribly palatable

---

25. Recall that traducianism is the view that human souls are passed down from parents to their children just as human genetic material is passed down from one generation to the next. God does not generate each human soul *ex nihilo*.

for theological reasons (why would God permit *that*?) is nevertheless, the simplest explanation given the assumptions involved in defending one of the Two Arguments. Alternatively, it might be thought that in such cases a true human individual is not generated, and the second, temporary twin is not ensouled. It is just a temporary, and anomalous fission of material from one 'parent' zygote, that later re-fuses with the 'parent' zygote, which continues to develop normally thereafter. If this way of thinking were opted for, then presumably, for the period of temporary fission, the 'second twin' (for it is only a twin for a short period of time) would remain soul-less, and simply be absorbed back into the ensouled 'parent' zygote when fusion takes place. Although this seems peculiar, it is not really that different from the possibility of removing one of my limbs for a short period, and then reattaching it at some later time. In sum, I suggest that the problems that monozygotic twinning poses for a defender of one of the Two Arguments are not insurmountable.

The second objection to consider is the too many wasted embryos objection. Some physicians estimate that as many as 50 per cent of human embryos do not survive the first few days after fertilization. If this is true – even if some percentage less than this is true, say between 5–50 per cent – it would involve vast numbers of embryos that do not successfully implant and gestate. If human embryos are human persons from conception, this has the unhappy consequence that many – perhaps as many as half of all embryos – are lost. But this means half the human persons that are generated perish before birth. And this seems to pose a very considerable problem of evil for those who believe human personhood begins at conception.

Without wishing to belittle this difficulty, it seems to me that this appears more problematic at first glance than it actually is. An analogy will help to explain this. Consider a developing country that has a high infant mortality rate. There are a number of such countries in the world today, and, for all I know there may be some whose infant mortality rate is as much as 50 per cent. Suppose there is at least one such country. In that country half the population never make it to adulthood. That is also a shocking statistic if true. But it serves to show that there is no *particular* problem of theodicy for those who think human personhood begins at conception. Similar problems beset theodicists quite apart from considerations of human embryology. In fact, the too many wasted embryos objection has the same logical form as what we might call the 'too many wasted infants' objection to infant mortality in developing countries. Of course, this is merely *ad hominem*: it does nothing to lessen the problem this objection poses. But it does show that this is not a problem that defenders of human personhood from conception have to face alone. It is, in fact, part of a larger problem of theodicy, to do with what has become known as concrete problems of evil. To that extent, solutions theodicists offer to other concrete problems of evil such as that posed by the too many wasted infants objection should apply, *mutatis mutandis*, to this particular way of thinking about the human embryo wastage issue.

The third objection I have called the no clear moment of conception objection. There is a particular moment at which syngamy takes place, when the gametes (human sperm and human ovum) fuse to form a new individual, which has his or her own particular genome. However, it might be objected that this does not necessarily mean that there is a clear moment at which conception takes place. In fact, as Norman Ford points out, there is a period of about twelve hours after syngamy during which the newly formed entity changes dramatically. It is during this period that the spermatozoon forms a nucleus and the genetic material of the two gametes is combined to form a new individual. But it is very difficult to state, so the objection goes, exactly the moment at which a new human embryo is conceived.

There are two things to say by way of response to this particular issue. The first is that, given the Christological assumptions motivating the Two Arguments, the moment of conception most naturally falls to the moment of syngamy. If, at the moment the gametes are fused a new genome begins to exist, a new individual begins to exist. It would appear to be Apollinarian to deny that Christ assumes a human nature from that moment, because from that moment onwards, a new genome has come into existence.

But there is a second way of thinking about this objection. Perhaps it is not clear exactly when conception takes place in the twelve-hour window between syngamy and the emergence of an identifiable new zygote. This does not mean there is no such moment. It just means we may not be able to establish when that moment is in every instance. So this does not necessarily rebut the claim that there is a moment of conception. Perhaps the best option is to 'play safe' and allow that, although we do not necessarily know exactly when, during this twelve-hour period conception occurs, it occurs at some moment in that period, and from that moment a new human person begins to exist. It is even consistent with one of the Two Arguments to claim that this moment of conception might occur at different times in the twelve-hour window in different cases, provided it is borne in mind that, whatever moment is the moment of conception during this period, is also the moment of ensoulment. Advocates of the Two Arguments have to guard against any temporal separation of the moment of conception from the moment of ensoulment. However, although this may seem to be the way of least resistance, I think that, given the fact that it raises the spectre of Apollinarianism with respect to the conception of Christ's human nature, the safer option here is the first response, where syngamy is the moment of ensoulment as well as the moment the gametes are fused.

Our fourth objection is from developmental accounts of human personhood. Such accounts suggest that human embryos are not persons from conception, but become persons after some period of development has taken place. This could be *in utero*. Sometimes, the emergence of the primitive streak is considered the moment from which a human person is present. Or perhaps it is when a heartbeat is discernable. But it need not be during gestation: if, say, ratiocination is thought to be a necessary condition of personhood (which seems dubious to me), it might be thought that even new born infants are not persons, and will not achieve personhood until some time after birth. When applied to the Two Arguments, this sort of reasoning yields the following objection. Suppose the metaphysical story about the Incarnation that lies behind the Two Arguments is true. Human persons are human beings (entities with a complete body-soul composite of the right kind), unassumed by the Word at conception. This characterization may supply some of the necessary conditions for human personhood, but it does not give all the conditions sufficient for personhood. For, plausibly, human personhood requires other conditions such as the capacity for conscious thought and experiences, including self-consciousness and self-reflection. But it should be clear from the foregoing that nothing I have said denies that the conception of personhood informing the Two Arguments supplies the necessary and sufficient conditions for personhood, just what is required for the metaphysics of the argument to make sense. Moreover, the fact that embryos do not have the capacity for conscious thought is no objection to embryos being persons. All humans are unconscious each time they sleep, but most people uncorrupted by philosophy do not suppose that when they sleep they cease to exist. If I am a person when I sleep, I am an unconscious person with the capacity or disposition to have conscious thoughts when awake.

But the objection could be refined to overcome this response. Embryos may have the capacity to develop into entities that are capable of sustaining conscious thought. The point is that, at conception and for some period thereafter, embryos are not capable of exercising this capacity because the hardware necessary for such thought (e.g., a brain) is not fully developed for some time after conception. In this respect they are significantly unlike unconscious adult human persons. What are we to say to this? Well, the point about undeveloped hardware is undeniable. Embryos do not have brains. At the early stages of development, their cells are totipotent (able to differentiate into all sorts of tissue). But I take it that no theist is willing to concede that possession of a certain piece of organic hardware, like the brain, or central nervous system, is necessary for personhood, because at least one person, God, does not possess a brain. And if there are angels and demons, I suppose they are persons without brains too. And, depending on what one thinks about the metaphysics of human persons, disembodied human souls may be persons as well, even if they are persons in some diminished state. I see no good reason to abandon this deliverance of Christian theology. So I can see no reason to concede to the developmentalist that the presence of a particular bodily organ is necessary for human personhood.

5. *Coda*

Often in theological discussion of the status of the embryo, something like 'benefit of the doubt' reasoning is applied: the embryo is treated 'as if' it were a human person for purposes touching its moral status, although commitment to the personhood of human embryos is withheld.[26] There are good reasons for doing so. In the case of Roman Catholic discussions of the matter, this is often because of a belief that the moral status of the embryo is theologically underdetermined, coupled with an agnosticism regarding the deliverances of philosophical arguments for personhood from conception. However, if the burden of this chapter is correct, then there are good theological reasons for thinking human embryos are human persons from conception (with the exception of Christ). This would have important implications for a range of bioethical technologies for example, IVF, stem-cell research and early-stage abortions. Greater clarity about the moral status of the human embryo does not present a ready-made solution to any of the moral issues these technologies raise. If anything, it may complicate matters further. But it does give a more theologically satisfactory reason for thinking that humans are persons, even in the womb.

26. Compare the report of the Congregation for the Doctrine of the Faith, *Declaration on Procured Abortion 13* in *Acta Apostolicae Sedis* 66 (1974): 739, which states 'From the moral point of view this is certain: even if a doubt existed concerning whether the fruit of conception is already a person, it is objectively a grave sin to dare to risk murder.'

Chapter 6

WAS CHRIST SINLESS OR IMPECCABLE?

Why do you call me good? No one is good but One, that is, God.

Mt. 19.17

It has been the almost unanimous view of classical Christology that Christ was not merely without sin, though he might have sinned, but that he was incapable of sin.[1] In keeping with tradition, let us call the former of these two, *the sinlessness view*, and the latter, *the impeccability view*. However, in the last few centuries, an increasing number of theologians have distanced themselves from the stronger, impeccability view, opting instead for the idea that Christ was merely sinless. That is, Christ was capable of sinning, and might have sinned had he chosen to do so, although he did not choose to, and, as a matter of fact, remained sinless throughout his earthly career. Endorsement of this sinlessness view has come from some unexpected quarters. One example from the nineteenth century is the Princetonian theologian – and (otherwise) stalwart defender of Chalcedonian orthodoxy – Charles Hodge. In discussing the offices of Christ he says this:

> The Mediator between God and man must be sinless. . . . A sinful Saviour from sin is an impossibility. He could not have access to God. He could not be a sacrifice for sins; and He could not be the source of holiness and eternal life to his people. This sinlessness

---

1.   Compare Ludwig Ott, *Fundamentals of Catholic Dogma* (Rockford, IL: Tan Books, 1955), Bk. III, § 2, ch. 26. Wolfhart Pannenberg offers a brief overview of the historical background in his *Jesus – God and Man*, pp. 354–364. Regrettably, his assessment is skewed by his belief that Christ possessed a fallen human nature, and that Christ is impeccable only in light of his resurrection – which is equivalent to the teaching of Theodore of Mopsuesta, condemned by the Fifth General Council of Constantinople in AD 553 (Theodore taught that Christ is only impeccable after the resurrection). To illustrate: Johnson can be shown to be the winner of the race after he has completed it in first place. But the relevant question here is whether Johnson (and, *mutatis mutandis*, Christ) will *inevitably* or *certainly* win the race. Whereas the former is a merely contingent matter, the latter is not. But only if we can say Christ certainly could not and would not sin, can we say he was impeccable. And this is just what Pannenberg denies. Another recent historical overview of this material can be found in John Elton McKinley's thesis, 'A Relational Model of Christ's Impeccability and Temptation', PhD Dissertation, The Southern Baptist Theological Seminary, 2005, chs. 1–3. For biblical-theological argument concerning the doctrine of Christ's sinlessness, see Gerald O'Collins, *Christology*, pp. 268–271.

of our Lord, however, does not amount to absolute impeccability. It was not a *non potest peccare*. If He was a true man He must have been capable of sinning. That He did not sin under the greatest provocation; that when He was reviled He blessed; when He suffered He threatened not; that He was dumb as a sheep before its shearers, is held up to us as an example. Temptation implies the possibility of sin. If from the constitution of his person it was impossible for Christ to sin, then his temptation was unreal and without effect, and He cannot sympathize with his people.[2]

Similar sentiments can be found amongst some contemporary Anglo-American theologians who are, in other respects, defenders of classical Christology. For instance, the American Baptist theologian, Millard Erickson, in his monograph on the Incarnation, says this in commenting on Hebrews 4.15:

> The thrust of the passage is that he is able to intercede for us because he has completely identified with us; this seems to imply that his temptation included not only the whole range of sin, but the real possibility of sinning.

Later in the same passage he goes on: 'There are conditions under which he [Christ] could have sinned, but that it was certain those conditions would not be fulfilled. Thus Jesus really could have decided to cast himself from the temple pinnacle, but it was certain that he would not.'[3]

In the United Kingdom, the Anglican theologian Trevor Hart takes a similar view. He asks whether, in drawing a line between Jesus' truly human experience and ours that precludes the possibility of Christ sinning, we are not thereby removing from Christ's human purview some crucial element of what constitutes part of the make-up of a human being:

> If we draw that line in such a way that it removes from Jesus all possibility of sinning, are we not thereby precisely robbing him of the experience of 'being tempted in all things as we are'? Is the genuine potential for sin not analytic in some way in the very notion of temptation? Certainly it would seem to be basic to human temptation as we know and experience it.[4]

Note that the claim being made here is a fairly weak one: that some prominent theologians of the past two hundred years or so who are otherwise advocates of a broadly Chalcedonian Christology have taken this sinlessness view. There are, of course, a large number of theologians in the nineteenth,

---

2. Charles Hodge, *Systematic Theology, Vol. II* (London: James Clarke, 1960) p. 457.

3. Millard Erickson, *The Word Became Flesh: A Contemporary Incarnational Christology* (Grand Rapids, MI: Baker, 1991) pp. 562 and 563 respectively.

4. Trevor Hart, 'Sinlessness and Moral Responsibility: A Problem in Christology' in *Scottish Journal of Theology* 48 (1995): 38. Compare McKinley, 'A Relational Model', ch. 3, where he also notes the way in which some theologians, including the three listed here, advocate a sinlessness view of Christ's human nature.

twentieth (and early twenty-first) centuries that would dissent from the sinlessness view. Nevertheless, this is, I suggest, an important development in Christology in the same period, and, as we have just seen, one not restricted to those who are of an otherwise theologically liberal or revisionist persuasion. In this chapter, I wish to take issue with the notion that Christ could be sinless, rather than impeccable. It seems to me that only the traditional view, that Christ is impeccable, makes sense. The alternative suggested by these, and other, theologians, though stemming from a laudable desire to affirm the full humanity of Christ, actually ends up undermining the very view of the Incarnation they seek to defend.

We proceed in two stages. In the first, I shall address several central issues concerning the nature of temptation, as they bear upon the question of Christ's moral state. I do not claim these issues offer a complete description of temptation, only that these are central issues in an adequate account of temptation. It seems to me that, on inspection, these considerations tell against the sinlessness view, and in favour of the impeccability view. In a second section, I argue that the sinlessness view suffers from two serious and debilitating objections arising from misunderstanding of what the impeccability view entails, and from modal considerations applied to the Incarnation. The impeccability view does not involve these problems and is able to account for the central concern expressed by defenders of the sinlessness view, to wit, that Christ has the capacity to sin (though he is incapable of sinning). For these reasons, it seems to me that there is no good reason to prefer the sinlessness view before the impeccability view, and several good reasons in favour of the traditional notion that Christ was impeccable, rather than the revisionist view that he was merely sinless.

1. *Aspects of the Nature of Temptation*

We begin with one aspect of Trevor Hart's concern, which is surely a concern motivating many who take the sinlessness view, that if Christ is incapable of sinning, then he cannot be said to be truly tempted as we are, yet without sin, which would be contrary to the teaching of Hebrews 4.15.[5] Behind this assertion there is often, I think, a wider concern, to do with the picture of Christ that one finds in the canonical Gospels. There we see a human being who hungers and thirsts, weeps, is capable of suffering, and goes through agonies as he struggles to remain true to his messianic mission in the temptations of the wilderness and the Garden of Gethsemane. The Jesus of the New Testament is

5.   Compare Hugh Ross Macintosh, writing at the beginning of the twentieth century. He asks 'are the temptations of the sinless real? In such a nature, what door can open and let in the base allurement? How can evil find resonance where there is neither inherited bias to evil, nor weakness due to previous transgression?' In, *The Doctrine of the Person of Jesus Christ*, p. 401.

also said to be sinless (see Jn 8.46; 2 Cor. 5.21; 1 Pet. 2.22 and 3.18; Jas 5.6; 1 Jn 3.5).

But, as Wolfhart Pannenberg points out, the New Testament statements about Christ's sinlessness are all directed towards establishing that Christ *in fact* committed no sin.[6] They do not offer a metaphysical theory about Christ's sinlessness that would establish whether it was inevitable that Christ would resist temptation, or not. It might be thought that the reason for this is that the writers of the New Testament were convinced that prior to the completion of his mission, Christ's continued sinlessness was not a foregone conclusion. This would certainly comport with the sinlessness position. But it is not the only theory that fits the data. It is perfectly possible that the writers of the New Testament thought Christ was impeccable.

Alongside the concern for a biblically satisfactory account of Christ's sinlessness, there is sometimes a distaste expressed for theories about Christ's resistance to temptations that are considered too abstruse, or metaphysical in nature.[7] Take, for instance, the picture of Christ that one finds in the high medieval discussions of the Incarnation, where the human nature of Christ is so hedged about by metaphysical arguments concerning the nature of the divine grace he was blessed with (preventing him from sinning) and the beatific vision he enjoyed (rendering him, like the Glorified in heaven, incapable of sinning) which ensure Christ's impeccability, that (so it might be thought) the frailty of Christ's humanity is, for all practical purposes, obliterated.[8]

Such aspersions are, it seems to me, quite unfair, and often (as above) unsubstantiated by anything approaching a watertight argument (either historical or theological).[9] It is true that the reader of the great medieval doctors will find more by way of metaphysical sophistication in the arguments about the

---

6.   Pannenberg, *Jesus – God and Man*, p. 356. Otto Weber makes a similar point in *Foundations of Dogmatics, Vol. 2*, pp. 38–39. Cf. 141: 'Jesus enters into solidarity with man who is a sinner. And it is in that very fact that his freedom from sin lies.'

7.   This is how I understand the following comments by Colin Gunton concerning what is often called 'Christology from above', that is, a Christology which begins from the premise of Christ's divinity, not his humanity: 'If an eternal being or hypostasis . . . takes to himself a body, can the resulting being be truly human?' Gunton is here setting out one of two 'dogmas' (the other concerning the 'historical Jesus') that he thinks bedevil modern theology. See 'Two Dogmas Revisited: Edwards Irving's Christology' in *Scottish Journal of Theology* 41 (1988): 359.

8.   Weber seems incredulous about some of these aspects of the medieval view in *Foundations of Dogmatics, Vol. 2*, p. 121 and following. For a brief and lucid account of Thomas's theory of the Incarnation, see Nicholas M. Healy, *Thomas Aquinas, Theologian of the Christian Life* (Aldershot: Ashgate, 2003) pp. 92–94. For a sophisticated account of the metaphysics of the incarnation in several important medieval theologians, see Richard Cross, *The Metaphysics of the Incarnation*, passim. See also Ludwig Ott, *Fundamentals of Catholic Dogma*, Bk. III, § 2, ch. 26.

9.   Compare the sort of claim often made by contemporary political pundits in the media that the United States is an imperial power. This claim is fatuous. It is trivially true that the United States is not an imperial power precisely because it has not conquered and subjugated other nation states, which is a necessary condition for a nation state to be an imperial power.

Incarnation there than at any time prior to the advent of the school theology (with the possible exception of theologians like St Augustine of Hippo). But one should not mistake metaphysical sophistication in argument for an implicit denial of the Christ we find in the New Testament. I suppose that all the medieval doctors of the Church believed implicitly in the picture of Christ we find in the canonical Gospels, and never once thought they were deviating from that picture, but rather considered their own work as offering a sort of metaphysical underpinning of that very New Testament understanding of Christ.[10] After all, the Incarnation is about as metaphysically sophisticated an event as one can conceive. If the Christ to whom the Gospels bear witness is in fact the Word made Flesh, then there are some difficult, convoluted but important issues that need to be explored by the responsible theologian. It is the glory of the medieval and post-Reformation scholastic traditions in theology that they did not shy away from such hard questions but embraced them. And all in the name of making clearer the nature of the Incarnation – with a healthy regard for the fact that this, like other central Christian doctrines, is mysterious in many important respects. So it seems to me that it is a mistake to think that commitment to a biblical picture of the person of Christ is incompatible with a sophisticated account of the metaphysics of the Incarnation. It is no more incommensurate than being both a lover of nature and a scientist with a detailed understanding of the complexities of biological life.[11]

The real problem, as Hart points out, has to do with the fact that being capable of sinning 'would seem to be basic to human temptation as we know and experience it'. Yet, *prima facie*, it would seem that an impeccable Christ has no such capacity. Someone who is incapable of doing a particular action cannot be said to be tempted to perform such an action. Like all human beings, I am a featherless biped, incapable of flight. So it is no real temptation to say to a human being who is *compos mentis*, 'why don't you try to fly off the top of that tall building?' Only someone in a precarious mental state would find such a 'temptation' appealing, because any sane human being knows that he or she is just not capable of performing such an action.[12] Similarly, it might be thought that Christ can only be tempted if he is capable of succumbing to that which is offered to him as a temptation.

---

10.   Of course, they may have been gravely mistaken in this undertaking. But that is another matter entirely. The question here concerns what the medieval school theologians thought they were doing in their Christology, not what they actually achieved.

11.   One of the virtues of Nicholas Healy's account of Thomas's theology is that he points out how Thomas connects his theological reflection with homiletics and doxology. Thus Healy: 'His [Thomas's] effort [in Christology] is directed towards showing the reasonableness, coherence and wisdom of what Scripture says about Jesus Christ. His goal is to help his readers preach the Gospel fruitfully and without misleading the faithful.' *Thomas Aquinas,* p. 94.

12.   Saying, in all seriousness, 'I would really love to be able to fly' as small children often do, is whimsical.

In this connection we need to distinguish *succumbing to a particular tempta-tion* from *the capacity to succumb to temptation*. The former requires the latter. To succumb to temptation I must have the capacity to succumb to temptation. But the latter need not entail the former. I may have a capacity to succumb to temptation, but withstand it on a particular occasion. Theologians like Hart (and, it seems, Erickson and Hodge) are suggesting that, like us, Christ must have the capacity to succumb to temptation as such, in order to be truly human. And, of course, someone who has this capacity may well resist temptations on one or more occasions – in the case of Christ, on all occasions. The point these authors are making (or ought to be making) is that he must have this capacity in order to be *truly* tempted. Otherwise any purported instance of temptation is really a charade.

This important issue is often thought to tell against the impeccability view. An impeccable person is constitutionally incapable of succumbing to tempta-tion on any given occasion. This suggests that an impeccable person cannot have the capacity to sin. If this is the case, then there is good reason to prefer the sinlessness- over the impeccability view. It seems to me one reason why this way of thinking persists in contemporary Christology is that theologians overlook certain unique features of the hypostatic union that make Christ sig-nificantly unlike other human beings. It would make perfect sense to say that if an individual is fully and merely human as well as being impeccable, then he or she is incapable of sin. But the same cannot be said of Christ, for two reasons. First, he is fully but not merely human – he is also a divine. Secondly, Christ is only incapable of sin in the relevant sense if he has no capacity or disposition to sin as a human being in abstraction, as it were, from the hypo-static union. However, one traditional account of the Incarnation suggests that the Divine Son of God assumes a sinless but peccable human nature, which, by virtue of being united to the Son, is rendered incapable of sin. If this is right, then this strand of classical Christology has the resources to deal with the 'no-capability to sin' objection that is raised by the advocates of the sinlessness view. We shall return to this matter in the latter section of the chapter.

There is a second aspect of temptation that is relevant here. A prerequisite of temptation is that one has the right 'psychological configuration' to desire an object of temptation. Consider the case of a person who has a strong psy-chological aversion to eating flesh. It is perfectly *physically* possible for this person to consume meat. He or she has, let us suppose, no allergy to flesh or inability to metabolize meat. In other words, there is no physiological reason preventing him or her from consuming the cooked flesh of other animals. Yet it would be reasonable to suppose that, for such an individual, the psychological impediment trumps the physical capacity to eat flesh on every occasion they are free to choose what they eat. Consequently, if such a person were presented with the opportunity to consume a hamburger, and he or she is fully aware that it is meat they are being presented with (and assuming the choice is a free one), it would hardly constitute a temptation in the way we conventionally use the term. The reason for this is that one central component of temptation concerns the fact that a person tempted by a particular thing feels the 'pull' of that temptation. They really desire the end to which the temptation is the means, and they know that, in some sense, that goal is less than the best, or, perhaps, an illicit, or sinful one.

So there is an important psychological element to temptation, which is independent of whether or not a person is physically capable of acting upon that temptation.[13] It might be thought that for Christ to be truly tempted, he too must have the right psychological configuration (whatever that may be) in order to feel the 'pull' of a particular temptation. In which case, he cannot be impeccable, because an impeccable person would not feel the 'pull' of temptation. He or she would not have the right psychological configuration in order to be in a position to feel the 'pull' of the temptation, any more than the person with an aversion to eating meat can be said to have the right psychological configuration to be carnivorous. This seems to be a more promising line of attack against the impeccability view.

Speculating about the psychology of the incarnation is theologically hazardous because the hypostatic union is *sui generis:* how can we know what it was like for Jesus of Nazareth to be God Incarnate? This is one way in which the Incarnation remains a divine mystery. However, it might be permissible to construct a thought experiment that tells a story that is consistent with Christ being impeccable and having a 'psychological configuration' that is consistent with feeling the 'pull' of the temptations the New Testament reports him enduring. Such an undertaking is not without peril, but the theologian is shielded from accusations of improper metaphysical speculations concerning the Incarnation if he couches his explanations in terms of such a story, rather than as the sober truth of the matter (of course, it might be that the story concerned is the sober truth of the matter, but that is not a requirement here).

Here is such a story: Christ, *qua* human, is constitutionally peccable (in abstraction from the hypostatic union). His human level of consciousness is aware of being very hungry (after his forty-day fast in the wilderness at the commencement of his public ministry) and of being tempted by the Devil to turn stones into bread. He is aware, again, in his human range of consciousness that turning the stones into bread would constitute a violation of one or more duties, such as to keep his fast, to obey the will of God, or whatever. Yet he is also aware that his body requires nourishment and that he is physically weak through abstinence. Finally, he is aware that he has the power to perform the requisite task and turn the stones into bread. This seems to be consistent with

---

13. Some theologians are deeply sceptical about arguments about the Incarnation that depend on appeals to Christ's psychological states, for example, Herbert McCabe in *God Matters* (London: Geoffrey Chapman, 1987) p. 58. My point here is just that there is an important psychological component to temptation. This is true even if we cannot establish what Christ's psychological state was when he was tempted.

the notion that, at the moments in which Christ has these thoughts in his human range of consciousness, he is in the right 'psychological state' to find turning stones into bread tempting. And this is also consistent with him feeling the 'pull' of such a temptation (as a human being). Thus far, our hypothetical scenario is consistent with either the sinlessness or the impeccability view.

To give some indication of how this is consistent with the impeccability view, we can extend the story as follows. Christ's divine nature would ensure that his human nature never sins, were his human nature about to sin. However, in the context of this particular temptation (to turn stones into bread), Christ's human nature is able, through the power of the Holy Spirit, to resist the temptation without the intervention of Christ's divine nature. Thus, Christ withstands the temptation 'in his humanity', as it were, yet he is impeccable because his divine nature would have ensured this outcome if his human nature had not managed to withstand it.

This story is not new. It is told, in a slightly different way, by Thomas Morris in his fine defence of Chalcedonian Christology, *The Logic of God Incarnate.*[14] But it does give some indication (I put it no more strongly than that) of how a defender of the impeccability view might respond to the idea that Christ must be in the right psychological state to feel the 'pull' of (at least one) temptation, contrary to what some defenders of the sinlessness view suppose.

This leads to a third element in the notion of temptation, having to do with the disposition of a person's moral nature. A number of Christian theologians have claimed that there is a distinction to be made between 'innocent' and 'sinful' temptations.[15] An innocent temptation is, roughly, a temptation that does not require the person being tempted to be in a prior state of sin. But a sinful temptation does require this. It is difficult to cash out just what an innocent or sinful temptation might consist of.[16] Perhaps acting against a divine command (or some sorts of divine commands) does not require a prior sinful condition, whereas committing premeditated murder does. If this is right, then the biblical Adam might be a paradigm case of a sinless human being who succumbs to temptation of an 'innocent' variety, by disobeying a divine command. His son Cain might be thought of as a paradigm case of a sinful human being who succumbs to temptation of a 'sinful' variety, and murders his brother Abel.

---

14. Thomas V. Morris, *The Logic of God Incarnate*, ch. 6. Nor is Morris the first to espouse something like this view.

15. For instance, the nineteenth-century American Presbyterian theologian, William G. T. Shedd in his *Dogmatic Theology, Third Edition,* ed. Alan W. Gomes (Phillipsburg, NJ: Presbyterian and Reformed, 2003) p. 665 and following. Richard Swinburne speaks instead in terms of Christ being able to subject himself to temptations to do lesser goods, but not to do evil. See Swinburne, *The Christian God* (Oxford: Oxford University Press, 1994) p. 207. But this is difficult to square with the New Testament. Is worshipping Satan a temptation to do a lesser good (Mt. 4.9)?

16. I have pointed this out in the context of William Shedd's Christology in Oliver D. Crisp, *An American Augustinian: Sin and Salvation in the Dogmatic Theology of William G. T. Shedd* (Milton Keynes: Paternoster Press and Eugene, OR: Wipf and Stock, 2007) ch. 4.

Another traditional way of distinguishing different sorts of temptations depends on the difference between external and internal temptations on the basis of James 1.12-15. This passage explains that those who are tempted are drawn away by their own desires and enticed, they are not tempted by God. Christ cannot tempt himself because he is divine, and God tempts no one – presumably, not even himself. Nor can he be tempted by his own desires for the same reason, and also because he is without sinful desires. Only things external to him can provide avenues of temptation (e.g., the Devil).[17] Combined with the distinction between 'innocent' and 'sinful' temptations, it becomes clear that the only class of temptations Christ could feel the 'pull' of consisted in innocent temptations that were external to Christ (i.e., not generated directly by Christ, but by some other agent, e.g., Satan).[18]

Applied to Christ, this would mean that a person who is sinless cannot be in a morally vitiated state. But if this is the case, then it would seem that Christ is not capable of being tempted by at least one sort of temptation in precisely the way you or I are. For Christ cannot feel the 'pull' of sinful temptations in quite the same way as a sinful human being can. In order to feel the 'pull' of, say, premeditated murder, or adultery, one has to be in a position to find such actions appealing – have the right psychological configuration to do so. But Christ does not have the psychological configuration necessary to find such actions appealing because one would have to be in a state of sin in order for this state of affairs to obtain. And this seems true even if the larger question of determining the conditions under which a particular temptation counts as 'sinless' or 'sinful' are far from clear. So it would seem that the defender of the sinlessness view needs to have in place a sufficiently discriminating notion of the sort of temptation Christ may find appealing, in order to preserve a doctrine of Christ's sinlessness.

For the sake of argument, let us grant that a coherent version of such a circumscribed notion of the conditions under which a temptation may be appealing to Christ can be had (which is not, as I have already intimated, a trivial matter).

17.　Naturally, if one ignores James 1, then it is perfectly possible to say that God is a tempter, and this does make sense of a number of Old Testament passages, such as Genesis 22.1, 2 Chronicles 32.31 and 2 Samuel 24.1. But I take it this is not a live option for the Christian. A. T. Nuyen ends up taking just such a view in 'The Nature of Temptation', in *Southern Journal of Philosophy* 35 (1997): 102.

18.　An objection: If God 'tempts no one', as James tells us, and therefore cannot tempt himself in the person of his Son, can he bring about the temptation of his Son through other agents like Satan? In other words, can God cause someone else to tempt a third party, and can he tempt someone else to tempt himself? Well, if one has a robust doctrine of divine providence that includes the idea that God brings about all things that take place (perhaps through divine *concursus*, as with the Thomists), then it looks like God does do both of these things. In which case, he cannot tempt anyone (directly) but he can cause someone to tempt another or tempt himself, and thereby bring about a circumstance of temptation indirectly. Some may think this a rather casuistical way of construing James 1.12-15. But it does not seem inconsistent with the *letter* of the Epistle.

This may obtain in some form even if we are unable to determine what the necessary and sufficient conditions are for such a class of temptations. Then we might ask, is the act of being tempted itself morally culpable? An affirmative answer means that the very idea Christ can be tempted by any alleged source of temptation collapses. If the person being tempted is morally culpable for the very act of being tempted, then neither the defenders of the sinlessness view, nor of the impeccability view, can make any headway.

This is a difficult problem to which I do not pretend to have a completely satisfactory answer. Nevertheless, several things can be said by way of clarification that may go some way towards assisting the defenders of Christ's sinlessness and/or impeccability at this juncture. First, we must distinguish between the circumstances giving rise to an instance of temptation and the subjective state of being tempted. Plausibly, one might be being tempted and yet not culpable for finding oneself in circumstances in which temptation arises. To return to our earlier example: being tempted by another to break a fast and eat some bread. But are there circumstances in which an individual is not culpable for *being in the subjective state of being tempted*? If I am tempted to break my fast, is the very state of being thus tempted, a culpable one? I do not see how it can be. It may be true that someone who entertains or harbours a temptation, turning it over in his or her mind, and taking a kind of perverse pleasure in being titillated by the temptation (and its subject matter) may be culpable for so acting. But that, I take it, is hardly the same as being tempted by some external agent to perform a particular act that one finds tempting, but which one wishes to withstand. It might be that for some, or, perhaps all temptations that require the person being tempted to be in a prior state of sin, the person so tempted is culpable just for finding the object of temptation tempting, even if that person does not succumb to the temptation in a given circumstance.[19] But this is not relevant to Christ because he cannot be in a state of sin, on account of being free from sin.

So I suggest that, for at least some class of temptations, sometimes designated 'innocent temptations', a person may be in a state of temptation (where they feel the 'pull' of that temptation, and that temptation is an 'external' one) and yet not be culpable for being in that state. If this makes sense (and some might think that this is a rather big 'if' where the notion of 'innocent' and/or 'external' temptations are concerned), then Christ can be said to be tempted by such 'innocent' temptations and not be culpable for being in the subjective state of being tempted by the object of such temptations. Those who dissent from this sort of view, but who wish to defend either Christ's sinlessness or his

---

19. The idea here is that if Dean is in a sinful state when he is tempted to commit adultery (say), then he is (a) culpable for being in that state of sin (according to a classical notion of original sin) and (b) culpable for finding tempting that which only someone who is already in a fallen state would find appealing. In which case, he would seem to be culpable for being in a subjective state of temptation, irrespective of whether or not he acts upon that temptation, and sins.

impeccability, must find some other way of accounting for the fact that Christ's temptations are not in-and-of-themselves such as to render Christ morally culpable for being subjectively tempted by them. This is no small theological matter.

2. *Problems with the Sinlessness View*

According to the Roman Catholic theologian Gerald O'Collins, 'Christ's sin-lessness *de facto* almost inevitably raised a question *de iure*: in principle could he have sinned?' Upon which O'Collins offers the following comment:

> Was Christ personally impeccable *de iure*? The answer must be yes. Otherwise we would face the situation of God possibly in deliberate opposition to God; one divine person would be capable (through his human will) of committing sin and so intention-ally transgressing the divine will. The possibility of Christ sinning seems incompatible with the divine identity of his person.[20]

If Christ is *vere deus*, as well as *vere homo*, then he cannot sin – according to the sort of classical conception of the divine nature with which O'Collins aligns himself. But the fact that Christ cannot sin does not entail that he may not have the capacity to sin, which is the crucial issue upon which much of the force of the sinlessness argument turns and the problem with which we began our consideration of temptation in the previous section of the chapter. St Anselm made the same point in *Cur Deus Homo II. X,* where he points out that Christ could and could not tell a lie. Anselm unpacks this comment as follows: Christ had the capacity to lie (Jn 8.55), but he was incapable of exercising this capacity. This can be cashed out in terms of reduplication (although Anselm does not do so in this passage). In which case, we can say that, *qua* human Christ had this capacity, but *qua* divine he was incapable of sin. Those who take the sinlessness view seem to think the impeccability view requires that Christ may not have the capacity to sin, but this is certainly not the position of defenders of Christ's impeccability like Anselm.[21] The claim that Christ may be capable of sin in one sense, and yet incapable of sinning all things consid-ered is no more incoherent than the notion that a fragile champagne glass may be protected from being shattered by being surrounded in polystyrene packing. We might say that the glass has the disposition to shatter if handled roughly, but that, provided it remains in the polystyrene packing, it will never 'realize' this dispositional property and be shattered. Similarly, Christ's human nature may have the disposition or capacity to sin (in abstraction from the

---

20.   Gerald O'Collins, *Incarnation* (London: Continuum, 2002) pp. 85 and 86 respectively.
21.   At the very least Hart's comments about the potential for sin being part and parcel of Christ's moral nature suggest that the alternative, impeccability view does not include such a capacity.

incarnation, as it were), and yet be rendered incapable of sinning by being in personal union with his divine nature.[22]

This means that the real issue between the sinlessness and impeccability views is not whether Christ has the capacity to sin. Nor does it concern whether he feels the 'pull' of temptation. Christ may be tempted by 'innocent temptations' (clearly not by 'sinful' ones) because, as a human being he really does feel the pull of certain sorts of temptation, just as unfallen Adam could feel the pull of such temptations, and yet be without sin. (Perhaps he has the right 'psychological configuration' to feel the 'pull' of temptation, along the lines of the metaphysical story, outlined earlier.) It is rather like an invincible pugilist battling it out in the ring with an opponent. The outcome is a foregone conclusion if our pugilist is invincible; but that does not mean the he does not have to put up a real fight in the ring. Similarly, when Christ is tempted in the desert to turn stones into bread (Lk. 4.1–4) he really feels the 'pull' of that temptation, he really wrestles with it, having fasted for forty days, although the outcome is certain: there is no possibility of him succumbing to temptation. Hence, the real issue between the two views of Christ's moral status with respect to temptation is whether Christ could actually have sinned when presented with ('innocent') temptation, not whether he had the capacity to sin, or felt the 'pull' of temptation. Both the sinlessness and impeccability views can offer some accounting of these latter two issues.

This raises a second, modal problem for the sinlessness view. According to the logic of this account, Christ might have sinned, but did not in fact sin (a fact only established at the resurrection, according to Pannenberg). But then, there are possible circumstances in which Christ would have sinned, though he did not in fact sin. And this means that, possibly, the incarnate Second Person of the Trinity could have sinned (hence, a *modal* problem for the sinlessness view). Recall that both defenders of the sinlessness view and of the impeccability view can affirm that Christ has the capacity to sin, as a human being. But, as has already been pointed out, having the capacity to do a thing is not the same as doing a thing (which one has a capacity to perform). The sinlessness view cannot stop at suggesting Christ had the capacity to sin as a human being, though he never exercised this capacity, the reason being that, as it stands, this statement is ambiguous, given that the advocate of the impeccability view can say the same thing. To distinguish the sinlessness view from the impeccability view, the defender of the sinlessness position has to offer something more, by way of explanation. To have purchase, she or he must affirm that there are possible situations in which Christ would have sinned (though he did not actually sin). But this poses a very real difficulty for the defender of the sinlessness view. As H. R. Macintosh observed, 'faith cannot

---

22. A similar point is suggested by Richard Sturch in *The Word and The Christ, An Essay in Analytic Christology* (Oxford: Oxford University Press, 1991), Excursus IV, pp. 263–264.

acquiesce in the thought that conceivably the Divine redeeming plan might have been frustrated; yet frustration would have been had Jesus yielded to temptation even once.'[23]

Consider a hypothetical situation in which Christ has to make a morally responsible choice between two alternatives: to sin or to do the right thing. Suppose Christ chooses to do the right thing. What does it mean to say Christ might have chosen to sin? The defender of the sinlessness view surely means this: Christ could have chosen to sin, though he did not, as a matter of fact, choose to sin. But if this means anything, it surely means Christ could have exercised a different choice than the one he did. He could have acted differently.[24]

Christ can only have acted differently and sinned if, in a given circumstance, he had the power to sin (he could have chosen to sin) and there was nothing preventing him from acting in a way consistent with that option, had he so chosen (though he did not so choose). In other words, the sinlessness view seems to involve the following claims:

1. There were alternate possibilities open to Christ when tempted (e.g., to turn the stones into bread, or to refrain from turning the stones into bread).
2. Christ was able to make a morally responsible choice between these alternatives that was, in some sense, free, not a forced or coerced.
3. Christ could have chosen the alternative to what he did choose, though, as a matter of fact, he did not.
4. Had he so chosen, Christ would have sinned, though, as a matter of fact he did not.

The defender of the sinlessness view cannot claim, as the defender of impeccability may, that Christ has the capacity to sin (*qua* human) but is incapable of ever exercising that capacity, because, say, his divine nature prevents such an outcome or would prevent it, if it became necessary, though such an eventuality never in fact arose. To remain consistent, the defender of the sinlessness view must affirm that Christ (a) had the capacity to sin (*qua* human) and (b) had the capacity to sin (*qua* divine). To affirm the first without the second is to play into the hands of the advocates of Christ's impeccability. In short, if Christ really could have sinned – but did not – then he must have been able to choose to sin *as the God-Man*. The logic of the sinlessness position drives in this direction.

The upshot of this is that Christ has the capacity to sin as a divine being. Moreover, if Christ has the capacity to sin *qua* divine, then it is a very short step

23.   *The Doctrine of the Person of Jesus Christ*, p. 413.
24.   Thus, it seems that the defender of the sinlessness view is committed to the notion, beloved of libertarians, that Christ had a significantly free moral choice between alternatives in the case of his temptations. Conversely, for advocates of Christ's impeccability, Christ could not choose to sin, even if his human nature, being peccable, felt the 'gravitational pull' of that temptation.

from here to the view that the Triune God can sin.[25] Some contemporary philosophers have embraced the notion that God is capable of sin as a theological virtue.[26] But I do not see how this is viable. If God is necessarily good – a view that is certainly deeply ingrained in Christian theology and spirituality, to the extent that it is the default view in the tradition – then, as a simple matter of logic, he cannot be able to sin. I suppose one could simply stipulate that God is not necessarily good in some sense, but this is surely indicative of the theological dilettante.

To extrapolate: A distinction is often made between God's metaphysical and moral goodness. I take it x is metaphysically good just in case x is desirable, and God is the supremely desirable thing, so God is supremely good (perhaps 'goodness itself', if one follows Thomas).[27] But one might also say 'God is supremely morally good'. This is a different claim. Could one stipulate that God is necessarily supremely desirable (because perfect), and yet not necessarily supremely morally good? Well, I suppose so, but it seems an odd thing to say, and whether it amounts to a coherent claim would have to be argued. Could one claim the opposite, that God is not necessarily ontologically supremely good, but that he is necessarily supremely morally good? Again, yes, one can *claim* this. But does it make much sense? And even if it does make sense, does it reflect the Christian conception of these things? I am deeply dubious about both of these alternatives, although I cannot argue against them here. What does seem clear to me is that God need not be able to sin in order to be morally or metaphysically perfect: God can choose between alternatives (we might think). He is, after all, free. But one or more of those alternatives cannot be evil. In that regard, John Calvin is surely right when he says

> suppose some blasphemer sneers that God deserves little praise for his own goodness, constrained as he is to preserve it. Will this not be a ready answer to him: not from violent impulsion but from his boundless goodness comes God's inability to do evil?[28]

---

25. There is a short step involved because one could argue the divine person of the Word has the capacity to sin, but neither of the other divine persons does. Then, 'being able to sin' would be a property or predicate of the Second Person of the Trinity, but not a property or predicate of the divine essence.

26. See for instance Nelson Pike, 'Omnipotence and God's ability to sin' in *Divine Commands and Morality*, ed. Paul Helm (Oxford: Oxford University Press, 1981); Vincent Brümmer, 'Divine Impeccability' in *Religious Studies* 20 (1984): 203–214; and Keith Yandell, 'Divine Necessity and Divine Goodness' in Thomas V. Morris ed. *Divine and Human Action: Essays in the Metaphysics of Theism* (Ithaca, NY.: Cornell University Press, 1988). There are other examples, but these are representative.

27. *Summa Contra Gentiles*, I, 38.

28. John Calvin, *Institutes of the Christian Religion,* trans. Ford Lewis Battles, ed. John T. McNeill (Philadelphia, PA: Westminster Press, 1960), II. iii. 5, cited in Edward R. Wierenga, *The Nature of God, An Inquiry into Divine Attributes* (Ithaca, NY: Cornell University Press, 1989) p. 212. Wierenga's discussion of these issues is very useful. See ch. 7 of his work.

I suppose one could deny that God is necessarily morally or metaphysically good. But this looks even less plausible than the other two claims (a God who only *happens* to be morally and metaphysically good?). In short, it seems to me that God is necessarily metaphysically and morally good, and this is no constraint on the divine nature. It also seems to me (though, admittedly, no argument for this claim is offered here) that taking leave of a necessarily good God involves relinquishing something essential to Christian theology.[29] Yet this sort of theological revisionism is what the sinlessness view is driven to – which is the crucial issue here, and which I imagine those committed to an otherwise classical Christology will find a quite unappealing consequence of their adherence to the sinlessness view. For these reasons, the sinlessness view seems to me to be wholly inadequate. Moreover, much of the dialectical force of the sinlessness view is reduced once it is clear that a defender of Christ's impeccability may agree that Christ has the capacity to sin, but cannot sin, as St Anselm, amongst others, maintained.

Given these considerations, I see no need to abandon the view that Christ is impeccable, and several very serious reasons for steering clear of the modern theological predilection for reducing Christ's impeccability to mere sinlessness. The arguments sometimes offered for the sinlessness view and against the impeccability view that we have canvassed here are no grounds for thinking that an impeccable Christ may not be truly tempted, if, in order to be tempted one must have the capacity to be tempted, and feel the 'pull' of temptation. For, there is nothing about the nature of impeccability that precludes these things.

---

29. Compare Psalm 52.1 and Matthew 19.17. I suppose one could argue that such passages teach only God's goodness, not his necessary, or essential, goodness (and yet, what of passages like Habbakuk 1.13, or 1 John 1.5? Surely these imply that God's goodness is *essential*). But it seems to me that even if these passages do not imply divine necessary goodness, they fit best with such a doctrine. And, in any case, if one revises this divine attribute, it cannot but have implications for other divine attributes (and therefore, for a doctrine of the divine nature). If God is not essentially good, then whence divine holiness, love, compassion, trustworthiness to give but four of the most obvious examples? It also raises questions about God's worthiness of worship: ought we to worship a being who is only contingently good, and who may choose to do evil?

Chapter 7

MATERIALIST CHRISTOLOGY

A child of five would understand this. Send someone to fetch a child of five.
                                                                    Groucho Marx

A number of recent Christian biblical scholars, theologians and philosophers have rejected a substance dualist account of human persons. This is the view that human beings are normally composed of two substances, a soul that has some intimate relationship to a body. In its place, they have opted for various versions of materialism about human persons, that is, the notion that human persons are essentially material beings. Commitment to materialism about human persons should be distinguished from what is often called *global materialism*: the idea that all existing things are essentially material things; there are no immaterial entities.[1] Clearly, this latter, global materialism is incompatible with orthodox Christian belief. But defenders of materialism about human persons who are also Christian thinkers are not committed to global materialism. Their contention is simply that human persons are material beings, not that there are no immaterial beings. Any classical theist, let alone any Christian theologian, will want to affirm the existence of at least one essentially immaterial entity: God. And Christian theologians of an orthodox variety will agree that many more such essentially immaterial entities exist, the most obvious case in point being the class of angelic beings.

We might say that global materialism is a species of monism, the view that there is only *one sort of thing*, in this case matter, of which all existing things are composed. (This should not be confused with the idea that everything that exists is composed of *one thing*, or one substance, like Spinozistic pantheism.[2]) Idealism is another sort of monism, because the idealist says only mental things, that is, minds and their ideas, exist and everything is composed of such mental things. But clearly, the Christian who is a materialist about human

---

1. Of course, global materialism is compatible with the idea that some essentially material objects have mental properties. What is objected to is the notion that some entities are essentially immaterial substances, like souls.

2. Benedict Spinoza advocated a version of pantheism: everything is part of one immaterial substance, God. But one could claim everything that exists is part of some massive single material substance. This we might call panmaterialism.

persons is not a monist. In fact, I take it that a necessary condition of Christian theism is what we might call *global substance dualism*, which is the idea that all existing things are composed of matter or spirit (or mind), or both matter and spirit. The idea here is that all existing things are composed of one or other, or perhaps both, matter and spirit, not that all existing things are, or must be, composed of *both* matter *and* spirit – clearly this view, equivalent to panpsychism, would be unorthodox.[3]

Global substance dualism is an entailment of theism, which includes the idea that at least one immaterial substance exists, that is, God. And all Christians are, of course, theists. So all Christians, Christian materialists included, must be global substance dualists. It is just that the Christian materialist presumes that material and immaterial substances do not co-exist, or interact, in the case of human persons. In short, Christian materialists are global dualists but local materialists, when it comes to consideration of the metaphysics of human persons. Presumably, those who are Christians and also favour some materialist account of human personhood do so not because they think there is something incoherent about the notion of an immaterial agent or substance as such, but because they are convinced on other grounds that human persons are material beings.

In what follows, when materialism is mentioned, I mean to refer merely to the idea that human beings are essentially material entities – that is, *local* or *restricted materialism*, or *materialism about human persons* (I shall use all these terms) – not to the broader, global materialism. Since the basic tenet of restricted materialism is that human persons are *essentially* material beings, the Christian materialist must say that if humans have an immaterial component at all, it is certainly not an immaterial substance, like a soul. A further point of clarification: when mention is made of substance dualism in the remainder of this chapter, I mean to refer to those who are substance dualists 'all the way down' so to speak, that is, those who espouse both *global* and *local substance dualism*, who think that substances are either material or immaterial (or some compound of both) and that humans are normally composed of a soul with some intimate relation to a body.

Those Christian thinkers who espouse one or other form of materialism often speak of this as a view which has many theological as well as philosophical advantages over versions of substance dualism. For instance, it is often claimed

---

3.   Richard Bauckham suggested to me that some Christians have thought God is no more immaterial than he is material. He is something unlike both, some third sort of unknown thing. I suppose this might be the case on a strong apophatic theology, but it is hardly in accordance with Scripture, which declares in numerous places that God is a spirit (e.g., Gen. 1.2; Isa. 42.1, and especially Jn 4.24). This is also enshrined in confessional documents, such as the *Westminster Confession* II. § 1 that states, 'There is but one only living and true God . . . a most pure spirit'. Likewise, the first of the *Thirty Nine Articles* of the Church of England says that God is 'without body, parts or passions'.

that, aside from the supposed problems for substance dualism that recent advances in our understanding of the neurosciences have raised, there are problems the biblical data pose. Passages that have traditionally been thought to support substance dualism fit better with some version of the materialist view of the metaphysics of human persons, or so it is claimed.[4] But such issues are moot. It is a matter of historical record that Christians down through the ages have been substance dualists – both globally and locally, that is, concerning the kinds of things that exist, and concerning the kinds of thing human persons are. Christian materialism may be an increasingly popular option amongst contemporary Christian thinkers, but it is a view that flies in the face of the entire Christian tradition. This, I suggest, is no small matter. Moreover, it is certainly not true to say that arguments in favour of restricted materialism have carried the day. In fact, there are an increasing number of Christian theologians and philosophers who have defended sophisticated versions of substance dualism, and some that have also argued that it is a consistently dualist position that best fits the biblical and scientific data.[5]

I do not intend to contribute to this debate directly. Instead, I want to consider whether restricted materialism is compatible with one central claim of classical Christology, namely, that Christ's humanity included his having a 'rational soul'. The so-called 'definition' of the theanthropic (God-Man) person of Christ given by the Fathers at the Council of Chalcedon in AD 451 remains the touchstone for orthodox accounts of Christ. Taking the Chalcedonian 'two-natures' doctrine as my point of departure, I argue that any account of the person of Christ that wishes to remain within the bounds of theological orthodoxy (as laid down by the Canons of Chalcedon), must give some explanation of the two-natures doctrine that makes sense of Christ having a fully human nature, consisting of a human body and a 'rational soul', as the Fathers of Chalcedon put it. Accounts of the metaphysics of human persons that are not able to make sense of this crucial constituent of catholic Christology cannot be creedally orthodox, an outcome that is usually thought to be unacceptable for any theological argument.

---

4. To give one recent example, see Joel Green's editorial introduction to *In Search of the Soul, Four Views of the Mind-Body Problem*, eds Joel B. Green and Stuart L. Palmer (Downers Grove, IL: Inter-Varsity Press, 2005) pp. 7–32. For detailed theological views that are critical of a traditional reading of the biblical material in this regard, see Wolfhart Pannenberg, *Systematic Theology, Vol. II* (Grand Rapids, MI: Eerdmans, 1991) pp. 181–202. Materialists often claim that New Testament passages like I Corinthians 15 support materialism, not dualism about human persons.

5. Amongst contemporary defenders of substance dualism Richard Swinburne and Alvin Plantinga have been prominent. See Swinburne, *The Evolution of the Soul, Revised Edition* (Oxford: Oxford University Press, 1997), and Plantinga, 'Against Materialism' in *Faith and Philosophy* 23 (2006): 3–32. The most sophisticated defence of substance dualism from a biblical-theological position to date is John W. Cooper, *Body, Soul and Life Everlasting, Biblical Anthropology and the Monism-Dualism Debate* (Grand Rapids, MI: Eerdmans, 2000 [1989]).

The argument proceeds in five stages. In the first, I set out the requirements of an orthodox understanding of the two-natures doctrine drawing on the Chalcedonian 'definition' of the person of Christ. The second section sketches out some of the differences between dualism and materialism. I suggest that the most obvious route that the materialist concerned to remain creedally orthodox might take is to offer some version of materialism consistent with property dualism. In a third section I consider some central issues pertaining to property dualism as it bears on Christian materialism. The fourth section applies the findings of the previous two, and in particular, the claim about property dualism, to the Incarnation, focusing on the claim that Christ had a 'rational soul' by way of an anti-Apollinarian argument. In a final section, I argue that the Christian theologian is faced with a cost-benefit trade-off when it comes to opting for one or other account of the metaphysics of human persons. It turns out, on the analysis offered in the fourth section, that material-ists that are property dualists can tell a story consistent with catholic Christology, given certain assumptions about human nature and what it means to say Christ had a 'rational soul'. But there are certain costs involved in opting for a version of materialism consistent with this Christological claim, just as there are other costs involved in opting for a substance dualist account of human persons. Nevertheless, even if the Christian materialist account of the Chalcedonian claim that Christ had a 'rational soul' is not convincing to all, the Christian materialist who is also a property dualist can show that his mate-rialism does not entail Apollinarianism. And this defuses one important objection to Christian materialist accounts of Christology.

1. *The Requirements of Catholic Christology*

What, then, are the requirements of catholic Christology that have a bearing upon the metaphysics of human persons? In a recent and theologically informed defence of the claim that the Christian hope does not presuppose substance dualism, Peter van Inwagen argues that the catholic creeds make no prejudicial judgment about whether some version of substance dualism or restricted materialism is orthodox. Citing relevant passages from the Apostles' Creed, the Nicene Creed and the Athanasian Creed he concludes, 'I contend only that there is nothing in the passages I have quoted to make the anti-dualist uncomfortable.'[6] He is undoubtedly right about this. The three creeds he refers to say nothing that would require the Christian to endorse some species of local

---

6. Peter van Inwagen, 'Dualism and Materialism: Athens and Jerusalem?' in *Faith and Philo-sophy* 12 (1995): 479. We could press the point about 'relevant information'. Van Inwagen cites two 'creeds', which, though ancient and venerable, are not strictly theologically binding, because they are not considered to be canons of an ecumenical council. I refer to the Apostles' Creed and the Athanasian Creed. It is surprising he does not consider the Chalcedonian definition, since this is normally understood to be one of the four great symbols of the Catholic Church.

dualism with respect to human persons. But this is a false economy because van Inwagen has not canvassed all the relevant information. When we turn to consider what the Council of Chalcedon says about the person of Christ a rather different picture emerges:

> Following, then, the holy Fathers, we all with one voice teach that it should be confessed that our Lord Jesus Christ is one and the same Son, the same perfect in Godhead, the same perfect in manhood, truly God and truly man, the same [consisting] of a rational soul and a body; *homoousios* [consubstantial] with the Father as to his Godhead, and the same *homoousios* [consubstantial] with us as to his manhood; in all things like unto us, sin only excepted, begotten of the Father before ages as to his Godhead, and in the last days, the same, for us and for our salvation, of Mary the Virgin *Theotokos* as to his manhood; One and the same Christ, Son, Lord, Only begotten, man known in two natures [which exist] without confusion, without change, without division, without separation; the difference of the natures having been in no wise taken away by reason of the union, but rather the properties of each being preserved, and [both] concurring into one *prosopon* [person] and one *hypostasis* [individual] – not parted or divided into two *prosopa* [persons], but one and the same Son and Only-begotten, the divine Logos, the Lord Jesus Christ; even as the prophets from of old [have spoken] concerning him, and as the Lord Jesus Christ himself has taught us, and as the Symbol [i.e., Nicene Creed] of the Fathers has delivered to us.[7]

The following statements can be derived from this deliverance of the Council that are pertinent to the present concern:

a. Christ has a fully human and fully divine nature.
b. These two natures are held together in a hypostatic union without confusion or mixture, or generation of a *tertium quid* (third sort of thing).
c. Christ's human nature consists of a human body and a 'rational soul'.
d. Christ's human nature is consubstantial (of the same sort of substance) as that of other human beings, sin excepted.

The first two statements set out two central requirements of a two-natures doctrine of the person of Christ. The latter two have to do with what it means to say Christ is fully, or truly, human. At first glance, it is the third statement above that appears to be most problematic for the Christian committed to restricted materialism. For possession of a 'rational soul' does not seem to be compatible with the notion that humans are purely, or even essentially, material beings. But, in fact, the fourth statement is equally problematic. For if Christ is consubstantial with us with respect to his human nature, then Christ's human nature is no different from our human nature in its composition, and we, like Christ, must have a 'rational soul'. So the problem posed by Christ's

---

7. Adapted from Aloys Grillmeier, *Christ in Christian Tradition, Vol. 1, From the Apostolic Age to Chalcedon (AD 451)* (London: Mowbray, 1965) p. 544.

'rational soul' for materialist accounts of human persons is, it turns out, a difficulty that concerns the composition of all human beings. From this it should be clear that van Inwagen is wrong if he thinks that there is no creedal impediment to being a restricted materialist. It is, I suggest, incumbent upon those materialists who are creedally orthodox Christians to find some way of making sense of these problems thrown up by Chalcedonian Christology. With this in mind, we turn to consider dualism and materialism in more detail.

2. *Dualism and Materialism*

Whatever view one takes on the metaphysics of human persons, the same data have to be accounted for. These are that humans have corporeal bodies of a certain sort, normally composed in a particular way, and that human persons enjoy a particular kind of mental life including the capacity for conscious thought. Substance dualists make sense of these data by proposing that human persons are normally composed of an immaterial part that is somehow related to some parcel of matter.[8] The immaterial component of a human person is a distinct substance that is somehow essential to the composition of human persons. This is true if one is a Cartesian, and thinks human persons are just souls that happen to be 'housed', as it were, in the bodies they possess – as we have already had cause to note in previous chapters. It is also true if one is a hylomorphist of the sort that thinks human persons are a compound of matter and form, or the product of such a compound, where the soul organizes, or gives form to, the matter of the body, thereby generating a human person. Without a soul, says the hylomorphist, there is no 'thing' to organize the matter of the body, and no person is present.[9] And the same would be true, *mutatis mutandis*, for other sorts of substance dualism one finds in the contemporary

---

8.   I say this advisedly. Some dualists say human persons are just souls (e.g., Cartesians). Others say humans are soul + body composites, or the product of such composition (e.g., hylomorphists). Although different in important respects, both sorts of dualists are committed to the notion that humans are normally composed of an immaterial part somehow related to a parcel of matter that is a human body. What distinguishes them is (a) whether they think human persons are essentially immaterial entities, and (b) how they construe the relation between the immaterial and material parts of humans. Some recent philosophical discussion denies that those who think humans are body + soul composites are dualists (e.g., Trenton Merricks, 'The Word Made Flesh: Dualism, Physicalism and the Incarnation' in Peter van Inwagen and Dean W. Zimmerman eds *Persons: Human and Divine* (Oxford: Oxford University Press, 2007) p. 282 n. 2). But here I am concerned to be as generous about dualist positions as possible. And certainly hylomorphists are traditionally thought to be dualists of a sort.

9.   This might be the case even if the hylomorphist thought human persons were the product of a soul + body compound, that is, some sort of *tertium quid*, or third sort of thing, that is produced when soul and body are conjoined. Then a human person is not a soul, nor is it a body (at least, not a body that has not been conjoined with a soul); it is the product of conjoining these two substances. But this product (whatever it is exactly) has a soul as a necessary component, just as oxygen is a necessary chemical component of water, although water is not identical with oxygen.

literature.[10] The phrase '*mutatis mutandis*', that is, 'the relevant changes having been made' is, of course, an important qualification here. Dualists do not agree amongst themselves about exactly what metaphysical arrangement of immaterial and material components is necessary for a human person to be present. The Cartesian thinks all that is required is a human soul, which may (or may not) be contingently related to a given body; the hylomorphist thinks that the soul without the body is not a person as such, although disembodied souls may exist in some diminished state. Still others think souls cannot function without a body, with which they are intimately 'connected' (Richard Swinburne has defended this notion). I am sure there are also those dualists who think souls depend for their continued existence on being rightly 'connected' to a functioning brain, or even that souls are just immaterial epiphenomena accompanying mental life, a kind of incorporeal by-product of conscious thought that is an immaterial substance, but that is, as it were, causally inert.[11]

Matters are rather different for the restricted materialist, of course. All materialists claim that human persons are essentially material beings. But they disagree amongst themselves about what that amounts to. We can divide restricted materialists into those who think the mental life of humans can somehow be reduced to some aspect of human corporeal life. This family of views is usually referred to as *reductive materialism*. Then there are those materialists who think that the mental life of humans cannot be reduced to some aspect of human corporeal life. Call this sort of view, *non-reductive materialism*.

Reductive materialists want to say that human persons are identical with their bodies, either as masses of matter, or as a certain sort of complex physical organism. But if that is right, how can we make sense of our mental life, which does not seem to be reducible to our physical life? One response is to say that mental events and states are identical to physical events and states.[12] Take, for example, the mental property 'thinking of a blue flower' that I have at noon today. The identity theorist says that this mental state is in fact identical in every respect to some physical thing occurring in my brain, such as the physical state

---

Is this position clearly dualist? Perhaps not if this *tertium quid* is the fusion of material and immaterial substances. But it does require a soul and body as components necessary to generate a human person, even if a human person is not composed of a soul and body, strictly speaking, but the compound, or fusion of these two things (whatever such a thing might be).

10.   William Hasker's emergent dualism, for instance, or Cooper's 'holistic' dualism.

11.   One might think souls cannot function without being 'plugged into' a body, but that they continue to exist in a non-functional state without a body. But this is not the same as saying a soul requires a body to continue to exist. An object may continue to exist even it is not functioning (e.g., a broken computer). But an object that depends upon some other object for its continued existence cannot exist without being rightly related to that other object, rather like the light generated by the sun.

12.   Here I am assuming that mental states involve the instantiation of a mental property in the mind at a particular time. A mental event is the instantiation of a mental property in the mind that occurs at a particular time, and has duration.

of having the property of a particular c-fibre firing at that particular moment in time. Thus, when we speak of c-fibre x firing at noon today, that physical state is identical to the mental state of possessing the thought of a blue flower at noon today. The firing of the particular c-fibre in the brain, the organic, chemical change that takes place at that moment in my head is all there is to my having the thought of a blue flower. In which case, 'mental' states and events just are 'physical' states and events; the former is reducible to the latter without residue. This is not to deny the reality of my mental life. But it is to deny that my mental life is distinct from my physical life in any way, just as saying Cicero is identical to Tully does not deny the existence of Cicero, but denies Cicero is anything other than Tully.[13]

We come to non-reductive materialism. One non-reductive view claims that human persons somehow supervene upon the corporeal parcel of matter, or some parts thereof, of which living human bodies, with the propensity or capacity for the requisite sort of mental life, are composed. On this sort of view, the mental life that properly functioning humans enjoy is something that arises from a certain sort of material organization. It is, in some basic and continuous way, dependent upon this material organization, although it is not reducible to it, unlike reductive versions of materialism. The *composition view* is one such non-reductive version of materialism. Advocates of the composition view say the relation of persons to their bodies is like the relation of the statue to a lump of clay. The statue is formed out of the clay when manipulated by the sculptor. It is composed of the lump of clay. Yet it is not identical to the lump of clay. Just so, human personhood, including the mental life requisite to human personhood, arises from the material organization of the body. Human persons are composed by their bodies but are not reducible to the matter of which their bodies are composed.[14]

From this it should be tolerably clear that there are a variety of different versions of dualism and materialism in the literature, and that negotiating these complex waters requires some careful intellectual navigation. What I want to suggest next is that commitment to some form of property dualism is, perhaps, the most obvious and economical way in which the materialist can attempt to

---

13.   This line of reasoning is indebted to Tim Crane's discussion in *Elements of Mind, An Introduction to the Philosophy of Mind* (Oxford: Oxford University Press, 2001) ch. 2. Type-type identity theorists claim that one type of thing, a mental event, is somehow identical to another type of thing, a physical event in the brain. This sort of materialism is straightforwardly reductionist. But a token-token identity theorist might hold that particular mental events (tokens) are identical to certain physical events (tokens) without commitment to type-type identity. Such a materialist might also be a property dualist. I owe this point to E. J. Lowe, 'The Problem of Psycho-physical Causation' reprinted in Timothy O'Connor and David Robb, eds *Philosophy of Mind, Contemporary Readings* (London: Routledge, 2002) p. 50.

14.   Kevin Corcoran sets out an explicitly Christian version of the composition view in *Rethinking Human Nature, A Chrisian Materialist Alternative to the Soul* (Grand Rapids, MI: Baker Academic, 2006).

make sense of the theological idea that Christ had a 'rational soul'. To begin with, I will set out one way in which the materialist might construe property dualism. Then, we can apply this to the deliverances of Chalcedon regarding the Incarnation.

3. *Property Dualism*

Before we answer the question, 'What is property dualism?' it might be appropriate to say something about properties and substances. Here I cannot offer anything approaching a complete account of either properties or substances. So I will content myself with saying this: Substances are things of a certain sort that can exist independently of other things of the same sort, have certain causal relations with other substances, and are the bearers of properties. Descartes held to something like this view and, in the recent literature, Richard Swinburne has repeated it.[15] But it is really very difficult to say much more than this about substances and even this is not incontestable.[16] I take it that properties are abstract objects that are typically universals. 'Blueness' is one such. It is a universal because it can be instantiated in more than one object, such as my blue shirt or the blueness of the sky. Some properties are not universals like this because they necessarily apply to only one object, such as 'being the Son of God'. There are other views about what properties are, even views about whether there are such things as properties, but the sort of view I have in mind, often called 'realism about properties' or 'platonism' is the one I shall opt for here. It is sometimes opposed to 'nominalism', the family of views that share a common scepticism about the existence of abstract objects that are universals, although some modern nominalists are happy to talk about properties, as long as 'property' does not mean 'universal'. (Here I think of so-called 'trope' theorists.)

So, in sum, substances are distinct things that can have causal relations with other things, like bodies, balls or bats, whilst properties are abstract objects instantiated in particular substances, like 'being large', 'being round', 'being red' or 'being thoughtful'. A substance is said to possess a property just in case it exemplifies that property. Thus, we might say that the substance that is my

---

15.   See Richard Swinburne, 'From Mental/Physical Identity to Substance Dualism' in Peter van Inwagen and Dean W. Zimmerman eds *Persons: Human and Divine* (Oxford: Oxford University Press, 2006) pp. 142–143. Swinburne cites Descartes as follows: 'The notion of a substance is just this – that it can exist by itself without the aid of any other substance'. From Rene Descartes, *Replies to the Fourth Set of Objections*, in *The Philosophical Writings of Descartes, ii* trans J. Cottingham, R. Stoothof and D. Murdoch (Cambridge: Cambridge University Press, 1984) p. 159, cited in Swinburne, ibid., p. 143 n. 2.

16.   At one point in a recent paper Peter van Inwagen admits 'I would really like to say something useful about substances or individual things. But I can't, not really.' See 'A Materialist Ontology of the Human Person' in Peter van Inwagen and Dean W. Zimmerman eds *Persons: Human and Divine* (Oxford: Oxford University Press, 2006) p. 202.

body exemplifies the properties 'being physical' and 'being extended in space'. These distinctions are common enough features of philosophical and theological literature to need little further introduction.

Now, we come to property dualism. This is usually characterized as the view according to which a substance has certain properties that are said to be 'physical' and other properties that are said to be 'mental'. But what makes a property a 'mental' or a 'physical' one? Properties in and of themselves are, given the foregoing, neither mental nor physical things, but abstract objects of some sort. And any two properties are, presumably, things of the same sort, that is, the same ontological kind of thing. So the property 'Thinking of Malchus', the servant of the high priest whose ear was chopped off by Peter in John 18.10, and the property 'having a body', such as I trust I have, are not different sorts of things, the one mental, the other physical. For both are properties, so both are abstract objects of the same ontological kind. In a similar fashion, a symphony and an oratorio are the same sort of thing, namely musical compositions, although the content of an oratorio and a symphony are quite different. By the same token, what distinguishes 'mental' and 'physical' properties respectively is the content of each. The first concerns something mental; the second, something corporeal. Thus the term 'property dualism' cannot mean that mental and physical properties belong to different ontological kinds of things, but only that there are properties the content of which has to do with something mental, and there are properties the content of which has to do with something physical. When I refer to 'mental' and 'physical' properties in what follows, the reader should bear these circumlocutions in mind, though for reasons of economy of expression I shall not repeat them each time I speak of properties that are either 'mental' or 'physical'.

Richard Swinburne has recently distinguished between 'mental' and 'physical' properties in terms of *accessibility*. I think this is a helpful distinction. He suggests that a mental property exemplified by a particular substance is something that only one substance has privileged access to, whereas a physical property is not restricted in this way. It is, we might say, accessible to things other than the substance that instantiates it.[17] Thus, the mental property 'thinking about Malchus' the servant of the High Priest from John's Gospel is a property I have as I write these words. I am thinking about Malchus; hence I exemplify this property. You could also be thinking of Malchus at the same moment, and exemplify the same property, 'thinking of Malchus'. So, the same

---

17.   Swinburne, says

> a mental property is one to whose instantiation the substance in whom it is instantiated necessarily has privileged access on any occasion of its instantiation, and a physical property is one to whose instantiation the substance necessarily has no privileged access on any occasion of its instantiation.

(In 'From Mental/Physical Identity to Substance Dualism', p. 143.)

property can be exemplified in more than one individual at a time. Still, you do not have access to Crisp's thought about Malchus. It is not a property you have access to, because it is something I am thinking and my thoughts are not in the public domain. However, everyone I come into contact with can see I have a body with a certain physical extension, height, weight and so forth. My having the properties 'being physical' and 'having a body with a certain extension in space' are, in one important respect, accessible to those who come into contact with me.[18]

So property dualism concerns properties that are distinct, and that refer to either the mental or physical life of a substance. Also, property dualists hold that the content of mental properties refers to something irreducibly mental, or immaterial, whereas the content of physical properties refers to something irreducibly physical. One way of making sense of this distinction is to parse it in terms of the accessibility of such properties. But thus far, what we have said about property dualism is not sufficient to generate some version of materialism. For quite obviously, substance dualism requires property dualism: material substances have material properties, like 'having extension in space' and immaterial substances have immaterial properties like 'thinking of a blue flower'. Furthermore, since Christian materialists of all varieties are global substance dualists, all Christian materialists are committed to some form of property dualism, what we might call *global property dualism*, which maps onto their global substance dualism. Thus, global property dualism is the view that there are substances with mental properties and substances with physical properties, and all substances have one or other or both sorts of properties. Because all Christian materialists are global dualists, they are *ipso facto* committed to a global property dualism as well. Naturally, some Christian materialists think property dualism does not apply to human persons as a particular ontological kind of substance. Such Christian materialists are global property dualists, but not local property dualists with respect to human persons, where local property dualism is the view that a particular sort of substance – in this case, human persons – has both mental and physical properties. Such Christian materialists will be mental reductionists of some sort, concerning human mental life, because they do not think there is metaphysical room for mental properties that are distinct from, or not reducible to, physical properties.[19]

---

18. Some properties are what Swinburne dubs 'neutral properties' because they are not obviously mental or physical, such as the disjunctive property 'being a zombie or thinking about Malchus'. But we do not need to trouble ourselves with such properties here. We are interested in property dualism, not 'neutral properties', although I suppose human persons exemplify certain sorts of properties Swinburne thinks of as 'neutral', such as the property 'being a substance'. This is 'neutral' because immaterial and material objects can be substances.

19. It is worth pointing out that some materialists will say that the fact that no humans have mental properties distinct from physical properties is a contingent modal fact. Things could have been otherwise; humans might have had mental properties distinct from physical ones. It is just that, in the actual world, this state of affairs does not obtain.

Christian materialists who are global and local property dualists, (though not, of course global *and local* substance dualists) can distinguish themselves from those who are substance dualists about human persons by claiming that human persons are essentially material beings, albeit material beings that have a certain sort of mental life (and, as a consequence, mental properties) that is generated by, but not identical with, the matter of which they are composed.[20]

So, to sum up, property dualism with respect to human persons is the view that humans are substances that have properties, some of which are what we call 'mental' properties, having to do with some aspect of the mental life or make-up of a human person, and some of which are 'physical' properties, having to do with some aspect of the physical life or make-up of a human person. Mental properties are not reducible to, or identical with, physical properties (hence property *dualism*). Access to such properties is restricted to the person in whom they are instantiated, whereas physical properties are not restricted in this way. And Christian materialists who are property dualists can claim that human persons are essentially material beings that have certain irreducibly mental properties including having the right sort of mental life necessary for being human, the capacity for consciousness and experience. I have not argued in favour of property dualism. Here I am concerned merely to show that property dualism about human persons is an obvious view for the Christian materialist to take, and one that may be used to make sense of the claims of Chalcedon – which is the aim of the next section. It is also a consequence of what has been said thus far that Christian materialists who are not property dualists about human persons have a great deal of explaining to do when it comes to their Christology.

4. *Property Dualism, Apollinarianism and Christ's 'Rational Soul'*

We are now in a position to apply the results of the foregoing section on property dualism to the findings of our first section, on what a creedally orthodox account of the Incarnation requires. I want to suggest that the Christian materialist who is a property dualist about human persons can tell a story that makes sense of the troubling issue concerning Christ's 'rational soul' that Chalcedon raises. This story depends upon a particular understanding of the reasons for the insertion of this phrase into the Chalcedonian 'definition', which has its roots in the Apollinarian crisis in fourth-century theology.

Peter van Inwagen characterizes Apollinarianism as follows:

> *Apollinarianism* (after Apollinarius (c. 310 – c. 390)) holds that Christ did not have a human mind or spirit or rational soul – that he lacked something that is essential to

---

20.   Here one might want to add something to the effect that mental properties are only and necessarily generated by matter organized in a particular, complex fashion.

human nature – and that God or some 'aspect' of God (such as the divine *logos*) was united to the human body of Jesus of Nazareth in such a way as to 'be a substitute for' or perform the function of the human mind or soul or spirit.[21]

In enumerating the various reasons why Apollinarianism was considered beyond the pale of orthodoxy by the Early Church, J. N. D. Kelly writes, 'It was man's rational soul, with its power of choice, which was the seat of sin; and if the Word did not unite such a soul with Himself, the salvation of mankind could not have been achieved.'[22] If the Chalcedonian requirement that Christ has a 'rational soul' means something like this, it appears that the restricted materialist is in considerable theological difficulty. Yet the crucial issue between the orthodox and the Apollinarians had to do with the *nous*, that is, that rational level or strata of the soul that Christ, they claimed, did not possess. There is more than one reason given in the literature for what motivated Apollinarianism. In one account, the Apollinarians wanted to say that the divine *Logos* might take the place of the human *nous* because he is the archetype of the *nous*. Thus, John Anthony McGuckin says that according to Apollinarius, the *Logos*,

> constituted humans as the image of God. The image was particularly located in the *nous*, the spiritual intellect. This was also the seat of personhood (mind and soul). In the case of Jesus the *Logos* did not need to assume a human mind (*logos* or rationality) as he himself was the archetype of all intellect. In this one case the image was not anthropologically needed as the original was present, replacing it.[23]

Here it is important to note that the *nous* is regarded as that part of human beings particularly identified with the *imago dei* of Genesis 1.26-27. The *Logos* is the archetype of the *nous* because he is that in whose image the *nous* is made. He cannot be the archetype of (say) the mental life of great apes in the same way, because the great apes do not have the image of God. This is a property possessed by no other species of creature, according to the Genesis narrative. And this, I presume, means that if the great apes have a *nous* (which is by no means a foregone conclusion), their *nous* is not made in the image of the *Logos* in the way that the human *nous* is.[24]

A second motivation sometimes mentioned is that there was no need for Christ to have a mental life other than the mental life of the Word, because the

21. Peter van Inwagen, 'Incarnation and Christology' in Edward Craig ed. *The Routledge Encyclopedia of Philosophy* (London: Routledge, 1998) p. 727.

22. J. N. D. Kelly, *Early Christian Doctrines, Fifth Edition* (London: A & C Black, 1977 [1958]) pp. 296–297.

23. John Anthony McGuckin, *The Westminster Handbook to Patristic Theology* (Louisville, KT: Westminster John Knox, 2004) pp. 21–22.

24. Of course, the modern concern about whether other animals have mental life similar to human beings, and whether they have souls, is a post-Enlightenment, even post-Darwinian concern, that the patristic authors would not have shared.

Word already possessed all the properties necessary to being human, barring possession of a body. Thus, J. P. Moreland and William Lane Craig state,

> God already possesses the properties sufficient for human personhood even prior to the Incarnation, lacking only corporeality. The Logos already possessed in his preincarnate state all the properties necessary for being a human self. In assuming a hominid body, he brought to it all that was necessary for a complete human nature. For this reason, in Christ the one self-conscious subject who is the Logos possessed divine and human natures that were both complete.[25]

These two issues, though closely related, are not the same. If the *Logos* is the archetype of the human *nous*, he might be able to 'stand in' for a human *nous*, so that the relation he bears to a particular human body is equivalent to the relation a human *nous* normally bears to a human body. In which case, the net result is that, in taking on a human body, the *Logos* comes to have a relation to his body that is sufficient for him to be fully human. The idea is rather like having a new computer without any software to run on it. If the manufacturer arrived at your doorstep and installed the prototype of the production-line software on your computer that runs just like the production-line software that is based on this prototype model, you might be forgiven for thinking that, once installed, you have all you need to run your computer correctly. Although the software installed is not a production-line model, the prototype software does everything the production-line version would, leaving you to get on using your computer. This is one motivation for Apollinarianism.[26]

The second motivation, drawn from Moreland and Craig, is that the *Logos* has all that is necessary to be a human, barring a body. So the Incarnation involves the *Logos* coming to own a particular human body, nothing more. This need not involve commitment to the idea that the Logos is some archetype of the human *nous*, which the Logos can 'stand in for' in the particular instance of the assumption of human flesh at the Incarnation. Return to our example of the computer software. On the Moreland–Craig account, the Logos is like a piece of Apple Mac software running on a Microsoft-compatible computer. It has all the properties of a Mac product, but also has all the properties requisite to make it compatible with a Microsoft-compatible computer. In order to run this software on a Microsoft-compatible computer, all you need to do is download it.[27]

25. J. P. Moreland and William Lane Craig, *Philosophical Foundations for a Christian Worldview* (Downers Grove, IL: Inter-Varsity Press, 2003) p. 609.

26. The computer example relies on some equivalence between an archetype and a prototype that might be disputed. Still, at least one dictionary definition of these two words has the idea of an 'original model'. This is what I had in mind, and I think this is sufficient for the example to be of use.

27. *Caveat lector:* this is not the same as the notion that at the Incarnation the Logos 'assumes' the property of being a human soul in addition to having a human body. This view, which has recently been dubbed the Alvinized view, for reasons I do not need to go into here, requires the

These two stories about what motivated Apollinarianism might both be true, of course. After all, one can install a prototype piece of Apple Mac software on a Microsoft-compatible computer, and it would work just as a production-line version of Microsoft software would. Nevertheless commitment to the first story does not necessarily involve commitment to the second, which means there is more than one motivation for being an Apollinarian.

Now, apply these two distinct, but related stories to the problem Chalcedon raises about Christ having a 'rational soul'. Notice first of all that the Christian materialist who is a property dualist concerning human persons is not committed to Apollinarianism because he does not deny that Christ has an irreducibly *human* mental life. Christ has mental properties consonant with his human mental life, just like any other human, and these properties are distinct from his physical human life. This is quite unlike our two metaphysical stories motivating Apollinarianism. Take the first story, indebted to McGuckin. On the Christian materialist and global + local property dualist account, is it sufficient for a fully human Christ to be composed of a human body and the Word of God, standing in as the prototype of the human *nous*? No, it is not. The Christian materialist and global + local property dualist says that to be fully human an entity must have the relevant sort of irreducibly mental life, including mental properties that are not identical to physical properties. In other words, this sort of Christian materialist says Christ must have a *human* mind. And, on his understanding 'human mind' means something like 'irreducibly mental properties requisite for the right kind of mental life normal humans enjoy', rather than a soul. But this effectively blocks the first motivation for Apollinarianism.

It also blocks the second, Moreland–Craig story, for the same reasons. The combination of Word of God + assumption of human body is not sufficient for an orthodox account of the Incarnation because it denies Christ has a human mental life distinct from his divine mental life. His human mental life just is his divine mental life. But the Christian materialist and global + local property dualist denies this, because he thinks Christ's fully human life must include an irreducible *human* mental life. So, on the Christian materialist and global + local property dualist combination of views, Apollinarianism is false: for something to be fully human that thing must have the relevant capacity for human mental life, including the relevant irreducibly mental properties requisite to such a life.[28] Christ has the relevant capacity for human mental life, including

---

addition of certain properties (i.e., human nature) in order for the Incarnation to take place. But the Craig–Moreland view does not require anything more than the addition of a human body for the Incarnation to occur. For this reason, their view is straightforwardly Apollinarian, whereas the Alvinized view is not. The Alvinized view is discussed in Oliver D. Crisp, *Divinity and Humanity*, ch. 2.

28.   Objection: Christ is fully human but he is not a human person on pain of Nestorianism. But the argument thus far turns on the concept of human personhood. Reply: orthodoxy claims Christ is fully human; he is a human being and has all those properties and parts other human beings do,

the relevant irreducibly mental properties requisite for such a life. So Christ is fully, but not merely, human.

Now, it may be that the Fathers of Chalcedon thought that the only way to rebut Apollinarianism was to fall back upon some version of substance dualism. But the restricted materialist would be right to point out that if this is true, the Fathers of Chalcedon were mistaken. For it turns out that restricted materialism is consistent with Christ having the requisite sort of irreducibly mental life necessary for being fully human, such that Apollinarianism is blocked. Yet restricted materialism postulates no human soul in order to do so. One might construe the Chalcedonian claim that Christ had a 'rational soul', that is, a human *nous*, to mean the mental part or component of a human being. (This seems consistent with some of the things McGuckin says.) But that, the materialist will point out, is consistent with the tenets of restricted materialism given local property dualism, and is also anti-Apollinarian. Such reasoning does justice to what Chalcedon says about Christ's 'rational soul', without appeal to an immaterial substance. And this, the restricted materialist might claim, is sufficient for his views about the metaphysics of human persons to be orthodox.

5. *The Cost-Benefit Analysis*

We have seen that at least some versions of restricted materialism are consistent with an orthodox Christology, provided one construes the Chalcedonian notion that Christ had 'a rational soul' in a particular way. But there are costs involved in such an undertaking, just as there are costs attending substance dualism.[29] The first and most obvious cost for the materialist is that the materialist understanding of Christ's 'rational soul' will not persuade those who think the Chalcedonian Fathers had substance dualism about human persons in mind when they framed their definition. Yet, the materialist can offer some explanation as to why his views are not equivalent to the Apollinarianism that was the target of the 'rational soul' phrase. Perhaps the materialist ought to opt for the weaker claim that his reasoning is not consistent with Apollinarianism, but is consistent with one understanding of what a 'rational soul' is, and this

---

bar human personhood. He cannot have human personhood because he is a divine person, and there is only one subject in the Incarnation (Christ does not have Multiple Personality Disorder!). But nothing in the above argument entails Nestorianism, and the relevant changes can be made to the argument with respect to human personhood and being fully human without damaging the main point being made throughout.

29.   One possible cost for substance dualism: If one is a Cartesian, it looks like embodiment is not necessary for human personhood, because humans are essentially souls that are only contingently related to their bodies. But then, it seems that embodiment – *incarnation* – is not necessary for the Logos to become a human being! There are ways this might be blocked: one is to opt for some other version of dualism that does not have this consequence; another is to point out that incarnation and personhood are not co-terminus terms.

means his views are not unorthodox. Let us call this the *Anti-Apollinarian cost* for Christian materialism.

A related, and not unsubstantial point for the theologian already noted is that restricted materialism *per se* is simply not the traditional view of human persons in the Christian tradition. This uncomfortable fact cannot be denied. And in the case of Christ, though he is not a human person in a strict and philosophical sense, he is fully human, that is, he has all that is requisite in order to be counted amongst the sons of Adam. For all orthodox classical Christian theologians after the Apollinarian controversy, this meant Christ has a human soul. This potential cost for materialist Christology we shall dub *the problem of tradition*. The materialist faced with this difficulty must simply admit that his view is not the default position in the Christian tradition as dualism is, whilst pointing out that the catholic Creeds do not preclude a materialist account of human persons and that Scripture is also commensurate with a restricted materialist position – all of which would have to be argued for. Perhaps the best way forward for the materialist on this particular issue is to side with Peter van Inwagen when he says,

> since God has allowed dualism to dominate Christian anthropology for two millennia I can only conclude that, if dualism represents, as I believe, a false view of our nature, this view is not perniciously false: a widespread acceptance of dualism does not distort or impoverish the Gospel.[30]

A third cost, closely related to the second, has to do with the development of the traditional, orthodox account of the theanthropic person of Christ. This is made clear in Maurice Wiles' essay 'The Nature of the Early Debate about Christ's Human Soul'.[31] Wiles argues that the cut-and-thrust of early Christological debates about whether Christ had a human soul depend in large part upon differing theological concerns. There are those, like Irenaeus or Origen who recognized the soteriological importance of Christ's human soul: if he does not have a human soul, there is some important part of human beings that is not 'healed' in the atonement. But there were other theologians, including, perhaps, Eusebius of Caeserea, and of course Apollinarius, who were much more concerned with making sense of the Incarnation and the unity of the resulting theanthropic person, and who questioned whether this event required the Second Person of the Trinity to assume a human soul in addition to a human body. Thus Wiles says:

> Our contention is that, from the very start, the mind of the Fathers was clear that when thinking soteriologically they must affirm the fact of Christ's possession of a human soul. On the other hand, when thinking of the unity of Christ's person they were

---

30. van Inwagen, 'Dualism and Materialism: Athens and Jerusalem?', p. 487.
31. In Maurice Wiles, *Working Papers in Doctrine* (London: SCM Press, 1976) pp. 50–65.

(with, as so often, the vigorous exception of the boldly individual mind of Origen) almost equally clear that the idea must be repudiated.[32]

The Chalcedonian definition comes out clearly in favour of the view that Christ had a human soul. To put it in the language of Wiles' essay, the soteriological argument trumped the argument from the unity of Christ's person. And even if the Fathers had a rather different understanding of the make-up of the human soul than do many contemporary substance dualists, the Chalcedonian definition shows that they thought that Christ has a fully human and fully divine nature held together in personal union where Christ's human nature is consubstantial (of the same sort of substance) as that of other human beings, although sinless, and consists of a human body and a 'rational soul'.

However, one might think that these historical considerations actually support the materialist because they indicate that Chalcedon was a sort of political compromise between different theological factions with quite distinct ideas about what being 'fully' human entailed. This is not the same as calling into question the veracity of the Chalcedonian settlement. The materialist can claim that (a) what Chalcedon says is orthodox and binding on Christian theologians, (b) Chalcedon was a political compromise document, the dogmatic content of which was superintended by the Holy Spirit, preventing it from containing serious error and (c) the phrase 'rational soul' is sufficiently hermeneutically porous to admit of more than one metaphysical explanation. Let us call the collection of problems thrown up by historical considerations centring on the early Christological disputes that culminated in Chalcedon, *the Chalcedonian-settlement problem for materialist Christology.*

These are some of the costs involved in opting for some version of materialist Christology. There may be others in the neighbourhood, but these seem the most pressing. Whether one finds the argument offered here in partial defence of materialism about human persons convincing, I think it is certainly true that the Christian materialist who is also a global + local property dualist is not an Apollinarian. In this way, one could run the Anti-Apollinarian argument of the fourth section of the chapter independently of the argument about whether the Christian materialist can satisfy the Chalcedonian claim that Christ has a 'rational soul'. Even this diminished return for the Christian materialist is of some theological benefit. For it removes one very important obstacle that I imagine many theologians think stands between commitment to some form of materialism about human persons, and a Christology that is not unorthodox. So I say, there may be more to Christian materialism than some traditionalist Christologists think. And this is a constructive contribution to the metaphysics of the Incarnation because it goes some way towards showing that there is more than one manner in which metaphysics can be used to underpin that which is dogmatically non-negotiable: that Christ is the Word made flesh.

---

32. Ibid., p. 64.

Chapter 8

MULTIPLE INCARNATIONS

Now the power of a Divine Person is infinite, nor can it be limited by any created thing.
Hence it may not be said that a Divine Person so assumed a human nature as to be
unable to assume another. For it would seem to follow from this that the Personality of
the Divine Nature was so comprehended by one human nature as to be unable to
assume another to its Personality; and this is impossible, for the Uncreated cannot
be comprehended by any creature.

St Thomas Aquinas, Summa Theologiae IIIa. Q 3. 7

Traditionally, Christians have affirmed that the Incarnation was the event in which the Second Person of the Trinity assumes a human nature in addition to his divine nature. But was that event unique and unrepeatable? Can one divine person assume two (or more) human natures? These apparently abstruse matters actually touch upon an important issue for any account of the Incarnation. For if it turns out that God could have become incarnate more than once then the Incarnation, though a singularly important event for the salvation of human beings, may not be a singular event, all things considered.[1]

In what follows I argue that multiple incarnations are metaphysically possible, contrary to the objections raised in the recent literature by the Anglican theologian Brian Hebblethwaite. However, although such a divine act is metaphysically possible – there is no metaphysical obstacle to God becoming incarnate on more than one occasion – there is good reason to think that the Incarnation is in fact a unique event in the divine life. Thus, the burden of this chapter is that God could have become incarnate more than once, but he has not done so.

---

1. There are other, related problems having to do with the possibility of multiple incarnations. In the *Summa Theologiae IIIa. 3*, St Thomas Aquinas maintains that more than one divine person could be incarnate in the same created nature and that more than one divine person could become incarnate, although there may be reasons why this is not entirely fitting. And in the recent literature there has been some discussion about whether a divine person would become incarnate in order to save some other race in a far-flung corner of the cosmos. See, for example Christopher L. Fisher and David Fergusson, 'Karl Rahner and the Extra-Terrestrial Intelligence Question' in *Heythrop Journal* XLVII (2006): 275–290, and C. S. Lewis's novel, *Perelandra* in *The Cosmic Trilogy* (London: The Bodley Head, 1989 [1943]).

The argument falls into five parts. In the first, I recap some of the metaphysical distinctions used earlier in the book, which are important for the subsequent sections of the chapter. Then, in a second part, Hebblethwaite's objection to the idea of multiple incarnations is explained, drawing, as Hebblethwaite does, upon the work of Thomas Morris. In the process of setting out Hebblethwaite's reasoning, I outline three assumptions that form the backbone of his objection. In the third section, I set out a metaphysical view that depends upon a particular account of the metaphysics of human persons, which I shall call the Cartesian account. In this section, I show that two of the three assumptions that underpin Hebblethwaite's objection to multiple incarnations are questionable, and do not provide sufficient reason to doubt that multiple incarnations are metaphysically possible. In a fourth section I show how someone committed to the Cartesian account of human persons could accept all three of Hebblethwaite's assumptions and still hold to a particular sort of multiple incarnations doctrine, where incarnation is taken to be equivalent to 'enfleshment'. Thus there are two independent, but related arguments against Hebblethwaite's analysis, and in favour of the possibility of a multiple incarnation doctrine. However, in a concluding section, I argue that the possibility of multiple incarnations should be distinguished from the actuality of multiple incarnations. There are important theological reasons for thinking that there is in fact only one incarnation, although God could have arranged matters otherwise.

1. *Comments on the Metaphysics of the Incarnation*

Two metaphysical assumptions we have already encountered in this volume underlie the argument of this chapter.[2] The first is that human natures, Christ's human nature included, are concrete particulars of a certain sort. Recall that a concrete particular is a discrete, real object, such as a table, a tortoise or a telephone. Some contemporary philosophical theologians maintain that natures, human natures included, are simply properties of things, like 'being red' or 'being west of London'. That is not the view I have in mind here, and I think I have much of the Christian tradition in my favour in this particular regard. As we have already had cause to note earlier in the book, there are a number of different views about the sort of concrete particulars human natures actually are, if they are concrete particulars. Some think humans are essentially souls that just happen to be 'housed', so to speak, in the bodies they 'own'. Others think human nature is a compound of a human body and soul, or is the product of such a compound, where the soul organizes the matter of the body in some way. Yet another view, which we have explored in the previous chapter, might be that human natures are simply a certain kind of material object. But it is the first of these conceptions of human natures as concrete particulars that is

---

2. As well as my previous work on this matter, in *Divinity and Humanity*, ch. 2.

assumed here, although I offer no argument for the superiority of this particular view or family of views over its rivals.

My second assumption drawing on the previous chapters of the book is this: Christ's human nature is a concrete particular that is a human being, but is not a human person, strictly speaking. Christ is fully human, according to creedal orthodoxy. But he is not merely human. What is more, his human nature is (we might say) 'owned' by the divine person of the Word of God. In this important respect, Christ's human nature is unlike my human nature. I have a human nature and am a human person. I am fully human, but I am merely human. My human nature is not the human nature of a divine person; it is my human nature. And I am a person. In fact, I am a human person. By contrast, Christ is fully human, but not merely human. His human nature is the human nature of a divine person; it is never the human nature of a human person distinct from the divine person of God the Son. Hence, he is a human being with a human nature, like me. But he is not a human *person* in the strict and particular sense I shall be using here for the very good reason that if Christ were a human person as well as a divine person, then Nestorianism would be true. But, of course, Nestorianism is a heresy; it cannot be true. This distinction, along with my previous remark about human natures being concrete particulars, is important for the argument of what follows.[3]

2. *Hebblethwaite's Objection Outlined*

Consider Brian Hebblethwaite. In a career which has involved a fair share of defending orthodox Christology, he has made the strong claim that it is not 'logically possible' for there to be multiple incarnations. In his most recent statement of this view, he says 'if God the Son is one divine subject, only one human subject can actually *be* the incarnate, human, form of that one divine life. Otherwise, we would be attributing a split personality to the divine Son.' He goes on to say, 'if Jesus was the same person as God the Son, so would other incarnations be. They would all have to be the same person. That makes no sense, least of all if they exist simultaneously in the eschaton.'[4] His reason

---

3.   Compare St Anselm who says at one point,

> those who cannot understand anything to be a human being unless an individual
> will in no way understand a human being other than a human person. For [so they
> think] every individual human being is a person. Therefore, how will they under-
> stand that the human being assumed by the Word is not a person, that is, that another
> nature, not another person, has been assumed?

(From *On the Incarnation of the Word* § 1 in *Anselm of Canterbury, The Major Works*, pp. 237–238.)

4.   Hebblethwaite, 'The Impossibility of Multiple Incarnations' *Theology* 104 (2001): 324 and 327 respectively. Hebblethwaite traces the development of his own views in the first section of this essay. See also his earlier reflections upon the question of multiple incarnations in response to Thomas Morris's work in *The Incarnation*, pp. 166–168.

for thinking this has much to do with what, following Thomas Morris, he calls the 'asymmetrical accessing relation' that obtains between the two natures of God Incarnate, as well as the 'unique metaphysical ownership' of the human nature of Christ by the Second Person of the Trinity.

These terms require some explanation. The idea seems to be this: The Second Person of the Trinity has immediate access to the conscious life of all created minds, including the mind of Jesus of Nazareth. But created minds do not have the same epistemic access to the divine mind. Nor, on this two-minds way of thinking about the hypostatic union, does the human mind of Jesus of Nazareth. According to the canonical Gospels, Christ appears unable to access certain information known only to the Father, including the time of his Second Coming. Hence, between the divine mind or consciousness and the human mind or consciousness of Christ there is an intimate, but not symmetrical relation, whereby God can know what Christ *qua* human knows, yet the human mind of Christ does not know all that his divine mind, or range of consciousness does. In short, the divine mind contains, but is not contained by, Christ's human mind.[5] This is Thomas Morris' 'asymmetrical accessing relation' that he concedes applies to all created minds, namely, the relation of such minds to the divine mind, Christ's human mind included. But this 'two-minds' Christology raises an immediate question, which is this: If this is the case, what distinguishes the epistemic access the Second Person of the Trinity has to the mind of Christ, as opposed to, say, the access he has to my mind? Morris allows that the Second Person of the Trinity enjoys a particular 'ownership' of Christ's human nature that does not obtain in the case of the divine relationship to my human nature. In short, Christ's human nature is the human nature of the Second Person of the Trinity.[6] Unlike Christ, my human nature is not hypostatically united to the divine nature and my human nature is not the human nature of God Incarnate. What is more, Morris sees no problem with maintaining that there is an asymmetrical accessing relation that obtains between the Word of God and Christ's human nature and that Christ's human nature is the human nature owned by the Word of God on the one hand, along with the idea that multiple incarnations are possible, on the other hand.

It is this Morrisian account of the possibility of multiple incarnations from which Hebblethwaite demurs. His objection to multiple incarnations depends upon three related assumptions. Although he does not declare them as such, the logic of his argument requires them in order for his objection to go through. They are as follows:

1. Any human nature assumed by a divine person is numerically identical with that divine person.[7]

---

5. Thomas V. Morris, *The Logic of God Incarnate*, p. 103.
6. Ibid., pp. 161–162.
7. 'For if God the Son is one divine subject, only one human subject can actually be the incarnate, human form of that one divine life. Otherwise, one would be attributing a split personality to

2. A divine incarnation has to be the same person, human as well as divine.[8]
3. A divine person can have at most one human nature.[9]

The first assumption is a commonplace in Christology: many theologians maintain that Jesus of Nazareth just *is* God Incarnate.[10] Hebblethwaite seems to think that the third assumption is implied by the second. But the second assumption is, it seems to me, false as it stands, and Hebblethwaite does not provide sufficient reason for endorsing the third assumption.

To see this, consider the following reasoning. First, as we have already noted, according to classical Christology Christ is a divine person with a human nature, that is, a theanthropic person. What is more, Christ *qua* human might not have existed had the Second Person of the Trinity not become incarnate. That is, Christ is truly but only contingently God Incarnate. For surely it is metaphysically possible for a given divine person to refrain from becoming incarnate, otherwise it would appear that God the Son is not free in his decision to become incarnate. Nor is it unorthodox to suggest that the Second Person of the Trinity might have taken a different human nature from the one he did take, although I grant that this is a more contentious Christological suggestion than the previous two. For instance, the Holy Spirit might have used a different ovum from which to form Christ's body in the womb of Mary *Theotokos* than in fact he did. In which case, the human body of God Incarnate would have been different from the one he did assume. This does not seem beyond the bounds of plausibility, and nothing in Hebblethwaite's argument is contrary to it.

But the crucial claim for present purposes has to do with whether, having decided to become incarnate as Jesus of Nazareth, the Second Person of the

---

the divine Son.' Hebblethwaite, 'The Impossibility of Multiple Incarnations', p. 324. This implies numerical identity between God the Son and his human nature. He makes similar comments elsewhere, for example, his essay 'The Uniqueness of the Incarnation' in Michael Goulder ed. *Incarnation and Myth: The Debate Continued* (Grand Rapids, MI: Eerdmans, 1979) p. 189.

8. 'Even he [St Thomas Aquinas, whose account Hebblethwaite is criticizing] does not take seriously enough the fact that a series of divine incarnations would have to be the same person, human as well as divine.' Hebblethwaite, 'The Impossibility of Multiple Incarnations', p. 326.

9. 'If Jesus was the same person as God the Son, so would other incarnations be. They would all have to be the same person. That makes no sense, least of all if they exist simultaneously in the eschaton.' Ibid., p. 327.

10. At least one commentator on Hebblethwaite's recent essay has overlooked this point. Peter Kevern remarks, 'if "Son of God" primarily designates a relationship rather than a separable self-conscious subject, Hebblethwaite's concern that the fullness of the Son's subjectivity be present in a particular incarnation becomes far less pressing.' But, of course, this can only be the case if the first of our three assumptions, affirmed by Hebblethwaite, is ignored. And in ignoring this, claiming instead that the Incarnation might be a 'relationship' rather than a 'self-conscious subject' Kevern denies the notion, shared by many catholic theologians, that Christ is identical with the Second Person of the Trinity. See Kevern, 'Limping Principles: A Reply to Brian Hebblethwaite on "The Impossibility of Multiple Incarnations"' in *Theology* September/October (2002): 346.

Trinity could have assumed another human nature *in addition to* the human nature of Jesus of Nazareth. Hebblethwaite says he cannot do so because any divine incarnation must be the same human and divine person on account of the fact that Christ is identical to the Second Person of the Trinity. In fact, he goes as far as saying 'the whole person of Jesus, his unique character and personality express God to us; for he is God the Son in person'.[11] But, according to catholic Christology no human *person* is generated or assumed by the Second Person of the Trinity at the Incarnation. Strictly speaking, Christ has a human nature; he is not a human person. He is a divine person with a human nature. We might speak with the vulgar and say Christ is a human person, when if we were speaking with the learned we would be more careful to say Christ was a *theanthropic* (i.e., God-Man) person.[12] I suppose this is what Hebblethwaite has in mind when he speaks of the need for any divine incarnation to be 'the same *person*, human as well as divine'.[13] However, his strong language about the 'unique character and personality' of Christ suggests at times that Hebblethwaite has something more in mind, namely that Christ and Christ alone has the requisite capacities and properties *qua* human to be God Incarnate. In which case, applying a principle of charity to Hebblethwaite's second assumption regarding his comments about Christ being a person, whilst taking seriously his strong claims about the uniqueness of Christ, we could construe Hebblethwaite to mean that the particular human nature that is assumed in the Incarnation is specially created for that purpose, to be the human nature of the divine person assuming it. Moreover, once a divine person 'owns' a particular human nature by assuming it in incarnation he cannot 'own' another human nature thereafter. It is 'part' of him from the first moment of assumption onwards. The relationship between the divine person and the human nature he assumes is a unique and unrepeatable one; a special sort of one-off metaphysical union between divine and human natures.

Were this all Hebblethwaite said on the matter of the theanthropic personhood of Christ, we could proceed accordingly to analyse whether this charitable reading of his second assumption makes sense. Unfortunately, at times he goes beyond even the stronger language about the uniqueness of the human nature of Christ just mentioned, to say the following sort of thing:

> But multiple incarnations of the same Person of the Trinity – in actuality, of the divine Son – are ruled out by considerations of logic. Here the very idea makes no sense. One individual subject cannot, without contradiction, be thought capable of becoming a series of individuals, or, a fortiori, a coexistent community of persons.[14]

---

11. Hebblethwaite, *The Incarnation*, p. 167.

12. This is precisely what St Thomas Aquinas does at times, as we have already had cause to note.

13. Hebblethwaite, 'The Impossibility of Multiple Incarnations', p. 326. Emphasis added.

14. Hebblethwaite, 'The Impossibility of Multiple Incarnations', p. 333.

Thus, it appears that there are three distinct aspects to Hebblethwaite's second assumption. The first is simply that Christ is a person, which we can charitably take to mean Christ is a theanthropic person. This is conjoined with a second notion, that the theanthropic person of Christ somehow uniquely represents God to us, because his human nature has been specially created in order to be the human nature of God the Son. The third notion is that the very idea of multiple incarnations of the same person is somehow illogical: it simply makes no sense when analysed.

There is quite a leap from the second notion just described, to the third. The trouble with the third notion as it stands is that it is, as it were, tilting at windmills. For one thing, referring to one of the persons of the divine Trinity as one 'individual subject', which Hebblethwaite does, seems problematic if one does not hold to a social model of the Trinity, where the divine persons of the Godhead are individuals bound together by a mysterious relation of mutual interpenetration or perichoresis.[15] But that aside, no creedally orthodox theologian would concede that the possibility of multiple incarnations implies that a divine person can become a series of individuals or a community of persons. In fact, Hebblethwaite seems to be confused about what the claims of classical Christology amount to. If an incarnation is simply the assumption of a human nature by a divine person, such that the divine person concerned comes to 'own' a particular human nature, no individual apart from the divine person exists, either before or after the first moment of incarnation. Nor can there be another individual on pain of unorthodoxy.[16] The point that Thomas Morris makes in relation to his own construal of a 'two-minds' Christology is that a divine person cannot be circumscribed by a human nature. Indeed, a divine person is capable of 'owning' more than one such human nature. Morris does not think of human nature as a concrete particular, but as a property. Yet even if human natures are concrete particulars, it does not seem *prima facie* 'logically impossible' for a divine person to 'own' more than one such concrete particular, given the sorts of metaphysical distinctions that Morris makes – aside from his particular construal of what a human nature is.[17]

15. But perhaps all Hebblethwaite means to say on this point is that the human nature assumed is an instrument of the divine person assuming it. As Thomas points out, 'the human nature . . . does not belong to the nature of the Word, and the Word is not its form; nevertheless the human nature belongs to his person.' *Summa Contra Gentiles* IV. 41. 12. The human nature is not assumed into the divine nature or essence, although it belongs to the divine person assuming it. This is a common distinction in medieval and post-Reformation scholastic theology.

16. Indeed, some medieval theologians were of the view that the human nature of Christ is necessarily such that it is sustained by a divine person. There is no possible world at which the human nature Christ actually assumes exists independent of God the Son, as a *suppositum,* or fundamental substance (a person). This, according to Alfred Freddoso, was Aquinas's position. See his fascinating essay, 'Human Nature, Potency and The Incarnation' in *Faith and Philosophy* 3 (1986): 27–53.

17. Aquinas makes many of the same distinctions as Morris and holds that human natures are concrete particulars. See, for example, *Summa Contra Gentiles* IV. 41. 13 and IV. 42. 3.

We could put it like this. In the Incarnation we are dealing with a divine person that has 'expanded', so to speak, to include a human nature. The 'expanded' divine person 'owns' his human nature, in a way similar to the manner in which I 'own' the limbs of my body. They are parts of me. In an extended or 'stretched' sense, the human nature of Christ is a 'part' of the Second Person of the Trinity.[18] But if this is the case, then there does not seem to be any reason why the Second Person of the Trinity cannot 'expand' in this way to assume more than one human nature. It would be like grafting more than one limb onto my body, where the limbs concerned have been specially prepared and grown for my body (rather than being removed from some donor before being attached to my body). Once grafted, the limbs become 'mine'. I 'own' them; they become 'part' of me.

Hebblethwaite's confusion is made clearest when he tackles Aquinas's well-known defence of the possibility of multiple incarnations.[19] In the *Summa Theologiae*, St Thomas makes clear his advocacy of the view that Christ's human nature, like all human natures, is a concrete particular. In this connection, he has this to say concerning the metaphysical possibility of multiple incarnations of one and the same divine person:

> Now the power of a Divine Person is infinite, nor can it be limited by any created thing. Hence it may not be said that a Divine Person so assumed one human nature as to be unable to assume another. For it would seem to follow from this that the Personality of the Divine Nature was so comprehended by one human nature as to be unable to assume another to its Personality; and this is impossible, for the Uncreated cannot be comprehended by any creature.

No divine person can be circumscribed by a human nature he assumes, says St Thomas, for the divine nature is infinite whereas human natures are finite. So it is not possible for a given human nature to somehow restrict the divine person that assumes it, in such a way as to prevent his assuming another human nature. Later in the same passage Aquinas goes on to clarify how one divine person can assume more than one human nature thus:

> For a man who has on two garments is not said to be *two persons clothed*, but *one clothed with two garments*; and whoever has two qualities is designated in the singular as *such by reason of the two qualities*. Now the assumed nature is, as it were, a garment, although this similitude does not fit at all points. . . . And hence, if the Divine Person

---

18.   Christ is a 'part' of God the Son in a 'stretched' sense because of the well-known objections to God having proper parts. For instance, defenders of divine simplicity deny God has any proper parts or properties. But aside from this, it might be problematic to think God has a human nature as a proper part. For then, God has a part that is physical. What is more, as many medieval theologians recognized, a being with parts is potentially fissile. But presumably God is necessarily non-fissiparous.

19.   See *Summa Theologiae*, IIIa. 3. 7.

were to assume two human natures, He would be called, on account of the unity of suppositum [i.e., the unity of his fundamental substance], one man having two human natures.[20]

This is not quite right, if we are thinking with the learned, rather than speaking with the vulgar. For, I take it that if a divine person were to assume more than one human nature, where a human nature is a concrete particular, the consequence of this would be one divine person, or one God-Man, having two human natures – not one *man* having two human natures as St Thomas puts it in this passage. But, as the saying goes, even Homer nods. And if Homer may nod and make the odd mistake in his epic poetry, perhaps the Angelic Doctor can be forgiven the odd slip too. This brings us to Hebblethwaite's objection to St Thomas's account of the possibility of multiple incarnations. In this regard, Hebblethwaite has the following to say:

> [O]ne cannot treat the human nature [of Christ] in a purely adjectival way, as a theoretically multipliable garment. Granted that there is only one ultimate metaphysical subject, namely God the Son, nevertheless, the human being God became is a human being, a personality, a subject, and a life that actually constitutes the human form of the divine life. One could even say that the human person is the divine person incarnate, though not, of course, an independent human person related to a divine person. Sadly, it is this generic, adjectival, talk of human nature being assumed that permits Thomas to envisage the possibility of multiple incarnations. Even he does not take seriously enough the fact that a series of divine incarnations would have to be the same person, human as well as divine.[21]

Now, given the foregoing sketch of St Thomas' views on this matter as a species of the notion that human natures are concrete particulars, coupled with an orthodox account of the assumption of human nature by the Son of God, the problems with Hebblethwaite's objection come into sharper focus. For one thing, how can God the Son be the one 'ultimate metaphysical subject' of the Incarnation, where his human nature is also a 'personality' and a 'subject', without positing two subjects and two 'personalities' in the hypostatic union? The fact that Hebblethwaite repeatedly speaks of the human nature of Christ as a person, albeit in a qualified fashion, does not help matters.[22] Aquinas and Morris both understand that there is only one metaphysical subject in the Incarnation, and that is God the Son. The language of two personalities or two subjects used by Hebblethwaite sounds rather unorthodox, and, in any case,

---

20. *Summa Theologica* IIIa. 3. 7, pp. 2043 and 2044, respectively. The first passage cited also appears as the superscript to this chapter.

21. Ibid., p. 326.

22. St Thomas does speak of Christ as a human person, but only in the 'vulgar' sense, not in the strict-and-particular sense I am using here. Hebblethwaite's language concerning Christ's personhood is much less clearly articulated than that used by St Thomas in this respect.

hardly helps to shore up Hebblethwaite's case against multiple incarnations if, in one respect, there are already two subjects in the canonical Incarnation without reference to other putative or possible incarnations! But more importantly, such inaccurate language muddies the theological waters. Once it has been made clear that a human nature is not a human person, and that the Incarnation is akin to the expansion of God the Son so as to assume a human nature – all of which is consistent with the burden of what St Thomas asserts – much of the force of Hebblethwaite's objection to the possibility of more than one such metaphysical arrangement dissipates. Nor is it true that St Thomas' metaphysics of the Incarnation commits him to an 'adjectival' account of human nature, as Hebblethwaite supposes. As the citations already given make clear, in context St Thomas is drawing an analogy between the assumption of human nature by a divine person and putting on a garment by a human person. He is clear that such an analogy is limited because 'this similitude does not fit on all points'. But such is the nature of an analogy. The point being made by St Thomas is much like the illustration used earlier of the expansion of a divine person, to wit, that a divine person can 'put on' or assume more than one human nature because no human nature can circumscribe or encompass the divine nature, nor a divine person.

Of course, analogies may be disputed, and perhaps it is the analogy St Thomas uses here that Hebblethwaite means to object to. Similarly, my analogy with a body onto which extra limbs are grafted could be disputed. The Incarnation is the assumption of a human nature that has a corporeal component by an essentially immaterial person. It is not the grafting of material components onto a material body. The two things are quite different, it might be thought. And this is true. In its place, let us construct a more adequate thought experiment that offers a model for thinking about multiple incarnations that rebuts Hebblethwaite's second assumption, and also has the advantage of suggesting an alternative way in which a doctrine of multiple incarnations could be set forth that avoids the problems Hebblethwaite sets out, which we shall pursue in the fourth section of this chapter.

3. *The Cartesian Account*

Substance dualism is undeniably the default option in the Christian tradition concerning the metaphysics of human personhood. According to substance dualists, humans are normally composed of a (human) body and soul. But there are a number of quite different philosophies of mind that go under the name 'substance dualism'. For present purposes we need only one: what I shall call the *Cartesian account*. For the sake of the argument it does not particularly matter whether Descartes actually held this view. It is sufficient that it is usually attributed to him in philosophical textbooks, and that it is usually thought of as the paradigm case of substance dualism in contemporary philosophy, even if it is not the only sort of substance dualism on offer.[23] The view in essence is this: a human is an essentially immaterial substance (i.e., a mind or soul) that is contingently related to a particular parcel of matter, which it 'owns' and by means of which it is able to act in the material world (i.e., a body). On this Cartesian account of substance dualism, the soul may be decoupled from the body at death. If the body perishes or is somehow annihilated, the human person continues to exist, since a human person is just a soul. Possession of a body is not a requirement for human personhood, on this view.[24] But it also appears that the Cartesian account is consistent with the idea that a human person (i.e., a human soul) on becoming decoupled from the body to which it was particularly related, might come into a new relationship of 'ownership' with respect to a different parcel of matter. That is, a particular human soul may be 'detached' from one human body and 'attached' to another body, whilst remaining the same person.[25] This is the case because, as we have already had cause to note, the Cartesian account presumes that embodiment is not a requirement of human personhood. If embodiment is a contingent matter, such that a human person may or may not have a body at a given time, then it would seem to be a small step to the conclusion that a particular human person (i.e., soul) may 'own' more than one body at different times, in succession.

On a certain construal of the general resurrection as reported by the Apostle Paul in passages like 1 Corinthians 15, this is just what we should expect to happen when the disembodied souls of the dead are given 'spiritual bodies' in the eschaton. My body perishes and rots. The matter that made it up is scattered over a certain area and becomes the matter that makes up other living things in due course. But this does not yield an objection to the general resurrection because, given the Cartesian account, God may generate a new body for my

23. Trenton Merricks points out that the majority of substance dualists hold to the thesis that is central to what I am calling the Cartesian account, namely, that human persons are identical with souls and only contingently related to a certain physical body, which is not a part of that human person. So, according to Merricks at least, if one objects to this central claim of the Cartesian account, one is objecting to a central claim of the majority of substance dualists. Some substance dualists deny that human persons are identical with souls. Instead, they posit that human persons are soul-body composites. But, says Merricks, this raises a serious problem for this minority 'composite' version of dualism. For 'the dualist who denies that a person is identical with a soul must say that there are two objects with mental properties (a person and her soul) where normally we think there is one'. See Merricks, 'The Word Made Flesh: Dualism, Physicalism, and the Incarnation', p. 282, n. 2.

24. This is not to say that the body to which a particular soul is 'attached' has no influence over 'its' soul. For presumably, the soul comes to have true beliefs about the world through the body to which it is 'attached'.

25. In this context, 'detachment' from one body and 'attachment' to another is just shorthand for the soul relinquishing certain causal relations it has with one body, which enables it to act immediately in the material world via that particular body, and beginning to have similar causal relations with another body. No notion of *physical* attachment is implied.

soul which is not composed of the matter of my old body, even if it is a facsimile in every other respect. For, on the Cartesian account, possession of the same body pre- and post-resurrection is not a persistent condition required for the identity across time of human persons.

Now, apply this to Hebblethwaite's objection to multiple incarnations. The Second Person of the Trinity is essentially divine, but only contingently human. He might not have become incarnate, and he might not have become incarnate as the particular human he did.[26] Yet, the Second Person of the Trinity did become Jesus of Nazareth. He 'owns' the human nature of Christ. It is *his* human nature in an important sense. But from the fact that the Second Person of the Trinity owns Christ's human nature in a special, even unique way (meaning, he is uniquely Jesus of Nazareth), it does not follow that the Second Person of the Trinity cannot become incarnate in some other human nature in addition to the human nature he possesses. For who is to say that a divine person cannot possess more than one human nature, just as, in a similar fashion, a human soul can possess more than one human body?

But at this point, an obvious difficulty will be raised. This is that the analogy drawn between the Cartesian account of the mind-body relationship and the Incarnation is tendentious. No classical theologian would agree that a human soul can 'own' more than one human body at any given time. Yet the argument just outlined presumes just this with respect to the Incarnation. So the analogy is not to the point.

This objection is partially right. The Cartesian account outlined above is consistent with the idea that a human soul can only 'own' one human body at any one time (although this is not made explicit in the account offered thus far). And, at least one of the problems in view on the question of the possibility of multiple incarnations has to do with whether there could be simultaneous multiple divine incarnations – that is, more than one such divine incarnation obtaining at a given time, or where there is temporal overlap between two different incarnations. But this objection is not fatal to the case in favour of the possibility of multiple divine incarnations, for two reasons. The first is that, although human souls have traditionally not been thought capable of 'owning' more than one human nature at any given time, it does not follow from this that the same conditions for 'ownership' of human natures (as opposed to human bodies) applies *mutatis mutandis*, to divine persons. For one thing, human

---

26. As I have already pointed out, some of what Hebblethwaite says about the nature of the Incarnation and the human nature assumed militates against the notion that God the Son could have assumed a human nature other than the one he did assume. But if Hebblethwaite grants that the assumption of human nature is a contingent matter, and that the human nature assumed is only contingently related to the divine person assuming it, it is a small step to say that some other human nature could have been prepared for God the Son to assume than the one he did assume. Surely, in the councils of God, this is not metaphysically impossible.

souls are not omnipresent as the Second Person of the Trinity is.[27] And, as St Thomas points out,

> whether we consider the Divine Person in regard to his power, which is the principle of the [hypostatic] union, or in regard to His Personality, which is the term of the [hypostatic] union, it has to be said that the Divine Person, over and beyond the human nature which He has assumed, can assume another distinct nature.[28]

For, to underline the point, the divine power of God the Son cannot be circumscribed by the human nature he assumes. Nor can the divine personhood of God the Son be limited by the human nature he assumes. The uncreated, as Thomas points out, cannot be comprehended by the created.[29] What is more, if the Incarnation involves an asymmetrical accessing relation between the divine mind of Christ and his human mind, and such a relation obtains between all created human minds and the divine mind, there does not seem to be any obstacle to the possibility of multiple incarnations, even if they are simultaneous, or temporally overlapping, rather than consecutive. As Thomas Morris points out, echoing his medieval namesake, there 'could be only one person involved in all these incarnations – God the Son – but this one person could be incarnate in any number of created bodies and minds, such as the body and earthly mind of Jesus'.[30]

It might be thought that this still does not adequately account for the 'unique metaphysical ownership' of Christ's human nature by God the Son, and that this is what lies at the heart of Hebblethwaite's objection. If the Second Person of the Trinity 'owns' Christ's human nature in a unique way, then there can be only one such incarnation. The problem with this is that it simply does not follow from the fact that a divine person has metaphysical ownership of a particular human nature that this must be a *unique* metaphysical ownership of one human nature. It is this matter that is in dispute between Hebblethwaite on one side, and St Thomas Aquinas and Thomas Morris on the other. In accordance with orthodoxy, both sides to the dispute are agreed that the metaphysics of the Incarnation means any human nature owned by a divine person is in a particular personal union with that divine person. But from metaphysical ownership alone nothing follows about how many such metaphysical arrangements a particular divine person may have at any one time, or across time. Orthodoxy presumes only that the Incarnation involves metaphysical ownership of a human nature by a divine person. But classical Christology is silent about

---

27. Even if one thinks souls are literally nowhere, having no spatial location, few will want to claim that created souls are omnipresent, even if this is not taken to imply some notion of physical location or co-location.
28. *Summa Theologica* IIIa. 3. 7.
29. Ibid.
30. Morris, *The Logic of God Incarnate*, p. 183.

whether such an arrangement is unique, and to presume this is the only viable position as Hebblethwaite does in speaking of it as a unique metaphysical arrangement, is to beg the question at issue. So the third assumption that underpins Hebblethwaite's reasoning seems dubious. It is not clear given the tenets of classical Christology that a divine person can have at most one human nature. Moreover, his second assumption also seems wide of the mark. The same *person*, human as well as divine is not involved in an incarnation according to classical Christology because any incarnation must involve the assumption of human nature by a divine person, not the assumption of a human person by a divine person or the generation of some hybrid divine-human person. Once the confusion at work in this aspect of Hebblethwaite's reasoning becomes clear, the second assumption collapses.

4. *The Twist in the Tale*

But more importantly, the Cartesian account provides a means of showing how, even if we concede to Hebblethwaite all three of the assumptions underlying his objection, the possibility of multiple incarnations is not precluded. For it could be that any human nature assumed by a divine person is numerically identical with that divine person; that a divine incarnation has to be the same 'person', human as well as divine; that a divine person can have at most one human nature; *and* that there are multiple consecutive incarnations.

To see this, let us return, once more, to the Cartesian account of the metaphysics of human persons. Recall that, on the Cartesian view, to be fully human the Second Person of the Trinity need only possess a human soul, even if, normally speaking, a human soul is 'attached' to a particular human body. Now, let us engage in a little theological make-believe. Suppose that at the Incarnation, the Second Person of the Trinity assumes the human body and soul of Christ. But according to this hypothetical story about the death of Christ, instead of Christ's body dying on the cross, it is burnt, the ashes of his body being scattered to the four winds. Yet, on the third day after his immolation, Christ appears to his disciples in a body that appears to have all the same physical characteristics of the body that was burnt three days previously. Christ's resurrection body in this counterfactual version of his death and resurrection is numerically distinct from his pre-resurrection body, which has been scattered as ash to the four winds.[31] Yet, given the Cartesian view of the metaphysics of human persons, this counterfactual resurrected Christ has the same human nature he had prior to the destruction of his pre-resurrection body, because

---

31. Objection: God could reassemble the ash of Christ's body and use it to reform a body for Christ. Well then, assume that Christ's pre-resurrection body is somehow annihilated. Then there would be no metaphysical possibility of his pre-resurrection body forming the material basis from which any post-resurrection body could be fashioned.

possession of a human body, let alone a particular human body, is not a requirement of human nature. Christ's human nature is essentially his soul that is
only contingently related to the body his soul is 'attached' to at a given time.
Furthermore, according to this story, Christ has two bodies, one prior to the
resurrection and one afterwards, but only one human nature because the same
human soul animates each body. One final caveat: As we have already noted,
catholic Christology requires that Christ has a human nature, but is not a human
person, strictly speaking. So the Cartesian account of human persons in view
here will need to be modified in the case of Christ so that it is clear that in this
particular case we are dealing with a complete human nature but not a human
person, strictly speaking. It is Christ's human nature that is in view here; were
the Cartesian account applied to some other human being who is also a human
person we would be able to speak of the human nature of that human person
consisting essentially of a soul contingently related to a particular body. But, of
course, this cannot obtain in the case of Christ, on pain of Nestorianism. So
who is said to 'own' the human nature in question is an important matter, and
Hebblethwaite is right to make this a central component of his own construal
of the Incarnation.

From this counterfactual story about the resurrection of Christ, consistent
with the Cartesian account and Hebblethwaite's three assumptions, we can
draw the following conclusion. This conception of the metaphysics of human
personhood, which appears consistent with the requirements of catholic Christology, is also consistent with the Second Person of the Trinity having at most
one human nature (i.e., human soul) as Hebblethwaite presumes. It is also
commensurate with the possibility of more than one incarnation, if by this is
meant the assumption by God the Son of more than one human body (i.e., more
than one 'enfleshment'). This is the case provided the multiple Incarnations
in question are consecutive, not simultaneous or temporally overlapping. And
if this is the case (if we have in view only consecutive, not simultaneous or
temporally overlapping incarnations), then on the Cartesian account, Christ
could be enfleshed in more than one body. In fact, he could be enfleshed in a
body located many miles and years away from the first century soil upon which
he trod.[32]

---

32. In the foregoing I have assumed that human souls cannot have metaphysical ownership
of more than one body at any given moment in time. But this assumption might be challenged.
If human souls have no location because they are essentially immaterial beings, then it might be
possible for one soul to have ownership of more than one body simultaneously, although, I admit
that I have strong intuitions against this view, having to do with the first-person perspective I currently enjoy in my body. (How can I enjoy a first-person perspective in two bodies simultaneously?)
But even if it turns out that, for some reason human souls cannot 'own' more than one body simultaneously, this can hardly apply univocally to God the Son, because he is omnipresent. In which
case, it would seem that there might be reason to think the Second Person of the Trinity can be
incarnate in more than one human body at-one-and-the-same-time, along the lines I have been
pursuing in this section.

5. *The Possibility, but not Actuality, of Multiple Incarnations*

We come to the final section of this chapter. In his monograph of collected essays on the Incarnation, Hebblethwaite observes that there is a distinction between the possibility and the actuality of multiple incarnations, and objects to both.[33] Thus far, I have provided two independent, though related, arguments for the metaphysical possibility of multiple incarnations. However, it seems to me that there are good theological grounds for thinking that in actuality there is only one Incarnation. First of all, there is some evidence from the New Testament that Christ's Incarnation has cosmic significance as a once-for-all event in which God is reconciling the whole of creation to himself, not merely human beings. Perhaps the most striking example of this can be found in Colossians 1.19-20, where the author says 'For it pleased [the Father that] in Him all the fullness should dwell, and by Him to reconcile all things [*ta panta*] to Himself, by Him, whether things on earth or things in heaven, having made peace through the blood of His cross'.[34] Taken at face value, this suggests the cosmic uniqueness of Christ's work, which would seem to render any further incarnation otiose.

There are also grounds independent of Scripture for thinking that the Incarnation is a unique occurrence. Here I have in mind what we might call the fittingness of only one Incarnation, given what God has ordained concerning the salvation of some number of humanity. This is hardly an overwhelming objection to the actuality of multiple incarnations. But it is, I think, an example of where considerations concerning what it is fitting for God to bring about, given his character and his commitments (such as creating the kind of world he did create), are important. Taken together, I think these considerations tell against the likelihood of multiple incarnations actually occurring.

Let us examine these claims more carefully. We begin with the biblical material. In his Bampton Lectures of the middle of the twentieth century, E. L. Mascall asserted that 'the arguments of both Ephesians and Hebrews rest upon the unquestioned, but also unformulated, assumption that there are no corporeal rational beings in the universe other than man.'[35] Such an objection could be expanded to include other New Testament passages relevant here (perhaps

---

33. Hebblethwaite, *The Incarnation*, p. 167.

34. There are other passages in the New Testament that might be thought to point in a similar direction, although they do not seem to me to be conclusively in favour of the once-for-all cosmic significance of Christ's work. For example, Luke 1.32-33 and Ephesians 1. However, Hebrews 2.8b sounds much more like Collosians 1. It says 'He [God the Father] put all in subjection under him, He left nothing that is not put under him. But now we do not yet see all things put under him.' Taken together with Collosians 1 this seems to present a strong *prima facie* theological reason for holding that Christ's work is cosmically unique.

35. E. L. Mascall, *Christian Theology and Natural Science* (London: Longmans, Green and Co., 1956) p. 45, cited in Christopher L. Fisher and David Fergusson, 'Karl Rahner and the Extra-Terrestrial Intelligence Question', p. 280.

even Colossians 1) since the main issue Mascall raises has to do with whether the New Testament authors he refers to thought that human beings were the *only* rational corporeal creatures in the cosmos to whom the work of Christ could be addressed. Perhaps this obtains in the case of all the New Testament writers – or at least all those writers whose work addresses this issue either directly or indirectly.

Let us expand Mascall's point to include all such New Testament authors. There are several things to be said by way of response to this. First, it might be thought that if Scripture is revelation, the question is impertinent. The issue is whether God intends to convey to us that Christ's work is cosmically unique, as at least Colossians 1 and Hebrews 2 seem to indicate. What the human authors of these passages believed about the unique place of human beings in the cosmos is irrelevant. The question has to do with what the divine author of these passages intended to convey through them to his church. But that aside, it seems to me that all we may safely say about the Ephesians 1 and the Colossians and Hebrews passages with regard to the existence of other corporeal intelligent creatures elsewhere in the cosmos is that as they stand these texts are commensurate with either the existence or non-existence of other such rational corporeal creatures. That is, these passages do not directly address this issue, nor do they imply a particular view of the existence of such creatures, because it does not seem to have been an issue these authors addressed, or even conceived of addressing. Mascall is guilty of over-reaching himself in stating otherwise.

But if the biblical material does not really address the question of whether or not there might be more than one incarnation, there may still be other reasons for thinking God only brings about one actual incarnation. It is here that considerations concerning the suitability of only one incarnation can be deployed. In order to make the case as simply and concisely as possible, I propose to set out one line of reasoning in favour of there being only one actual incarnation in terms of a theological 'just-so' story (with apologies to Rudyard Kipling). The story may not be the only way of making sense of the claim that God brings about only one actual incarnation. But it is one plausible way of thinking about this matter. Here it is.

It is a theological commonplace in much, though not all, classical theology to claim that God is free to create or refrain from creating this world, or any world. On this way of thinking, nothing compels God to create; nothing compels him to create the actual world he does create; and God creates the world he does intentionally. It is an act of sheer grace.[36] It is also common to find

---

36. There are, of course, exceptions to this rule. Jonathan Edwards is one such exception, Abelard another. Richard Muller does a good job of explaining the medieval debate in *Post-Reformation Reformed Dogmatics, The Rise and Development of Reformed Orthodoxy ca. 1520 ca. 1725, Vol. III* (Grand Rapids, MI: Baker Academic, 2003), ch. 1, especially pp. 35 and 69. There have been several recent discussions of Edwards on this matter. See for example William Wainwright's

classical theologians affirming that God has good reason to create this world, rather than some other world.[37] Suppose that is true. This is consistent with the possibility of multiple incarnations, because this is consistent with there being possible but not actual worlds at which God does become incarnate in more than one instance. But this only underscores our initial question: why think there is only one Incarnation? One reason has to do with the motivation for the Incarnation. Following those in the Anselmian tradition, let us assume that God deigns to create this world knowing that human beings will fall and require a mediator in order to bring about their reconciliation with God. The Incarnation is necessary, we might say, once God ordains to create this world, and to save some number of fallen humanity, in the knowledge that only a God-Man is able to bring about the reconciliation of human beings with God. According to this story, God cannot simply pass over or forgive sin without adequate satisfaction. Or, at least, if he could pass over or forgive sin without adequate satisfaction, he has good reason not to do this, and for ordaining the Incarnation and work of Christ instead.[38] For the Anselmian, the necessity attaching to the Incarnation is a kind of consequential necessity, because it depends upon God ordaining the creation of this world and the reconciliation of some number of fallen humanity through the saving offices of the God-Man. For many medieval and post-Reformation theologians, this sort of distinction would be a familiar subdivision of the larger distinction between the so-called absolute power of God, that is, what God has power to do in abstraction from any particular action he has ordained, and his ordained power, according to which God must act only in accordance with what he has ordained once he has ordained what he decrees.

Here endeth the narrative. This brief sketch of what we might call a consequentially necessary account of the Incarnation gives one reason for thinking that the primary motivation for the Incarnation is the reconciliation of some

---

essay 'Jonathan Edwards, William Rowe, and the Necessity of Creation' in *Faith, Freedom and Rationality, Philosophy of Religion Today*, eds. Jeff Jordan and Daniel Howard Snyder (Maryland: Rowman and Littlefield, 1996) pp. 119–133 and William Rowe, *Can God be Free?* (Oxford: Oxford University Press, 2004) ch. 4. Interestingly, in the recent literature William Mann has defended something like Abelard's thesis. See Mann, 'Divine Sovereignty and Aseity' in William Wainwright ed. *The Oxford Handbook of Philosophy of Religion* (Oxford: Oxford University Press, 2004) pp. 54–57.

37.   Discussion of what is entailed by having God having a good reason to create this world rather than another world would take us too far from our present concerns. However, it seems conceivable that God has a good reason for creating the world he does even if there is no best possible world. Thus, Muller, commenting on Aquinas's doctrine of divine freedom says, 'in the act of creation God necessarily wills his own absolute goodness as the end or goal of all his willing. Yet God freely chooses, without any necessity, the means by which he will communicate his goodness to creation.' Muller, *Post-Reformation Reformed Dogmatics III*, p. 60.

38.   Richard Swinburne has recently advocated a version of the satisfaction theory of atonement that presumes God could have foregone atonement, but that there are good reasons why God ordains atonement rather than foregoing it. See Swinburne, *Responsibility and Atonement* (Oxford: Oxford University Press, 1989).

number of humanity. If no human being had fallen, there would be no motivation for the Incarnation, on this view. Such an account of the motivation for incarnation can be found in the work of a number of Protestant as well as Catholic theologians, such as John Calvin, although Calvin is not entirely consistent in his application of this doctrine. Calvin maintains that 'the only reason given in Scripture that the Son of God willed to take our flesh, and accepted this commandment from the Father, is that he would be a sacrifice to appease the Father on our behalf'.[39] Let us assume, for the sake of argument and with theologians like Calvin, that this is what motivates the Incarnation. We can apply this to the question of the fittingness or suitability of there being only one Incarnation in actuality in the following manner, using the tenets of our just-so story as our theological frame of reference.

1. The creation of this world, or of any world, is an act of divine grace.
2. The Incarnation is consequentially necessary given that God ordains to create this world and reconcile some number of fallen human beings to himself (and God has good reason to bring this state of affairs about even if he could have simply forgiven sin without satisfaction).
3. The motivation for the Incarnation is the reconciliation of some number of fallen humanity, such that, without a fall there would have been no need for an incarnation.

To this we may add the idea that

4. The satisfaction offered by the God-Man has a value sufficient to the divine purpose of reconciling fallen human beings.

Now, it would seem that this provides a motivation for the Incarnation. But it also provides a reason for thinking that more than one Incarnation would be superfluous because the reason for the Incarnation – the reconciliation of some number of fallen human beings – is achieved through the Incarnation of Christ. If the Incarnation is motivated (at least in part) by a desire to bring about such reconciliation, and the Incarnation of Christ successfully achieves this end, another Incarnation is redundant. So it would seem most fitting for God to become man in only one instance, although multiple incarnations are metaphysically possible, given the Cartesian account of human nature outlined earlier.

---

39. Calvin, *Institutes* II. xii. 4, p. 468. Compare Galatians 4. 4, which Calvin cites in the course of his argument in *Institutes* II. xii. 7, p. 474. However, in *Institutes* II. xii. 1, p. 465, Calvin says 'Even if man had remained free from all stain, his condition would have been too lowly for him to reach God without a Mediator'. This runs contrary to everything Calvin goes on to argue against Osiander in the remainder of this chapter of the *Institutes*. It is difficult to know what to make of this, but it would appear to be a slip of the pen on Calvin's part.

Much of the dialectical force of the just-so story of a consequentially neces-sary incarnation depends on assumptions about the divine nature and the work of Christ that are now hotly disputed by contemporary theologians. Yet this story, or something very like it, has been espoused by a number of western theologians in what we might call the Anselmian tradition, broadly construed.

Swallowing this story without more by way of explanation of some of its key assumptions or assertions might be a tall order for some. And more would need to be said by way of dogmatic exposition in order for this story to withstand such criticism. Nevertheless, it seems to me that this offers one way of thinking about why a single incarnation might be most fitting, although multiple incar-nations are metaphysically possible. And that is all we set out to provide. But this does leave one final query in addition to the foregoing, having to do with the existence of other life forms in the universe that might also require recon-ciliation with God. The existence of such life forms is, of course, entirely speculative and there may be reasons to think that the likelihood of the emer-gence of corporeal intelligent life elsewhere in the cosmos is slim.[40] Be that as it may, some theologians have argued that if other cosmic life forms that also need salvation exist, it would be strange to think God has not provided some means of salvation for them too. And for all we know, this involves some sort of incarnation in addition to the Incarnation of Christ. If this is right, then there seem to be several possibilities with respect to the question of the salvation of some putative extra-terrestrial corporeal life form. The first is that God does not save such beings and the work of Christ does not apply to them. The second is that no additional incarnation is required because the scope of Christ's work includes them as things stand. So God does save these beings, but through the work of Christ. The third option is that the work of Christ might apply to them (it is cosmic in its scope) but God has not deigned to save any of these crea-tures. And the forth option is that the work of Christ does not apply to them, yet God has deigned to provide some means of salvation for these creatures. It is this fourth option that opens the door to the possibility of the applications of a multiple incarnation doctrine to the salvation of putative corporeal extra-ter-restrial intelligent life.[41]

Theological issues of such a speculative nature are difficult to adjudicate. Still, it would be strange to think God would not provide some means of salvation to such a benighted race of extra-terrestrials, and that God would not

40. See, for example, the evidence adduced by Fisher and Fergusson in 'Karl Rahner and the Extra-Terrestrial Intelligence Question'.

41. This fourth option is not restricted to a doctrine of multiple incarnations, however. It is consistent with some other means of salvation, as C. S. Lewis imagines in his novel, *Perelandra*. In this regard, God may simply forgive the sin of the fallen extra-terrestrial creatures without the need for an incarnation or atonement. But I shall leave this possibility to one side, since if this is true, then the doctrine of multiple incarnations is straightforwardly irrelevant to the question of the salvation of other fallen corporeal creatures that might exist elsewhere in the cosmos.

ordain the salvation of at least some of them. For the Christian God is gracious and merciful, a matter attested to by Scripture. Such theological considerations would mean discounting the first and third options given above. Of the remaining two, it seems to me that God could provide another incarnation. But granted considerations of fittingness as set forth in our just-so story, and the biblical evidence of the cosmic significance – even uniqueness – attributable to the (actual) Incarnation, my tentative conclusion is that the second, rather than the fourth, option, is the more likely, all things considered.

6. *Conclusion*

In their recent essay on Rahner's understanding of extra-terrestrial intelligence and its implications for the Incarnation, Christopher Fisher and David Fergusson claim that 'in a world of multiple incarnations, salvation must take place in ways other than through a single action of cosmic healing significance'. They go on to say that this 'raises the question of whether even one incarnation would be necessary, as opposed to multiple indwellings of conscious persons by the divine Spirit. A multiplicity of occurrence must inevitably compromise the singularity of the incarnation'.[42] Multiple Incarnations necessarily compromise the *singularity* of the Incarnation – that is analytically true. But multiple Incarnations might not compromise the saving significance of the work of Christ, if that work is restricted in its salvific scope to *homo sapiens* and there are other extra-terrestrial life forms God wishes to reconcile to himself. And it is surely this matter that is behind the sort of unease expressed by theologians like Fisher and Fergusson. Whether there are extra-terrestrial corporeal life forms in need of salvation, and whether God provides for this through an additional incarnation of some kind, is a matter of theological speculation. But this does emphasize the important modal distinction between the possibility and the actuality of multiple incarnations. In this paper I have argued that there are two arguments in favour of the possibility of multiple incarnations, *pace* Brian Hebblethwaite. Yet, there is reason to think that as a matter of fact, God has created this world with only one incarnation in mind; the cosmic significance of Christ's person and work spoken of in various places in the New Testament points in this direction. And there are other considerations, having to do with the fittingness of such an arrangement that may also be pressed into service here. Thus, on balance, I think that although Hebblethwaite is mistaken in thinking there is a logical or even metaphysical impediment to the possibility of multiple incarnations, there are good biblical and theological reasons for thinking that in actuality there is only one incarnation of the Son of God.

42. Fisher and Fergusson, 'Karl Rahner and the Extra-Terrestrial Intelligence Question', p. 282.

Afterword

There are theologians who think of philosophy as a discipline that has its own integrity and usefulness in the acquisition of knowledge. Thus Calvin, in the midst of a discussion on the nature of the soul, has this to say,

> But I leave it to the philosophers to discuss these faculties [of the soul] in their subtle way. For the upbuilding of godliness a simple definition will be enough for us. I, indeed, agree that the things they teach are true, not only enjoyable, but also profitable to learn, and skilfully assembled by them. And I do not forbid those who are desirous of learning to study them. (Inst. I. XV. 6)

Admittedly, not all divines have been as sanguine as Calvin about the relationship between philosophy and theology as this – and even Calvin on other occasions seems less than happy about certain sorts of philosophical theology he had encountered (particularly that of the faculty at the Sorbonne). But what shall we say about the value of analytic theology as a method that openly borrows tools of analysis from the analytical philosophers? Is this a legitimate plundering of the Egyptians, or the means to another potential Babylonian captivity of theology? By now it should be clear that I think analytic theology promises the former. William Abraham makes the point well, when he says,

> The subject matter of systematic theology has its own integrity. In the end the theologian must come to grips with the questions that arise in and around the activity of God in the great drama of creation, freedom, fall, and redemption. This is as true for analytic theology as it is for any other kind of theology. Within analytic theology the theologian will deploy the skills, resources, and virtues of analytic philosophy in clarifying and arguing for the truth of the Christian Gospel as taken up in the great themes of the creeds of the Church. No doubt the analytic theologian can develop and display other interests and skills as garnered, say, from biblical studies, historical investigation, and cultural commentary. Moreover, there is no reason why the analytic theologian cannot keep an eye on the role of theology in the fostering of deep love for God; indeed that should be a concern of any theology whatever its virtues or vices. There is ample evidence to hand to suggest that the time is ripe for the emergence of analytic theology; there is also sufficient evidence to suggest that this work will bear much fruit in the years ahead.[1]

---

1. Abraham, 'Systematic Theology as Analytic Theology' in *Analytic Theology*, p. 69.

In this volume I have tried to show how analytical theology as systematic theology might look when applied to eight dogmatic areas of Christology. In each case it has been clear that the sort of virtues this method possesses, virtues which make it ideally suited as an heir to much classical theological method in order to pursue properly theological conclusions that are substantive, are not somehow *enslaving* the theologian to an alien philosophical approach to Scripture or dogmatics.

There will be those sceptical of such an approach. But this should not be all that surprising. As Nicholas Wolterstorff observes in a different context,

> [l]earning is not some eternal essence that happens to enter history at particular times and places, but a long-enduring social practice whose goals, methods, standards of excellence, and legitimating and orientating frameworks of conviction change drastically over time and are often deeply contested.[2]

Some will contest the method deployed here just as others will contest the substantive dogmatic conclusions reached. But what I trust does emerge from this study is an approach to theology profoundly shaped by the Christian tradition and the various theological interlocutors of previous generations, that makes use of a method that can make a positive, doctrinal contribution to the literature today. Is that a *theological* theology? I think it is, as I hope the chapters of the present work have demonstrated.

---

2. Wolterstorff 'The Travail of Theology in the Modern Academy' in Miroslav Volf ed. *The Future of Theology, Essays in Honour of Jürgen Moltmann* (Grand Rapids, MI: Eerdmans, 1996) p. 37.

BIBLIOGRAPHY

Abraham, William *Crossing the Threshold of Divine Revelation* (Grand Rapids, MI: Eerdmans, 2006).

— 'Systematic Theology as Analytic Theology' in Oliver D. Crisp and Michael C. Rea, eds *Analytic Theology, New Essays in the Philosophy of Theology* (Oxford: Oxford University Press, 2009).

Adams, Marilyn McCord *What Sort of Human Nature?* (Milwaukee, WI: Marquette University Press, 1999).

— *Christ and Horrors* (Cambridge: Cambridge University Press, 2006).

St Anselm of Canterbury, *Anselm of Canterbury, The Major Works* eds Brian Davies and Gillian Evans (Oxford: Oxford University Press, 1998).

Aquinas, St Thomas *Summa Theologica,* trans. Brothers of the English Dominican Province (New York: Benzinger Brothers, 1948 [1911]).

— *Summa Contra Gentiles Vols. I–V* ed. Anton C. Pegis et al. (Notre Dame: University of Notre Dame Press, 1975 [1955]).

Armstrong, Brian G. *Calvinism and the Amyraut Heresy, Protestant Scholasticism and Humanism in Seventeenth-Century France* (Milwaukee, WI: University of Wisconsin Press, 1969).

Barth, Karl *Dogmatics in Outline,* trans. G. T. Thomson (London: SCM Press, 1949).

— *Church Dogmatics I/2* eds G. W. Bromiley and T. F. Torrance (Edinburgh: T&T Clark, 1956).

— *Church Dogmatics IV/1,* eds G. W. Bromiley and T. F. Torrance (Edinburgh: T&T Clark, 1956).

— *Church Dogmatics II/2,* eds G. W. Bromiley and T. F. Torrance (Edinburgh: T&T Clark, 1957).

Bauckham, Richard *God Crucified, Monotheism and Christology in the New Testament* (Grand Rapids, MI: Eerdmans, 1999).

Berkouwer, G. C. *Divine Election,* trans. Hugo Bekker (Grand Rapids, MI: Eerdmans, 1960).

Berry, R. J. 'The Virgin Birth of Christ' in *Science and Christian Belief* 8 (1996): 101–110.

Bloesch, Donald *Jesus Christ. Savior and Lord* (Downers Grove, IL: Inter-Varsity Press, 1997).

Boettner Lorraine *The Reformed Doctrine of Predestination* (Philadelphia, PA: Presbyterian and Reformed, 1963).

Bonhoeffer, Dietrich *Christology,* trans. John Bowden (London: Harper Collins, 1966).

The Book of Common Prayer (Cambridge: Cambridge University Press, 1968 [1662]).

Bromiley, Geoffrey W. *Introduction to the Theology of Karl Barth* (Edinburgh: T&T Clark, 1979).

Brown, David *The Divine Trinity* (London: Duckworth, 1985).

Brown, Raymond E. *The Virginal Conception and Bodily Resurrection of Jesus* (London: Geoffrey Chapman, 1973).

Brümmer, Vincent 'Divine Impeccability' in *Religious Studies* 20 (1984): 203–214.

Brunner, Emil *The Mediator, A Study of the Central Doctrine of the Christian Faith,* trans. Olive Wyon (London: Lutterworth Press, 1934).

— *The Christian Doctrine of Creation and Redemption, Dogmatics Vol. II*, trans. Olive Wyon (London: Lutterworth Press, 1952).

Calvin, John *Institutes of the Christian Religion,* trans. Ford Lewis Battles, ed. John T. McNeill (Philadelphia, PA: Westminster Press, 1960).

— *Commentary on Ephesians, Calvin's New Testament Commentaries Vol. 11*, trans. T. H. L. Parker, eds David W. Torrance and Thomas F. Torrance (Grand Rapids, MI: Eerdmans, 1965).

Clarke, F. Stuart *The Ground of Election, Jacobus Arminius' Doctrine of the Work and Person of Christ* (Milton Keynes: Paternoster, 2006).

Congregation for the Doctrine of the Faith 'Declaration on Procured Abortion 13' in *Acta Apostolicae Sedis* 66 (1974): 730–747.

Cooper, John W. *Body, Soul and Life Everlasting, Biblical Anthropology and the Monism–Dualism Debate* (Grand Rapids, MI: Eerdmans, 2000 [1989]).

Corcoran, Kevin *Rethinking Human Nature, A Christian Materialist Alternative to the Soul* (Grand Rapids, MI: Baker Academic, 2006).

Crane, Tim *Elements of Mind, An Introduction to the Philosophy of Mind* (Oxford: Oxford University Press, 2001).

Crisp Oliver D. 'On Barth's Denial of Universalism' in *Themelios* 29 (2003): 18–29.

— *An American Augustinian: Sin and Salvation in the Dogmatic Theology of William G. T. Shedd* (Milton Keynes: Paternoster Press and Eugene, OR: Wipf and Stock, 2007).

— *Divinity and Humanity: The Incarnation Reconsidered* (Cambridge: Cambridge University Press, 2007).

— 'On the *Letter* and *Spirit* of Karl Barth's doctrine of Election: A Reply to O'Neil' in *Evangelical Quarterly* LXXIX (2007): 53–67.

— 'Barth and Jonathan Edwards on Reprobation (and Hell)' in David Gibson and Daniel Strange eds *Engaging with Barth: Contemporary Evangelical Critiques* (Leicester: Apollos, 2008).

— and Rea, Michael eds *Analytic Theology, New Essays in the Philosophy of Theology* (Oxford: Oxford University Press, 2009).

Crisp, Thomas M. 'Presentism' in Michael J. Loux and Dean W. Zimmerman eds *The Oxford Handbook of Metaphysics* (Oxford: Oxford University Press, 2003).

Cross, Richard *The Metaphysics of the Incarnation, Thomas Aquinas to Duns Scotus* (Oxford: Oxford University Press, 2002).

Crossan, John Dominic *Jesus: A Revolutionary Biography* (New York: Harper One, 1995).

Descartes, Rene *Replies to the Fourth Set of Objections*, in *The Philosophical Writings of Descartes, ii* trans J. Cottingham, R. Stoothof and D. Murdoch (Cambridge: Cambridge University Press, 1984).

Donceel, Joseph 'Immediate Animation and Delayed Homization' in *Theological Studies* 31 (1970): 76–105.

Edwards, Jonathan *Treatise on Grace & Other Posthumously Published Writings* ed. Paul Helm (London: James Clarke, 1971).

Erickson, Millard *The Word Became Flesh: A Contemporary Incarnational Christology* (Grand Rapids, MI: Baker, 1991).

Fisher, Christopher L. and Fergusson, David 'Karl Rahner and the Extra-Terrestrial Intelligence Question' in *Heythrop Journal* XLVII (2006): 275–290.

Flint, Thomas P. 'Risky Business: Open Theism and the Incarnation' in *Philosophia Christi* 6 (2004): 213–233.

Ford, Norman M. *When Did I Begin? Conception of the Human Individual in History, Philosophy and Science* (Cambridge: Cambridge University Press, 1988).

Freddoso, Alfred J. 'Human Nature, Potency and the Incarnation' in *Faith and Philosophy* 3 (1986): 27–53.

Ganssle, Gregory ed. *God and Time: Four Views* (Downers Grove, IL: Inter-Varsity Press, 2001).

Gathercole, Simon 'Pre-existence, and the Freedom of the Son in Creation and Redemption: An Exposition in Dialogue with Robert Jenson' in *International Journal of Systematic Theology* 7 (2005): 36–49.

Gibson, David 'Reading the Decree: Exegesis, Election and Christology in Calvin and Barth' PhD Thesis, University of Aberdeen, 2008.

Green, Joel B. and Palmer, Stuart L. eds *In Search of the Soul, Four Views of the Mind–Body Problem* (Downers Grove, IL: Inter-Varsity Press, 2005).

Grenz, Stanley J. *Reason for Hope, The Systematic Theology of Wolfhart Pannenberg, Second Edition* (Grand Rapids, MI: Eerdmans, 2005).

Grillmeier, Aloys *Christ in Christian Tradition, Vol. 1, From the Apostolic Age to Chalcedon (AD 451)* (London: Mowbrays, 1965).

Grogan, Geoffrey 'Christology from Below and from Above' in Mark Elliott and John L. McPake eds *Jesus, The Only Hope: Jesus, Yesterday, Today, Forever* (Fearn: Christian Focus and Edinburgh: Rutherford House, 2001).

Gunton, Colin E. *Yesterday and Today, A Study of Continuities in Christology* (London: Darton, Longman and Todd, 1983).

— 'Two Dogmas Revisited: Edwards Irving's Christology' in *Scottish Journal of Theology* 41 (1988): 359–376.

Harrisville, Roy A. and Sundberg, Walter *The Bible in Modern Culture: Baruch Spinoza to Brevard Childs, Second Edition* (Grand Rapids, MI: Eerdmans, 2002).

Hart, Trevor 'Sinlessness and Moral Responsibility: A Problem in Christology' in *Scottish Journal of Theology* 48 (1995): 37–54.

Hasker, William *The Emergent Self* (Ithaca, NY: Cornell University Press, 1999).

Healy, Nicholas M. *Thomas Aquinas, Theologian of The Christian Life* (Aldershot: Ashgate, 2003).

Hebblethwaite, Brian 'The Uniqueness of the Incarnation' in Michael Goulder ed. *Incarnation and Myth: The Debate Continued* (Grand Rapids, MI: Eerdmans, 1979).

— *The Incarnation, Collected Essays in Christology* (Cambridge: Cambridge University Press, 1987).

— 'The Impossibility of Multiple Incarnations' *Theology* 104 (2001): 323–334.

— *Philosophical Theology and Christian Doctrine* (Oxford: Blackwell, 2005).

Helm, Paul 'God and the Approval of Sin', *Religious Studies* 20 (1984): 223–226.

— *Faith and Understanding* (Edinburgh: Edinburgh University Press, 1997).

— *John Calvin's Ideas* (Oxford: Oxford University Press, 2004).

— 'John Calvin and the Hiddenness of God' in Bruce L. McCormack ed. *Engaging the Doctrine of God, Contemporary Protestant Perspectives* (Grand Rapids, MI: Baker Academic, 2008).

Heppe, Heinrich *Reformed Dogmatics* (London: Wakeman Trust, n.d. [1950]).

Hodge, Charles *Systematic Theology, Vol. II* (London: James Clarke, 1960).

Hurtado, Larry *Lord Jesus Christ, Devotion to Jesus in Earliest Christianity* (Grand Rapids, MI: Eerdmans, 2003).

Jenson, Robert W. *Systematic Theology, Vol. 1, The Triune God* (New York: Oxford University Press, 1997).

— *Systematic Theology Vol. 2, The Works of God* (New York: Oxford University Press, 1999).

— 'For Us .. . . He Was Made Man' in Christopher R. Seitz ed. *Nicene Christianity, The Future for a New Ecumenism* (Grand Rapids, MI: Brazos Press, 2001).

— 'Response to Watson and Hunsinger', *Scottish Journal of Theology* 55 (2002): 230.

Jones, David Albert *The Soul of The Embryo: An Enquiry into the Status of the Human Embryo in the Christian Tradition* (London: Continuum, 2004).

Kelly, J. N. D. *Early Christian Doctrines, Fifth Edition* (London: A & C Black, 1977 [1958]).

Kevern, Peter 'Limping Principles: A Reply to Brian Hebblethwaite on "The Impossibility of Multiple Incarnations"' in *Theology* September/October (2002): 342–347.

Klauber, Martin I. '*Formula Consensus Helvetica*' in *Trinity Journal* 11 (1990): 103–123.

Lash, Nicholas 'Up and Down in Christology' in Stephen Sykes and Derek Holmes eds *New Studies in Theology 1* (London: Duckworth, 1980).

Leftow, Brian 'Souls Dipped in Dust' in Kevin Corcoran ed. *Soul, Body and Survival* (Ithaca, NY: Cornell University Press, 2001).

— 'A Timeless God Incarnate' in Stephen T. Davis, Daniel Kendall and Gerald O'Collins eds *The Incarnation* (Oxford: Oxford University Press, 2002).

Lewis, C. S. *The Cosmic Trilogy* (London: The Bodley Head, 1989 [1943]).

Locke, John *Essay Concerning Human Understanding* ed. Peter Nidditch (Oxford: Oxford University Press, 1975).

Lowe, E. J. 'The Problem of Psycho-physical Causation' in Timothy O'Connor and David Robb, eds *Philosophy of Mind, Contemporary Readings* (London: Routledge, 2002).

Machen, J. Gresham *The Virgin Birth of Christ* (London: Marshall, Morgan and Scott, 1930).

Macintosh, H. R. *The Doctrine of The Person of Jesus Christ, Second Edition* (Edinburgh: T&T Clark, 1913).

Macquarrie, John *Jesus Christ in Modern Thought* (London: SCM Press, 1990).

Mangina, Joseph L. *Karl Barth, Theologian of Christian Witness* (Aldershot: Ashgate, 2004).

Mann, William E. 'Divine Sovereignty and Aseity' in William Wainwright ed. *The Oxford Handbook of Philosophy of Religion* (Oxford: Oxford University Press, 2004).

Mascall, E. L. *Christian Theology and Natural Science* (London: Longmans, Green and Co., 1956).

McCabe, Herbert *God Matters* (London: Geoffrey Chapman, 1987).

McCormack, Bruce L. 'Grace and Being, The Role of God's Gracious Election in Karl Barth's Theological Ontology' in John Webster ed. *The Cambridge Companion to Karl Barth* (Cambridge: Cambridge University Press, 2000).

— *Orthodox and Modern, Studies in the Theology of Karl Barth* (Grand Rapids, MI: Baker Academic, 2008).

— 'The Actuality of God: Karl Barth in Conversation with Open Theism' in Bruce L. McCormack ed. *Engaging the Doctrine of God, Contemporary Protestant Perspectives* (Grand Rapids, MI: Baker Academic, 2008).

McGuckin, John Anthony *The Westminster Handbook to Patristic Theology* (Louisville, KT: Westminster John Knox, 2004).

McKinley, John Elton 'A Relational Model of Christ's Impeccability and Temptation', PhD Dissertation, The Southern Baptist Theological Seminary, 2005.

Merricks, Trenton 'The Word Made Flesh: Dualism, Physicalism and the Incarnation' in Peter van Inwagen and Dean W. Zimmerman eds *Persons: Human and Divine* (Oxford: Oxford University Press, 2007).

Milton, John *Ode on the Morning of Christ's Nativity,* reprinted in Helen Gardner ed. *The Faber Book of Religious Verse* (London: Faber & Faber, 1972).

Moltmann, Jürgen *The Crucified God*, trans. R. A. Wilson and John Bowden (London: SCM Press, 1974).

Moore, Jonathan D. *English Hypothetical Universalism: John Preston and the Softening of Reformed Theology* (Grand Rapids, MI: Eerdmans, 2007).

Moreland, J. P. and Craig, William Lane *Philosophical Foundations for a Christian Worldview* (Downers Grove, IL: Inter-Varsity Press, 2003).

Morris, Thomas V. *The Logic of God Incarnate* (Ithaca, NY: Cornell University Press, 1986).

Mozley, J. K. *The Doctrine of The Incarnation* (London: The Unicorn Press, 1936).

Muller, Richard A. *Dictionary of Latin and Greek Theological Terms, Drawn Principally from Protestant Scholastic Theology* (Grand Rapids, MI: Baker, 1985).

— *Christ and the Decree, Christology and Predestination in Reformed Theology from Calvin to Perkins* (Durham, NC: Labyrinth Press, 1986).

— *After Calvin, Studies in The Development of a Theological Tradition* (Oxford: Oxford University Press, 2003).

— *Post-Reformation Reformed Dogmatics Vols. I–III* (Grand Rapids, MI: Baker Academic, 2003).

Nuyen A. T. 'The Nature of Temptation' in *Southern Journal of Philosophy* 35 (1997): 91–103.

O'Collins, Gerald *Christology, A Biblical, Historical and Systematic Study of Jesus* (Oxford: Oxford University Press, 1995).

— *Incarnation* (London: Continuum, 2002).

Odo of Tournai, *On original sin and a disputation with the Jew, Leo, concerning the advent of Christ, the Son of God, two theological treatises,* trans. Irven M. Resnick (Philadelphia, PA: University of Pennsylvania Press, 1994).

O'Donovan, Oliver *Begotten or Made?* (Oxford: Oxford University Press, 1984).

Ott, Ludwig *Fundamentals of Catholic Dogma* (Rockford, IL: Tan Books, 1955).

Pannenberg, Wolfhart *Jesus – God and Man* trans Lewis L. Wilkins and Duane E. Priebe (London: SCM Press, 1968).

— *Systematic Theology Vol. II,* trans. Geoffrey W. Bromiley (Grand Rapids, MI: Eerdmans, 1994).

Peacocke, Arthur 'DNA of our DNA' in George J. Brooke ed. *The Birth of Jesus, Biblical and Theological Reflections* (Edinburgh: T&T Clark, 2000).

Pelikan, Jaroslav *The Christian Tradition, 1: The Emergence of the Catholic Tradition (100–600)* (Chicago, IL: University of Chicago Press, 1971).

Peterson, Michael L. and Vanarragon, Raymond J. eds *Contemporary Debates in Philosophy of Religion* (Oxford: Blackwell, 2004).

Pieper, Francis *Christian Dogmatics, Vol. III* (Saint Louis, MO: Concordia Publishing, 1953).

Pike, Nelson 'Omnipotence and God's ability to sin' in Paul Helm ed. *Divine Commands and Morality* (Oxford: Oxford University Press, 1981).

Plantinga, Alvin 'On Heresy, Mind and Truth' in *Faith and Philosophy* 16 (1999): 182–193.

— 'Can God Break the Laws?' in Andrew Dole and Andrew Chignell, eds *God and The Ethics of Belief: New Essays in Philosophy of Religion* (Cambridge: Cambridge University Press, 2005).

— 'Against Materialism' in *Faith and Philosophy* 23 (2006): 3–32.

Rahner, Karl *Theological Investigations Vol. IX,* trans. G. Harrison (London: Darton, Longman and Todd, 1972).

Rea, Michael C. 'Four Dimensionalism' in Michael J. Loux and Dean W. Zimmerman eds *The Oxford Handbook of Metaphysics* (Oxford: Oxford University Press, 2003).

Reed, Esther D. *The Genesis of Ethics, On the Authority of God as the Origin of Christian Ethics* (London: Darton, Longman & Todd, 2000).

Rehman, Sebastian *Divine Discourse: The Theological Methodology of John Owen* (Grand Rapids, MI: Baker, 2002).

Report of the Committee of Inquiry into Human Fertilization and Embryology (London: HMSO, 1984).

Robinson, John A. T. *The Human Face of God* (Philadelphia, PA: Westminster Press, 1973).

Rowe, William *Can God be Free?* (Oxford: Oxford University Press, 2004).

Saward, John *Redeemer in the Womb* (San Francisco, CA: Ignatius Press, 1993).

Schaff, Philip ed. *The Creeds of Christendom, With a History and Critical Notes, Vol. III, The Evangelical Protestant Creeds, Sixth Edition* (Grand Rapids, MI: Baker, 1983 [1931]).

Shedd, William G. T. *Dogmatic Theology, Third Edition,* ed. Alan W. Gomes (Phillipsburg, NJ: Presbyterian and Reformed, 2003).

Sonderegger, Katherine 'Election' in John Webster, Kathryn Tanner and Iain Torrance eds *The Oxford Handbook of Systematic Theology* (Oxford: Oxford University Press, 2007).

Song, Robert *Human Genetics, Fabricating the Future* (London: Darton, Longman and Todd, 2002).

Steinmetz, David *Luther in Context, Second Edition* (Grand Rapids, MI: Baker Books, 2002).

Strehle, Stephen 'The Extent of the Atonement and the Synod of Dort' in *Westminster Theological Journal* 51 (1989): 1–23.

— 'Universal Grace and Amyraldianism' in *Westminster Theological Journal* 51 (1989): 345–357.

Stump, Eleonore 'Non-Cartesian Substance Dualism and Materialism without Reduction' in *Faith and Philosophy* 12 (1995): 505–531.

Sturch Richard *The Word and The Christ, An Essay in Analytic Christology* (Oxford: Oxford University Press, 1991).

Swinburne, Richard *Responsibility and Atonement* (Oxford: Oxford University Press, 1989).

— *The Christian God* (Oxford: Oxford University Press, 1994).

— *The Evolution of the Soul, Revised Edition* (Oxford: Oxford University Press, 1997).

— 'From Mental/Physical Identity to Substance Dualism' in Peter van Inwagen and Dean W. Zimmerman eds *Persons: Human and Divine* (Oxford: Oxford University Press, 2006).

Tertullian, *Treatise on The Incarnation,* ed. and trans. Ernest Evans (London: SPCK, 1956).

Thomas, G. Michael *The Extent of the Atonement, A Dilemma for Reformed Theology from Calvin to the Consensus (1536–1675)* (Milton Keynes: Paternoster, 1997).

Tilley, Patrick *Mission* (New York: Time Warner books 1998 [1981]).

Torrance, Thomas F. 'The Doctrine of the Virgin Birth' in *Scottish Bulletin of Evangelical Theology* 12 (1994): 8–15.

Turretin, Francis *Institutes of Elenctic Theology, 3 Vols.,* trans. George Musgrave Giger, ed. James T. Dennison, Jr (Philipsburg, NJ: Presbyterian and Reformed, 1992–1997).

van Inwagen, Peter 'Dualism and Materialism: Athens and Jerusalem?' in *Faith and Philosophy* 12 (1995): 475–488.

— 'Incarnation and Christology' in Edward Craig ed. *Routledge Encyclopedia of Philosophy* (London: Routledge, 1998).

— 'A Materialist Ontology of the Human Person' in Peter van Inwagen and Dean Zimmerman eds *Persons: Human and Divine* (Oxford: Oxford University Press, 2006).

Vincent of Lérins, 'Commonitorium' in Philip Schaff and Henry Wace eds *A Select Library of Nicene and Post-Nicene Fathers of the Christian Church, Second Series, Vol. XI Sulpitius Severus, Vincent of Lerins, John Cassian,* trans. C. A. Heurtley (Grand Rapids, MI: Eerdmans, 1982 [1886–1889]).

Wainwright, William J. 'Jonathan Edwards, William Rowe, and the Necessity of Creation' in Jeff Jordan and Daniel Howard Snyder eds *Faith, Freedom and Rationality, Philosophy of Religion Today* (Maryland: Rowman and Littlefield, 1996).

Weber, Otto *Foundations of Dogmatics, Vol. II,* trans. Darrell L. Guder (Grand Rapids, MI: Eerdmans, 1983).

Webster, John *Holy Scripture, A Dogmatic Sketch* (Cambridge: Cambridge University Press, 2002).

— *Confessing God, Essays in Christian Dogmatics II* (Edinburgh: T&T Clark, 2005).

— 'Theologies of Retrieval' in John Webster, Kathryn Tanner and Iain Torrance eds *The Oxford Handbook of Systematic Theology* (Oxford: Oxford University Press, 2007).

Wierenga, Edward R. *The Nature of God, An Inquiry into Divine Attributes* (Ithaca, NY: Cornell University Press, 1989).

Wiles, Maurice *The Remaking of Christian Doctrine* (London: SCM Press, 1974).
— *Working Papers in Doctrine* (London: SCM Press, 1976).
Wilkinson, John 'Apologetic Aspects of the Virgin Birth of Jesus Christ' in *Scottish Journal of Theology* 17 (1964): 159–181.
Williams, D. H. *Evangelicals and Tradition* (Grand Rapids, MI: Baker Academic and Milton Keynes: Paternoster, 2005).
Witsius, Hermann *Economy of the Covenants Between God and Man in Two Volumes, Vol. I.* trans. William Cruickshank (Escondido, CA: The Den Dulk Christian Foundation, 1990 [London, 1822]).
Wolterstorff, Nicholas *Reason within the Bounds of Religion, Second Edition* (Grand Rapids, MI: Eerdmans, 1984 [1976]).
— 'The Travail of Theology in the Modern Academy' in Miroslav Volf ed. *The Future of Theology, Essays in Honour of Jürgen Moltmann* (Grand Rapids, MI: Eerdmans, 1996).
Yandell, Keith 'Divine Necessity and Divine Goodness' in Thomas V. Morris ed. *Divine and Human Action: Essays in the Metaphysics of Theism* (Ithaca, NY: Cornell University Press, 1988).
Zanchius, Jerome *Absolute Predestination* (Evansville, IN: Sovereign Grace Book Club, n. d.).

INDEX